SARATOGA NATURALLY:

Photographic Images of Saratoga's Most Beautiful Parks & Preserves

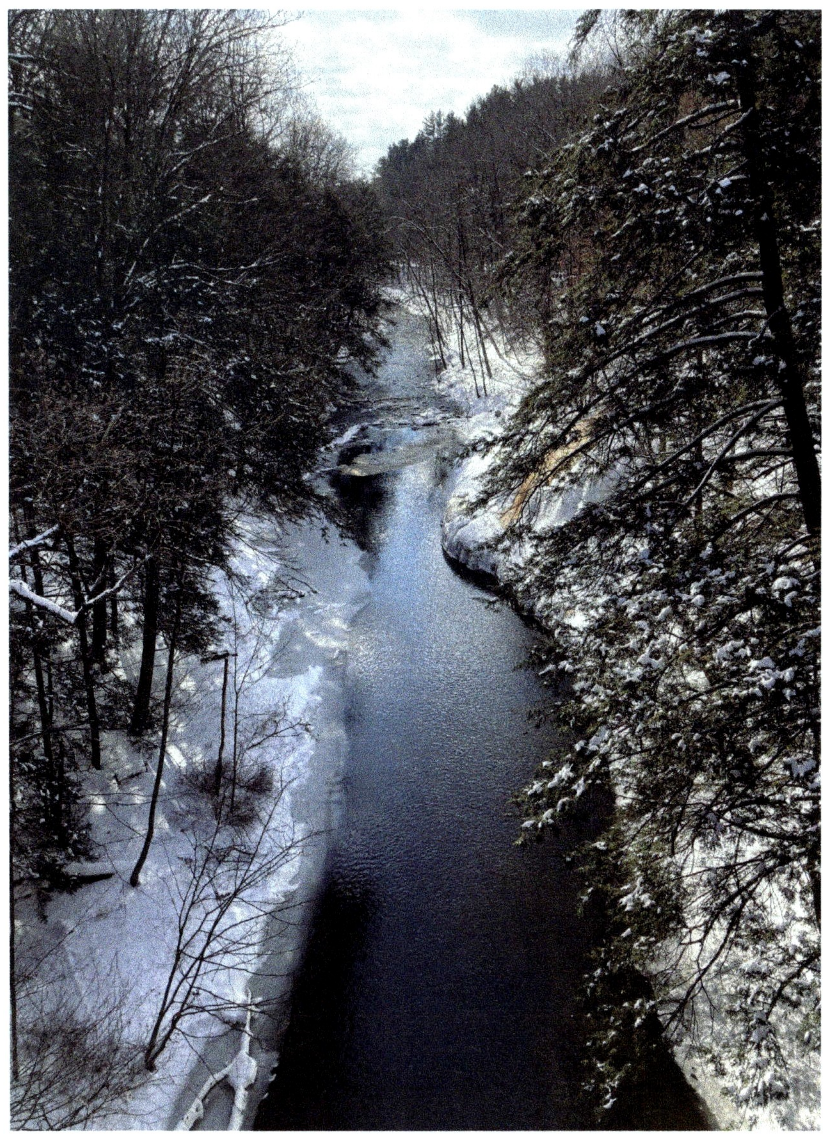

Photographs by Louis Valenti

Spa City Publishing – Saratoga Springs, NY
Paperback ISBN: 979-8-9854236-3-1
Hardcover ISBN: 979-8-9854236-2-4
Library of Congress Control Number: 2023905107
Saratoga Naturally: Photographic Images of Saratoga's Most Beautiful Parks & Preserves
Author: Louis Valenti
Digital Distribution | 2023
Paperback | 2023

Photography copyright © 2023 Louis Valenti
Valenti, Louis
Printed in the United States of America

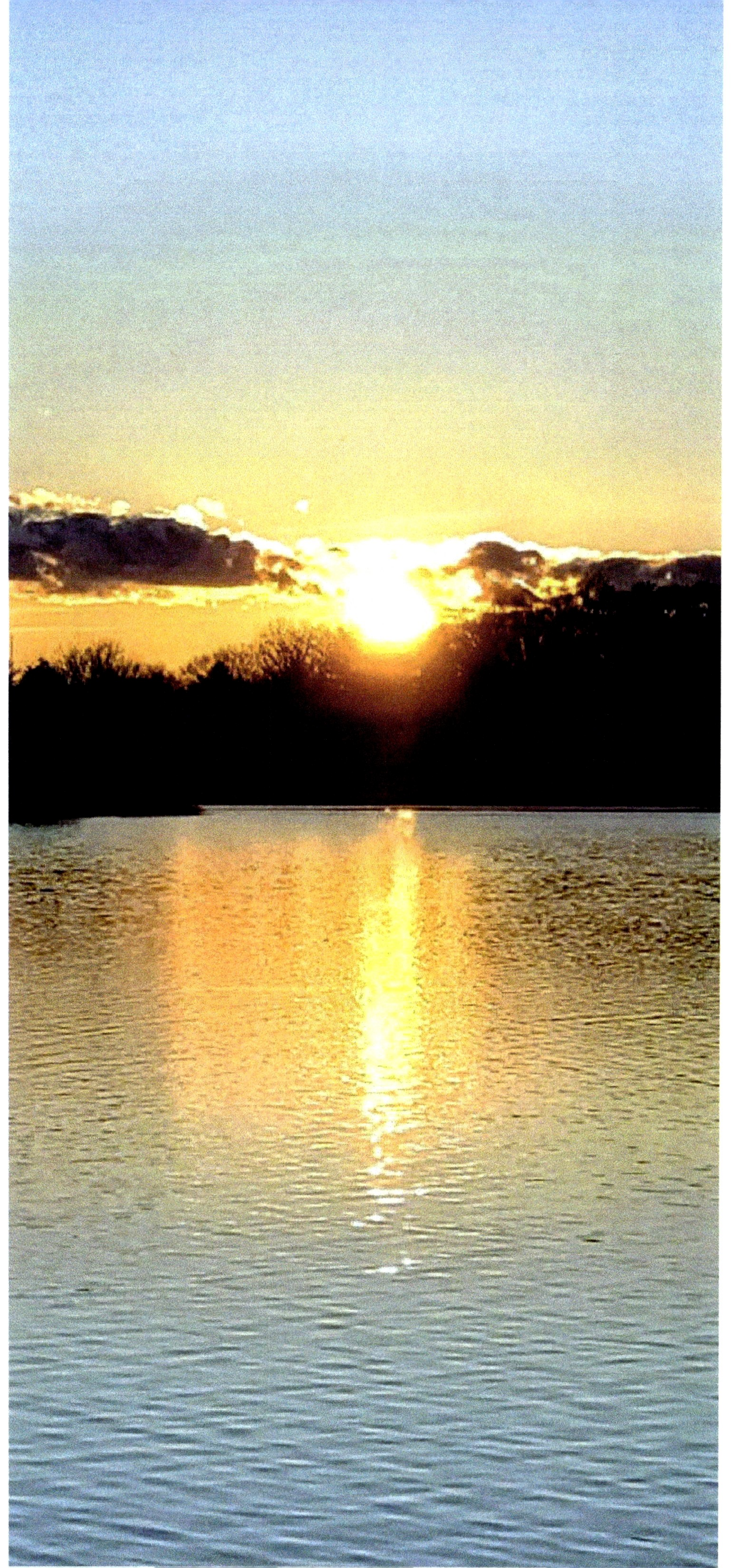

SARATOGA NATURALLY:

Photographic Images of Saratoga's Most Beautiful Parks & Preserves

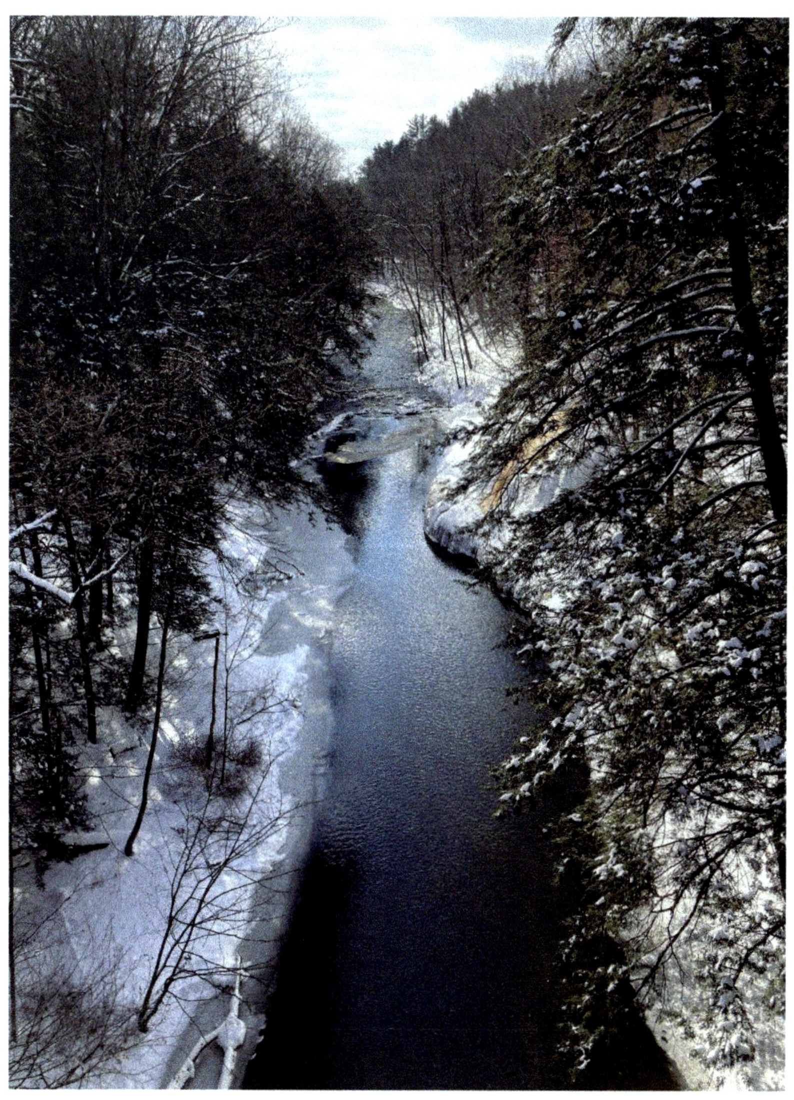

Photographs by Louis Valenti

Oh, Summer has clothed the earth.
In a cloak from the loom of the sun.
And a mantle, too, of the skies soft blue.
And a belt where the rivers run.

And now for the kiss of the wind,
And the touch of the air's soft hands,
With the rest from the strife and the heat of life,
With the freedom of lakes and lands . . .

So, long as the stream runs down,
And as long as the robins trill,
Let us taunt old cares with a mercy air,
And renew your joy of heart.

Paul Laurance Dunbar

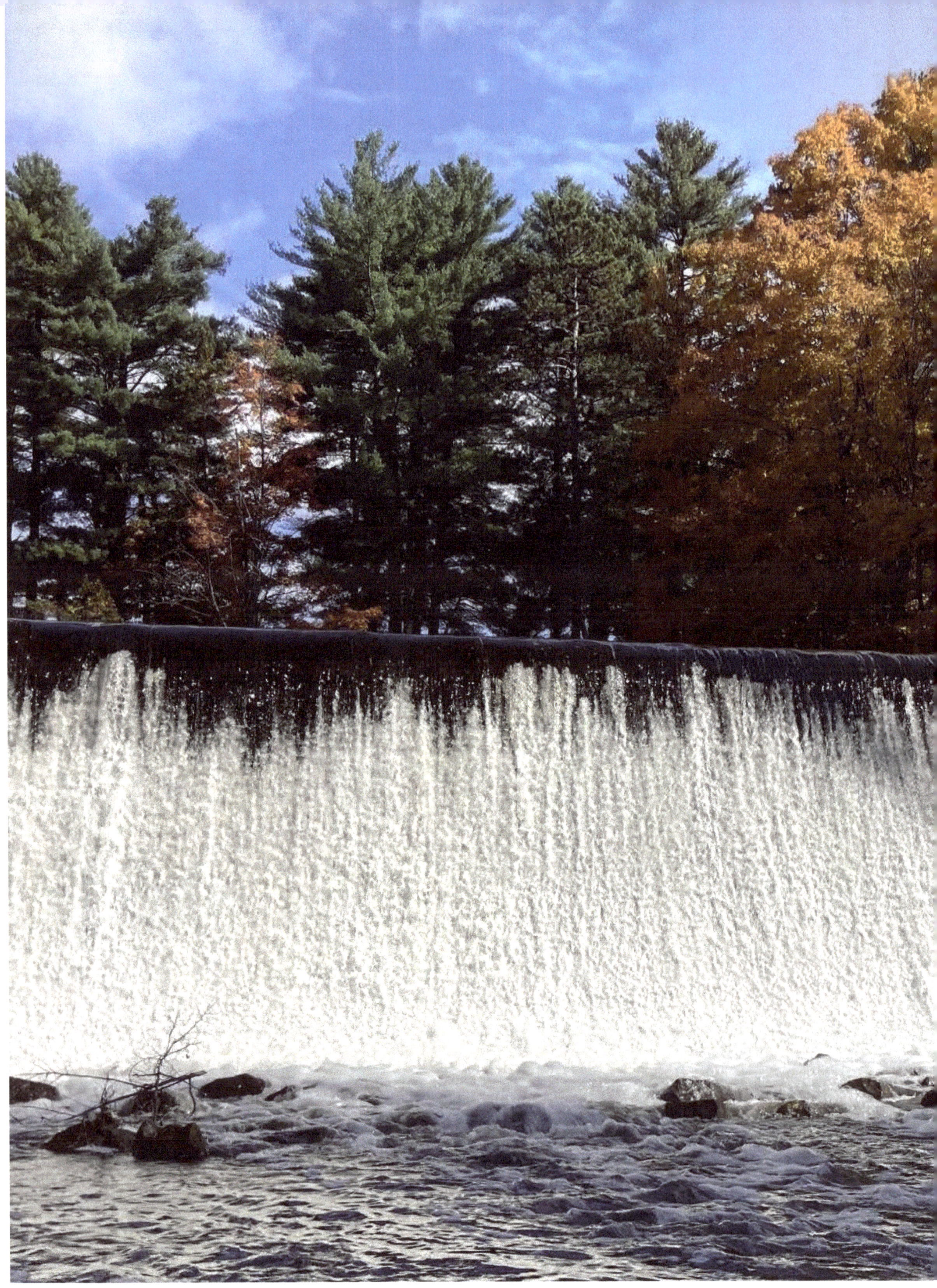

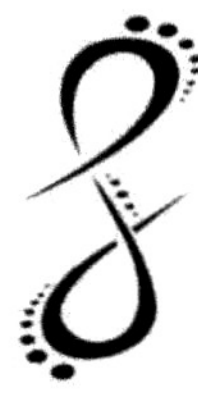

SARATOGA NATURALLY:

Photographic Images of Saratoga's Most Beautiful Parks & Preserves

Louis Valenti

Photographs by Louis Valenti

Acknowledgements

Once again, my heartfelt thanks and deepest appreciation to my amazing mother, Sandy, for a lifetime of love and support and for believing in me . . . always; Betty Friedlander, for her love and support and decades of wise counsel. I miss you both so very, very much. Special thanks to my life partner, Valerie, for her love and continued support in this second book that we have worked on together; her artistic brilliant mind, honest judgement, and meticulous general editing and photograph selection. Without them, Saratoga Naturally would not have been possible. I also thank all my family and friends and all those who have continuously encouraged and inspired me to do this second book and who have supported me with my first book, Seasons in the Pine Bush, of which this book is a reflection.

List of Photographs

Introduction

Saratoga Springs is home to several notable landmarks, including the Saratoga Race Course, Saratoga Performing Arts Center and of course, the famous mineral springs. Saratoga is also known as the Southern Gateway to the Adirondacks and features many beautiful parks and preserves offering more than 200 miles of multi-use trails for wildlife watching, hiking, running, mountain biking, birding, cross-country skiing, snowshoeing, and horseback riding encompassing more than 6,500 acres free and open to the public year-round.

*Saratoga Naturally features photographic images of five of Saratoga's most beautiful parks and preserves including **Saratoga Spa State Park; Colonel William F. Fox Memorial Saratoga Tree Nursery; Geyser Creek Trail; Bog Meadow Brook Nature Trail; and the Saratoga National Historical Park and Battlefield.** The **Saratoga Spa State Park** is stunningly beautiful. This is a large state park featuring six main trails that run near to the historic Gideon Putnam hotel, museums, two pool complexes, mineral baths, Saratoga Performing Arts Center, picnic areas, hiking trails, two golf courses, and numerous mineral springs. The **Colonel William F. Fox Memorial Saratoga Tree Nursery** in Saratoga is the oldest state forest tree nursery in the country. Established in 1902, the original priority was reforestation. The Nursery currently produces more than 1.5 million seedlings annually and maintains more than 200 acres of seed production areas and orchards located across the state. More than 6 million seedlings representing over 50 species are currently growing at the Nursery. By using local seed collected from around New York State, Nursery trees and shrubs are hardy and adapted to our state's climatic condition. The most popular Saratoga trail is the 2.9-mile **Geyser Creek Trail**, which goes directly past or very close to 12 open springs. The trail also features the Hayes Spring, Island Spouter, Waterfall and Tunnel, and Tufa Dome created by the Orenda Spring. **Bog Meadow Brook Nature Trail** is great for warm seasonal walks and cold season skiing, is a favorite among nature lovers. The path travels along an abandoned railroad that once connected the City of Saratoga Springs to various locations throughout the Northeast. The Meadowlark Preserve encompasses 174 acres of wetlands and woods that surround the trail. The **Saratoga National Historical Park and Battlefield** preserves the site of the Battles of Saratoga, the first significant American military victory of the American Revolutionary War. The park features many attractions including climbing the Saratoga monument, hiking through Victory Woods, hiking Wilkinson trail and tour of the Philip Schuyler Country Estate. The park is also famous for its outstanding views of the area's natural scenery and Vermont's Green Mountains in the distance.*

Saratoga Spa State Park

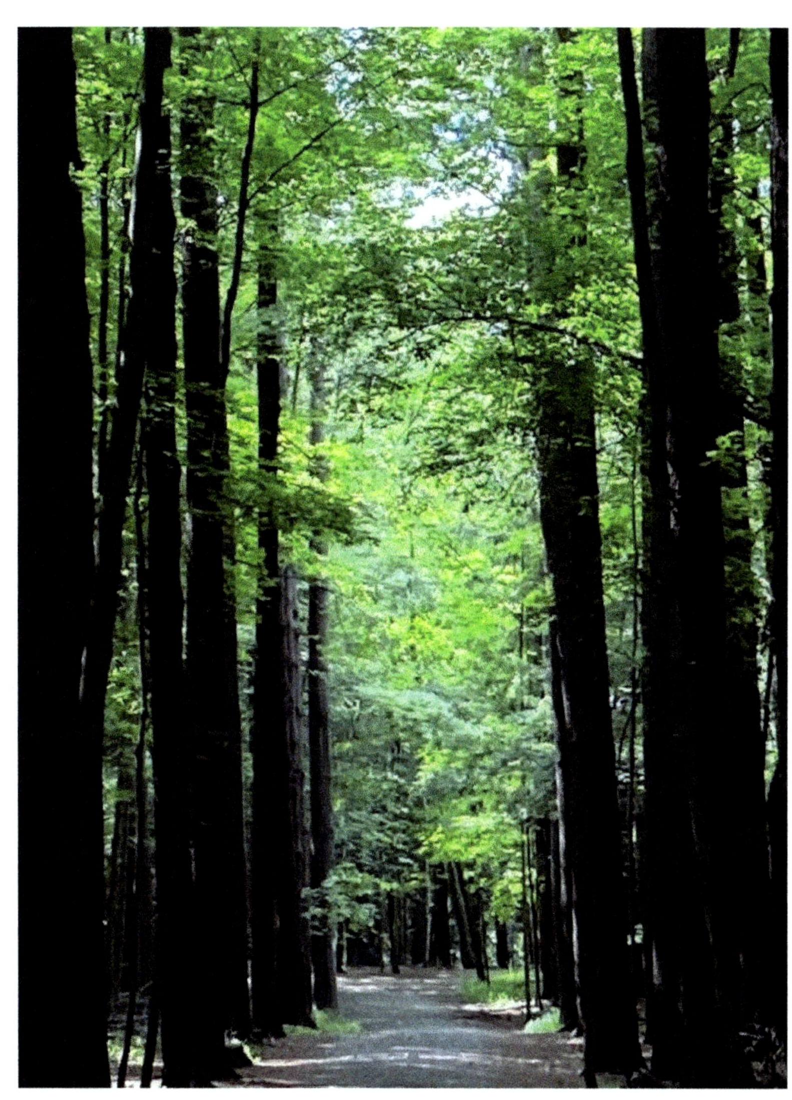

The secret to life . . .
Interest in the small things of
Nature, insects, birds, flowers,
And leaves. To be fully awake
To everything around you. And
The more you learn, the more
You can appreciate, and get
A full measure of joy and happiness
Out of life.

LeRoy Pollack

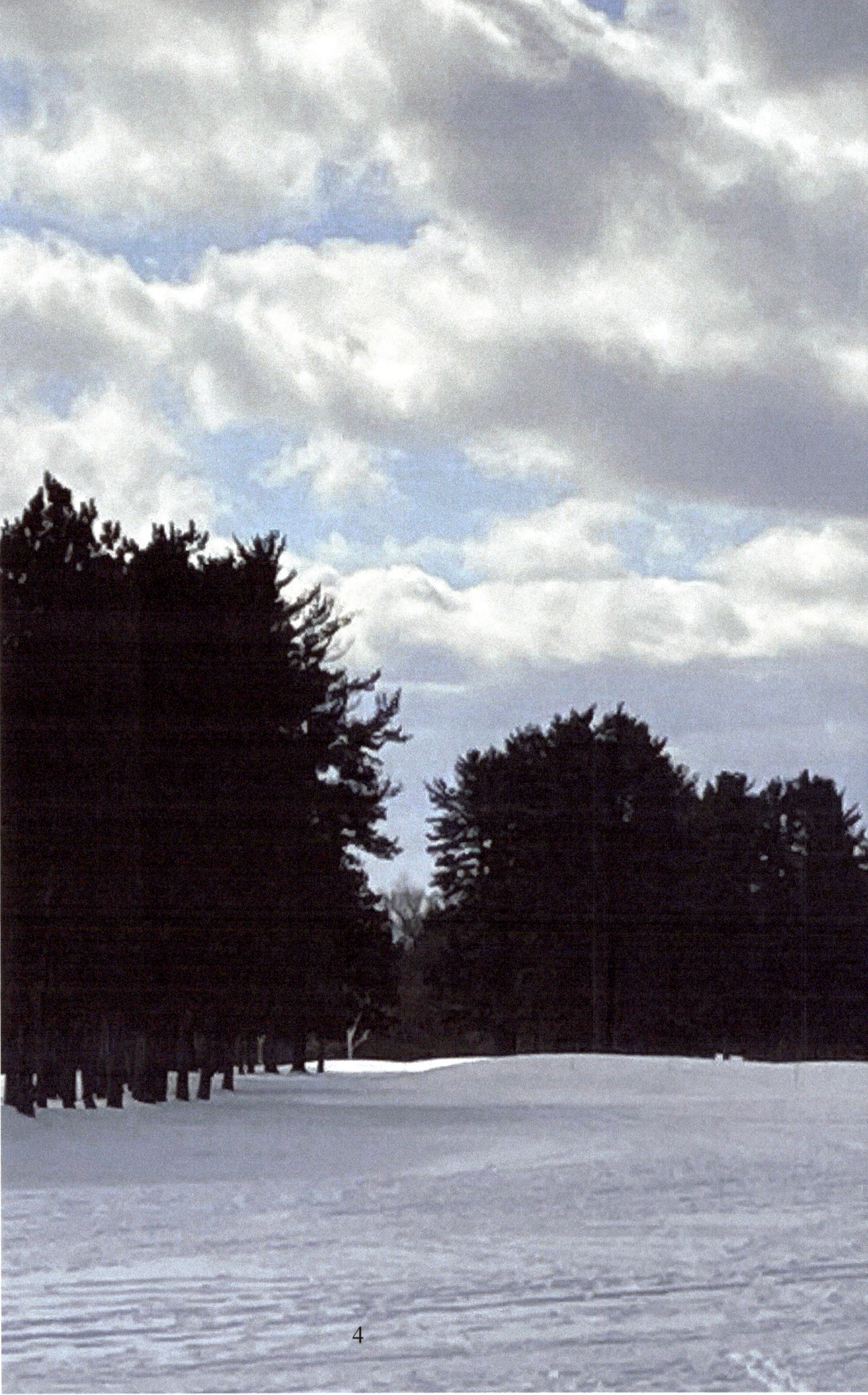

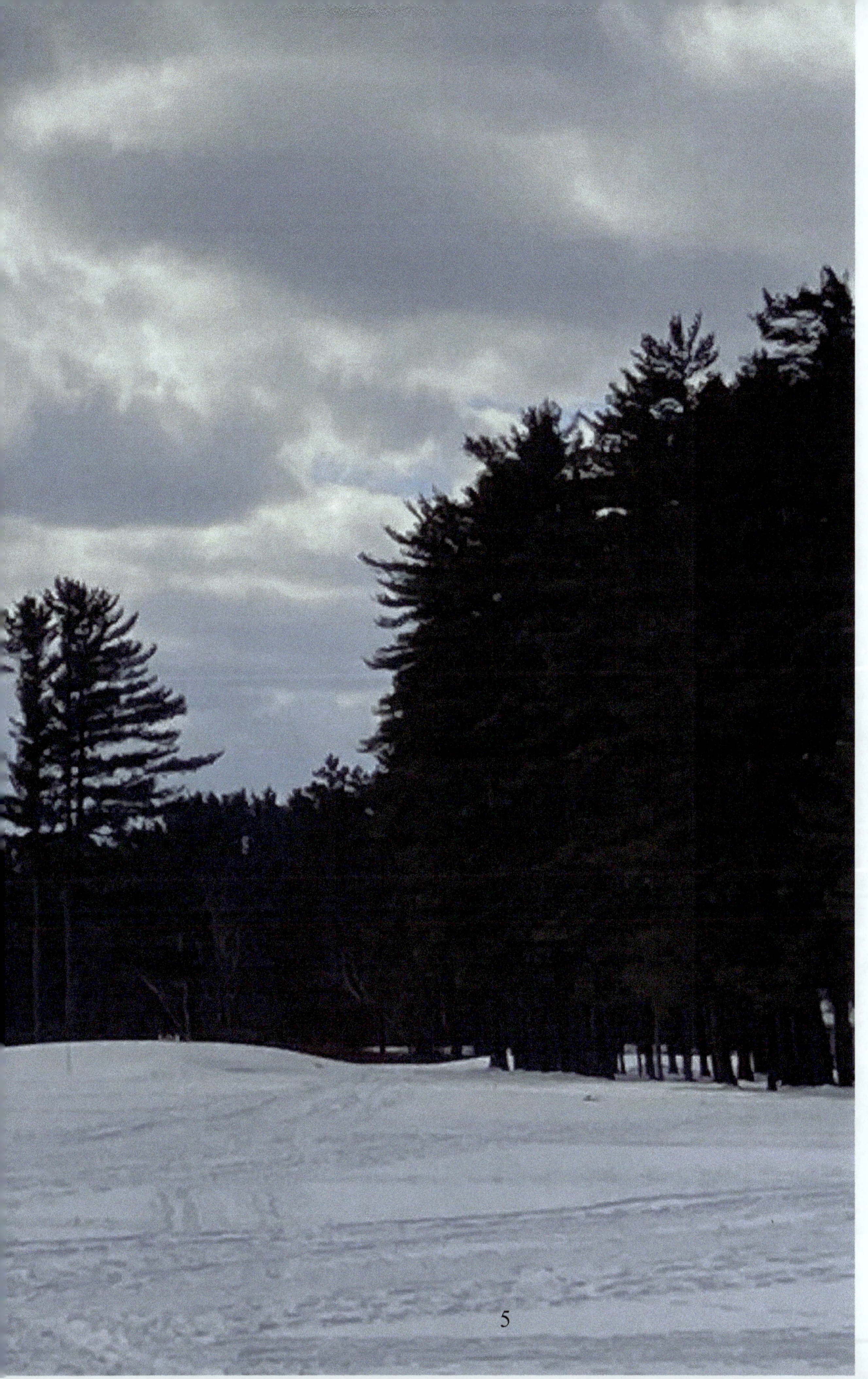

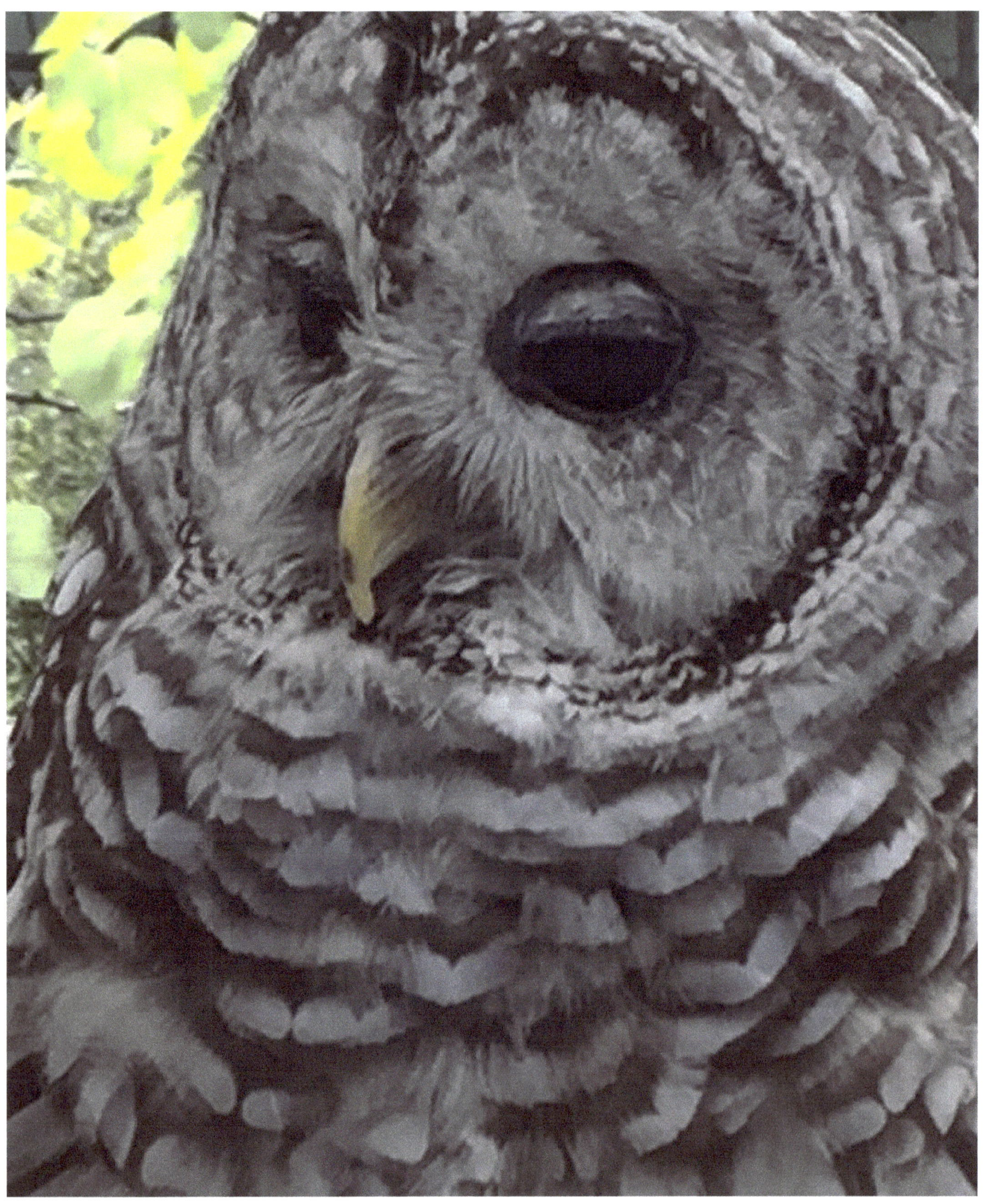

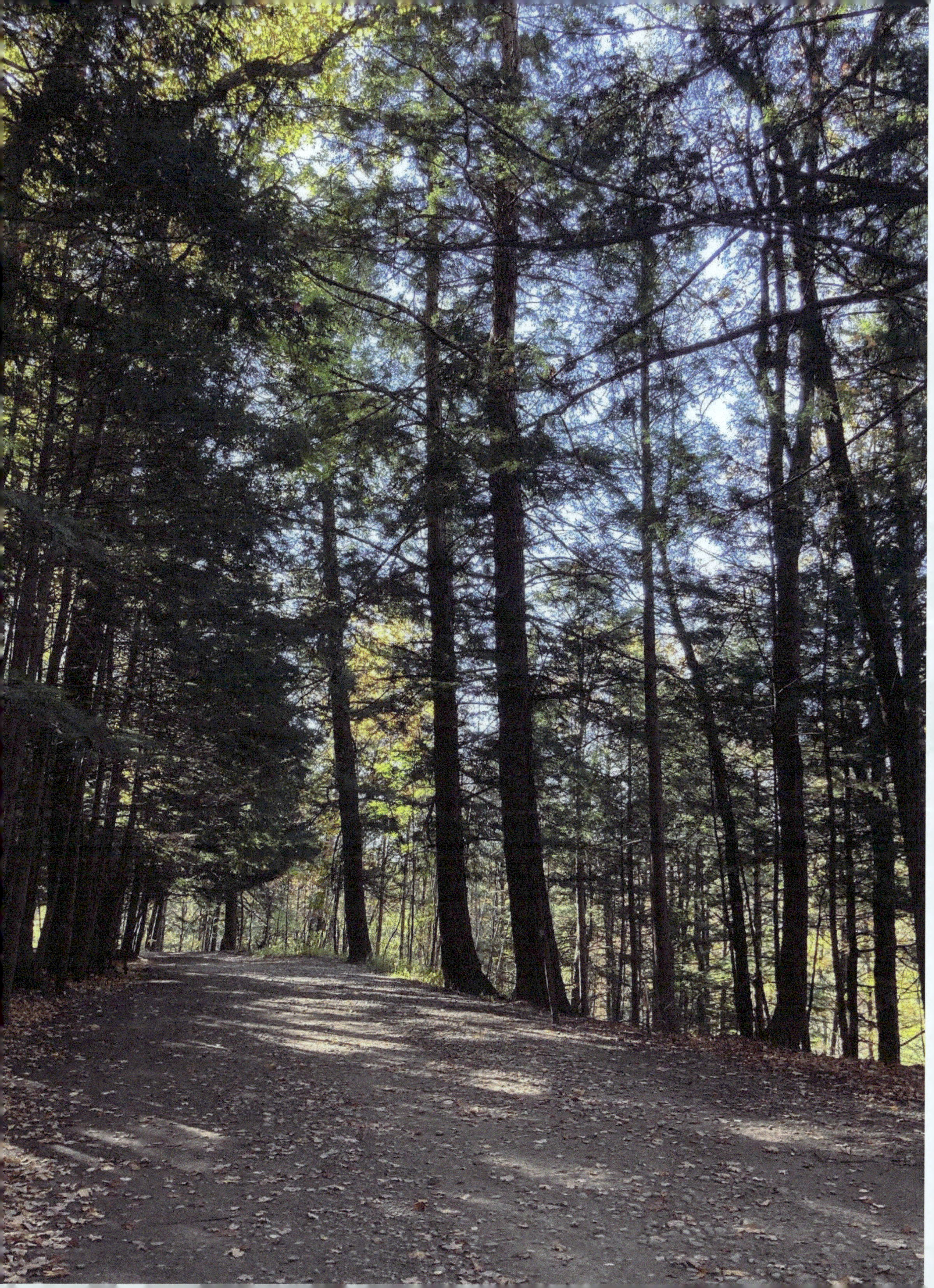

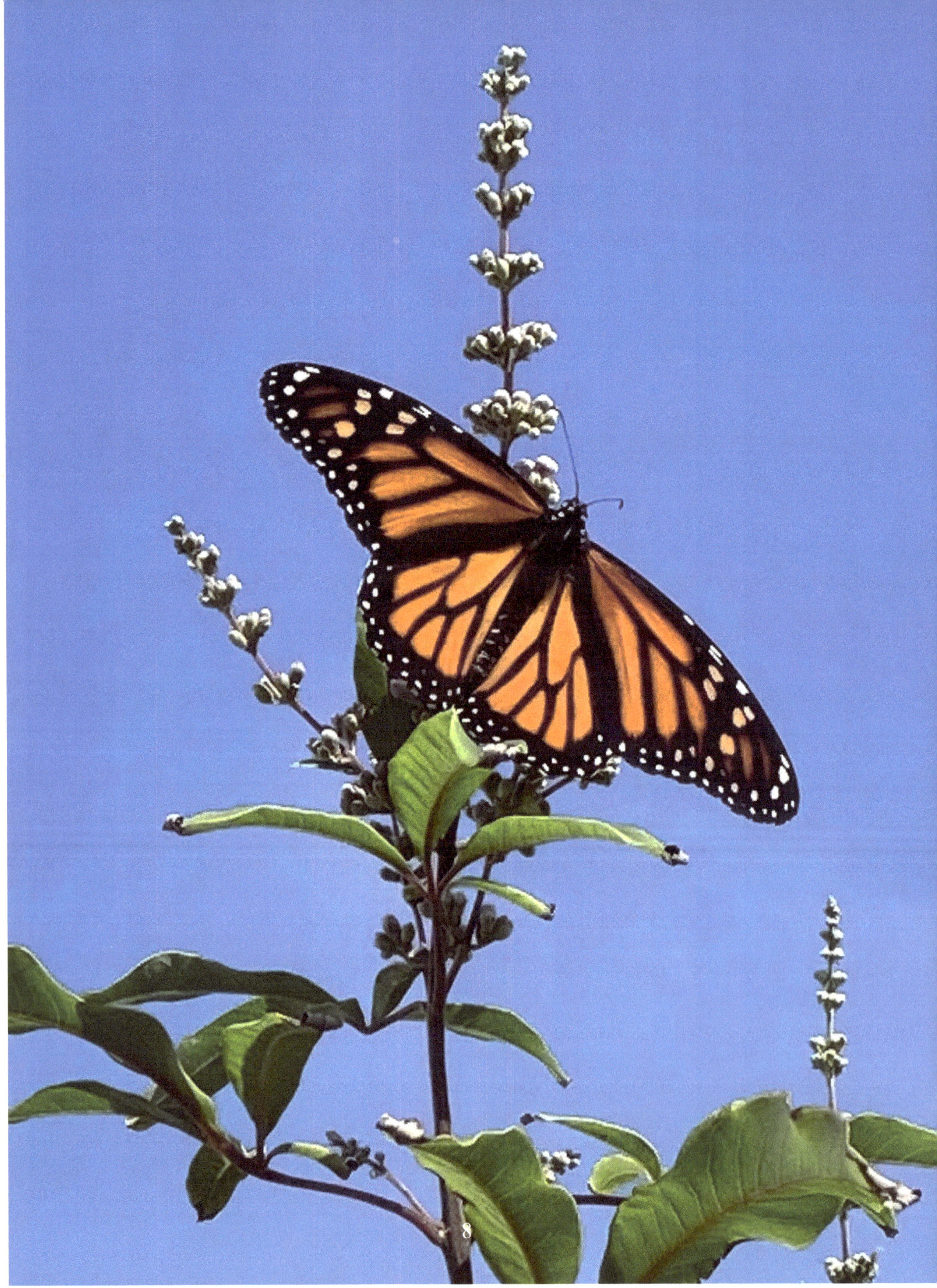

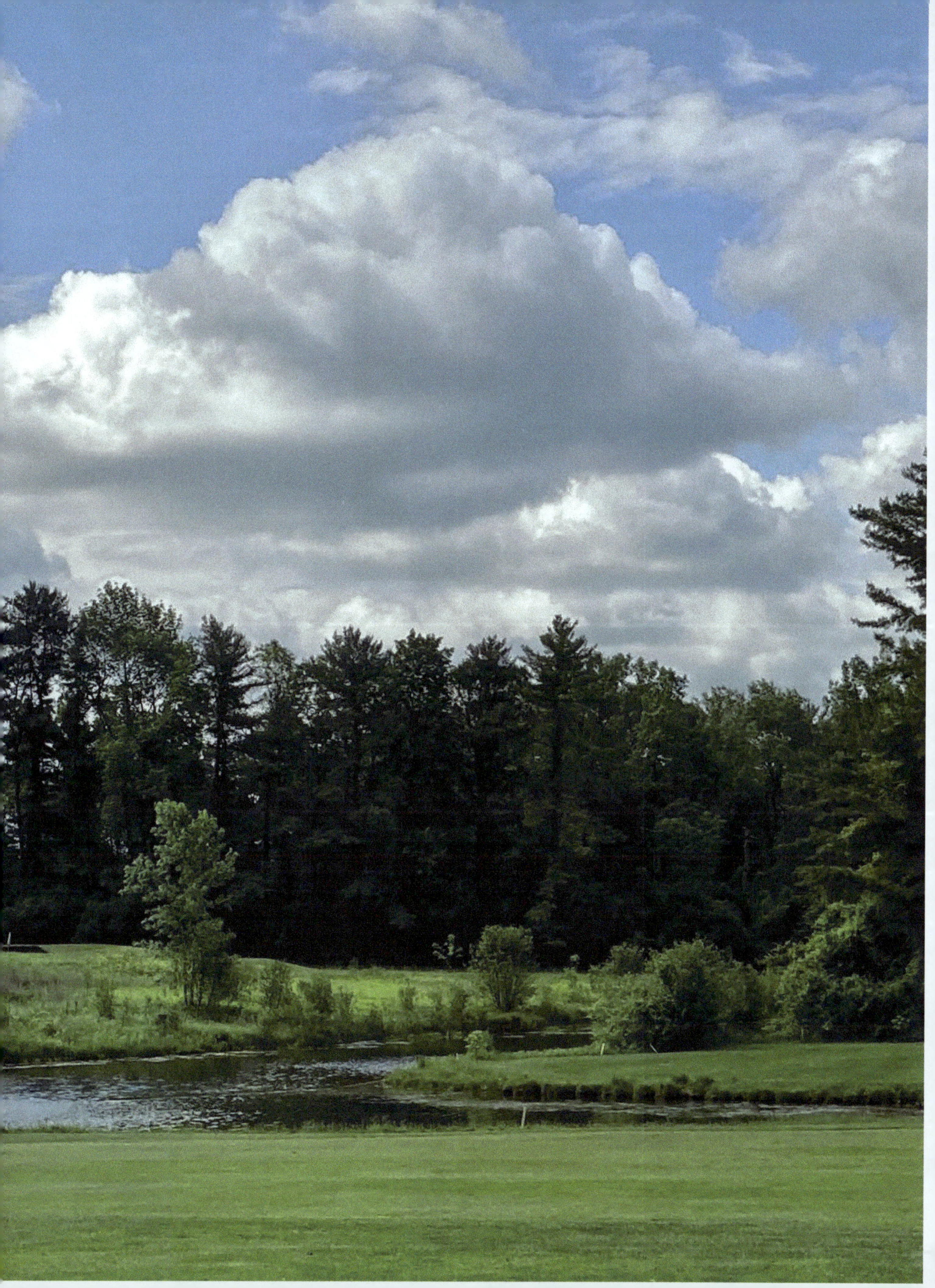

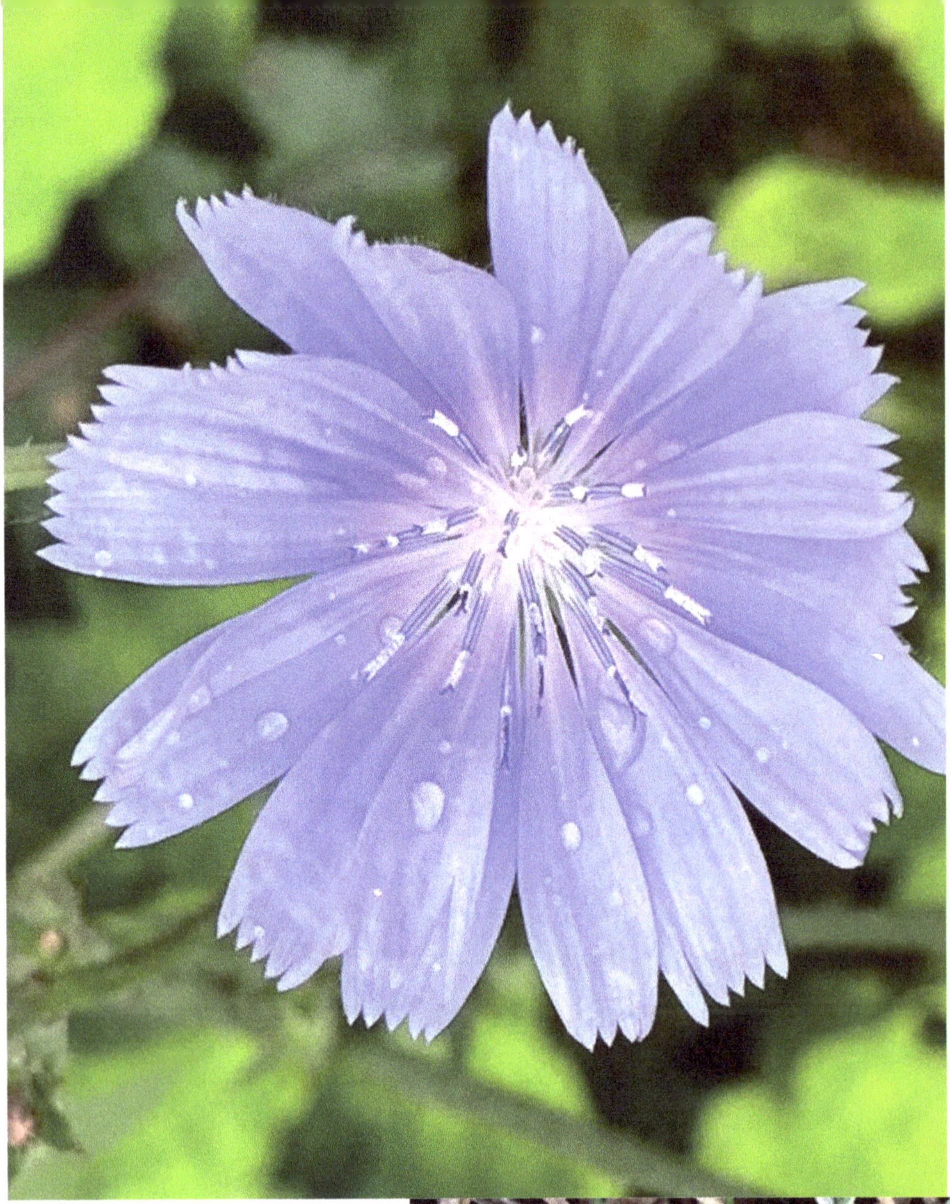

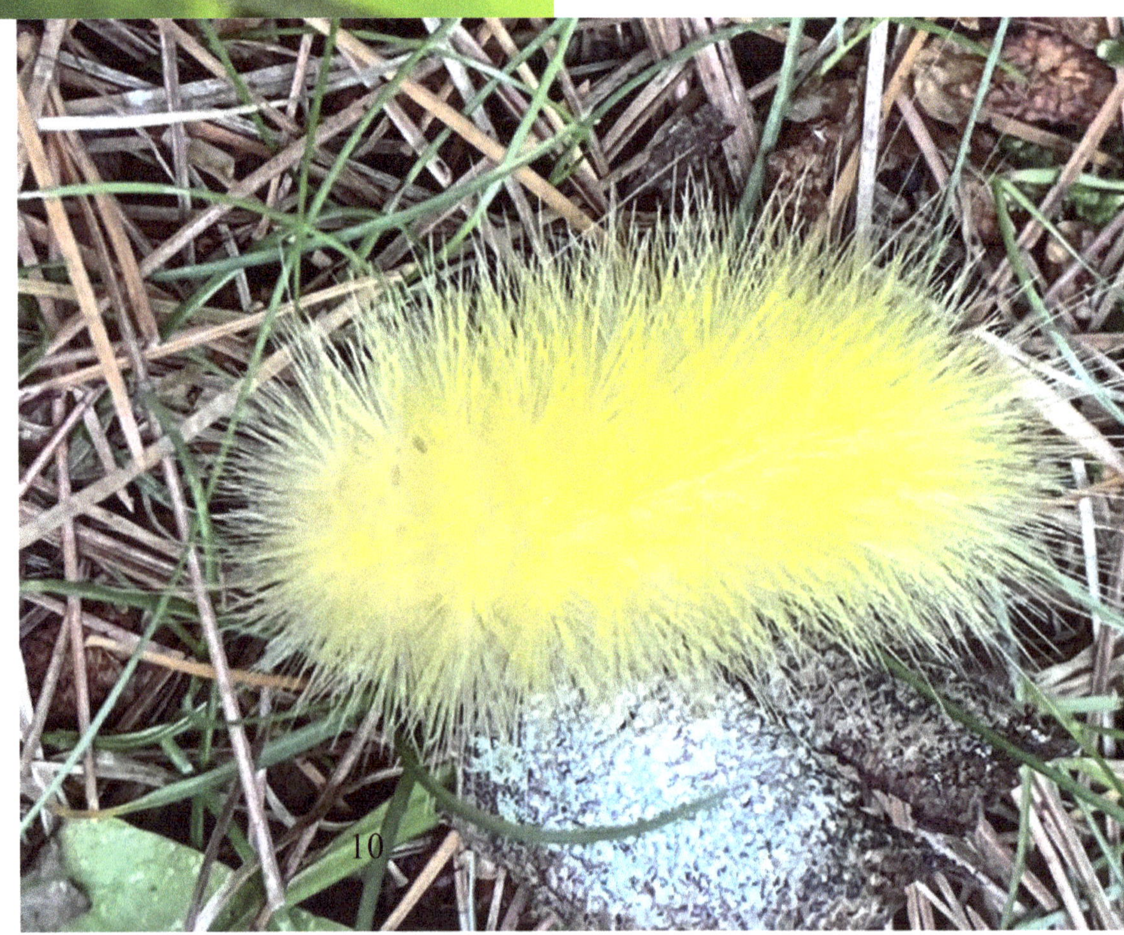

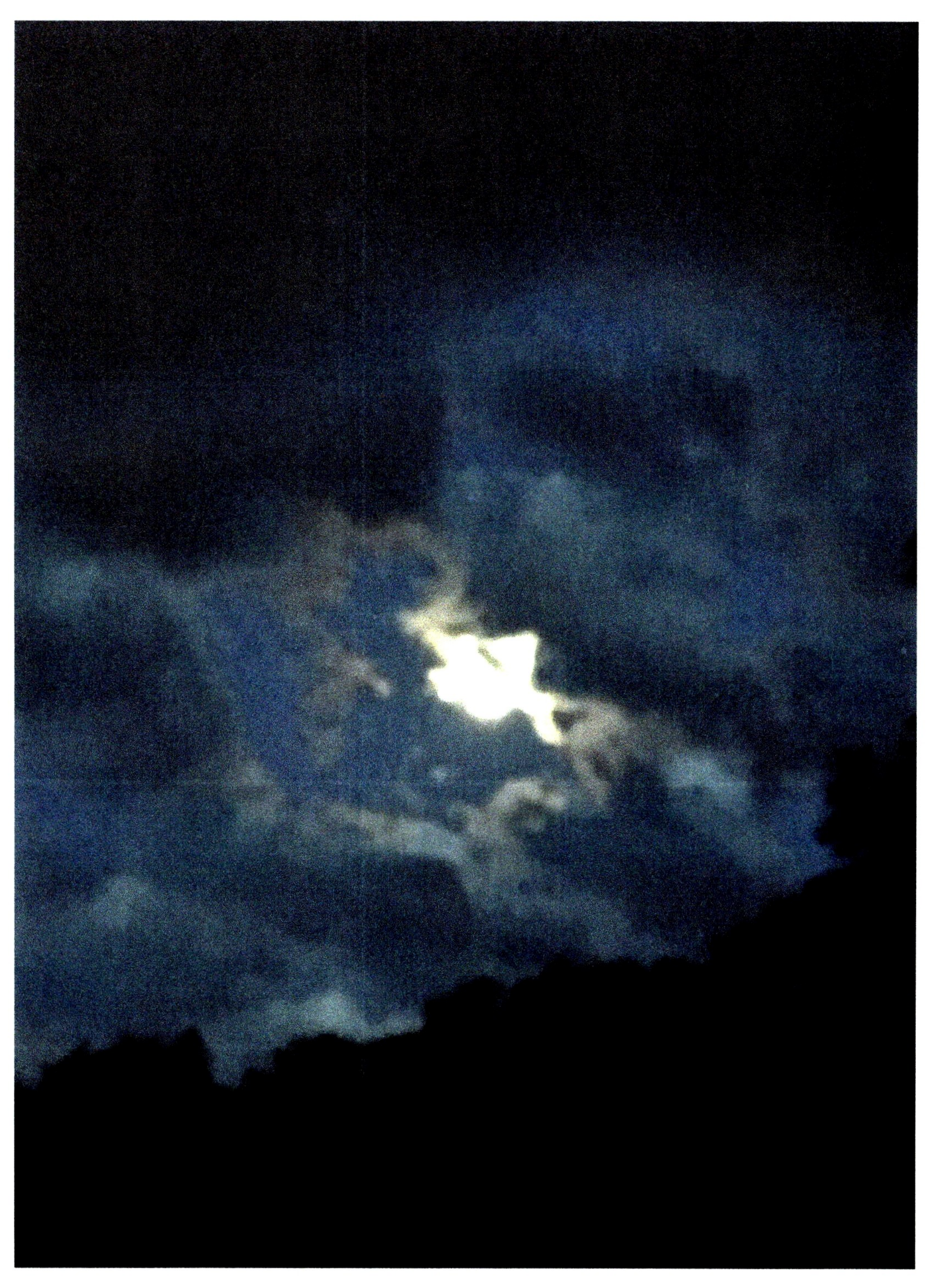

"The moon is magic for the soul and light for the senses."

Unknown

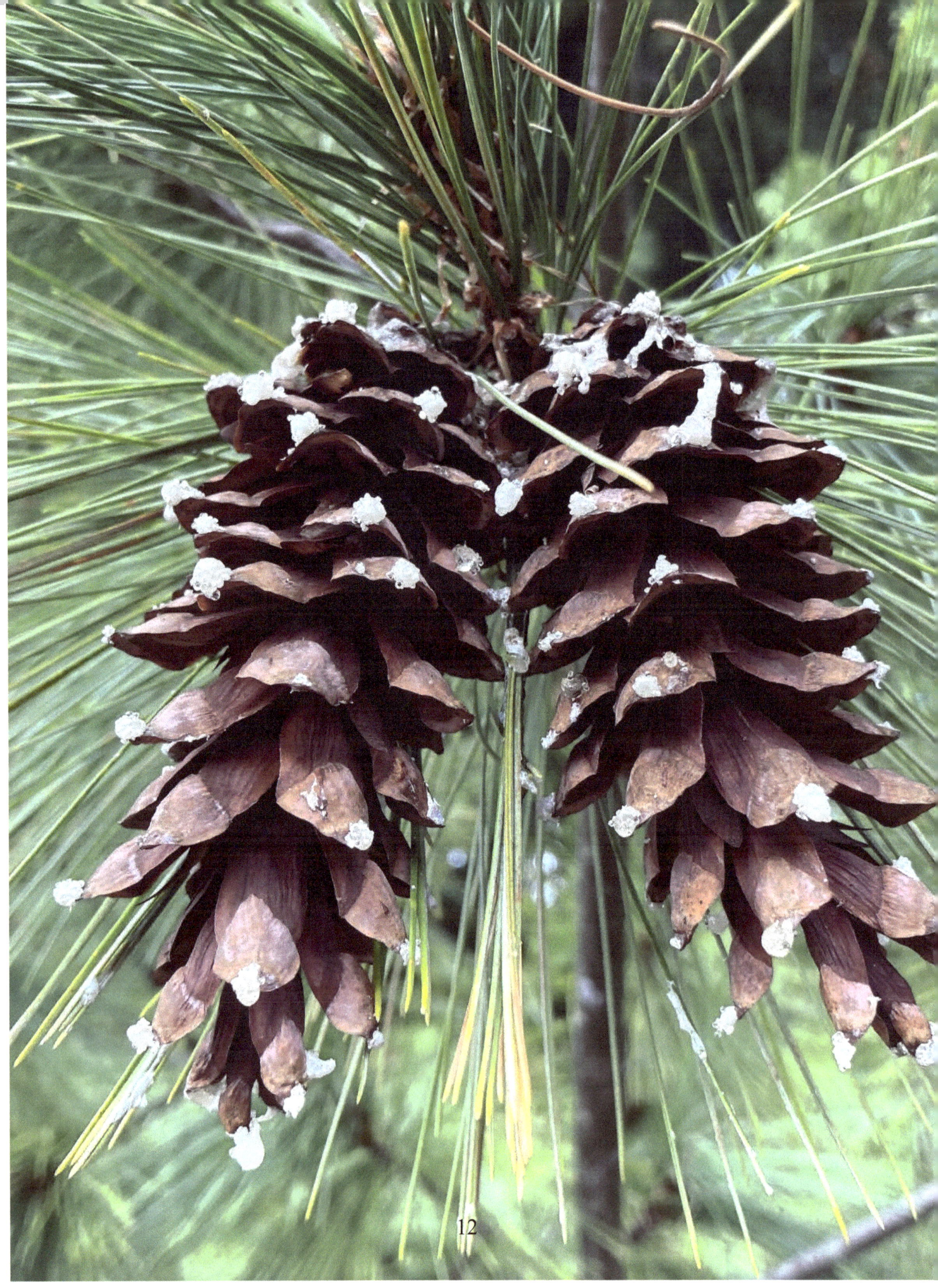

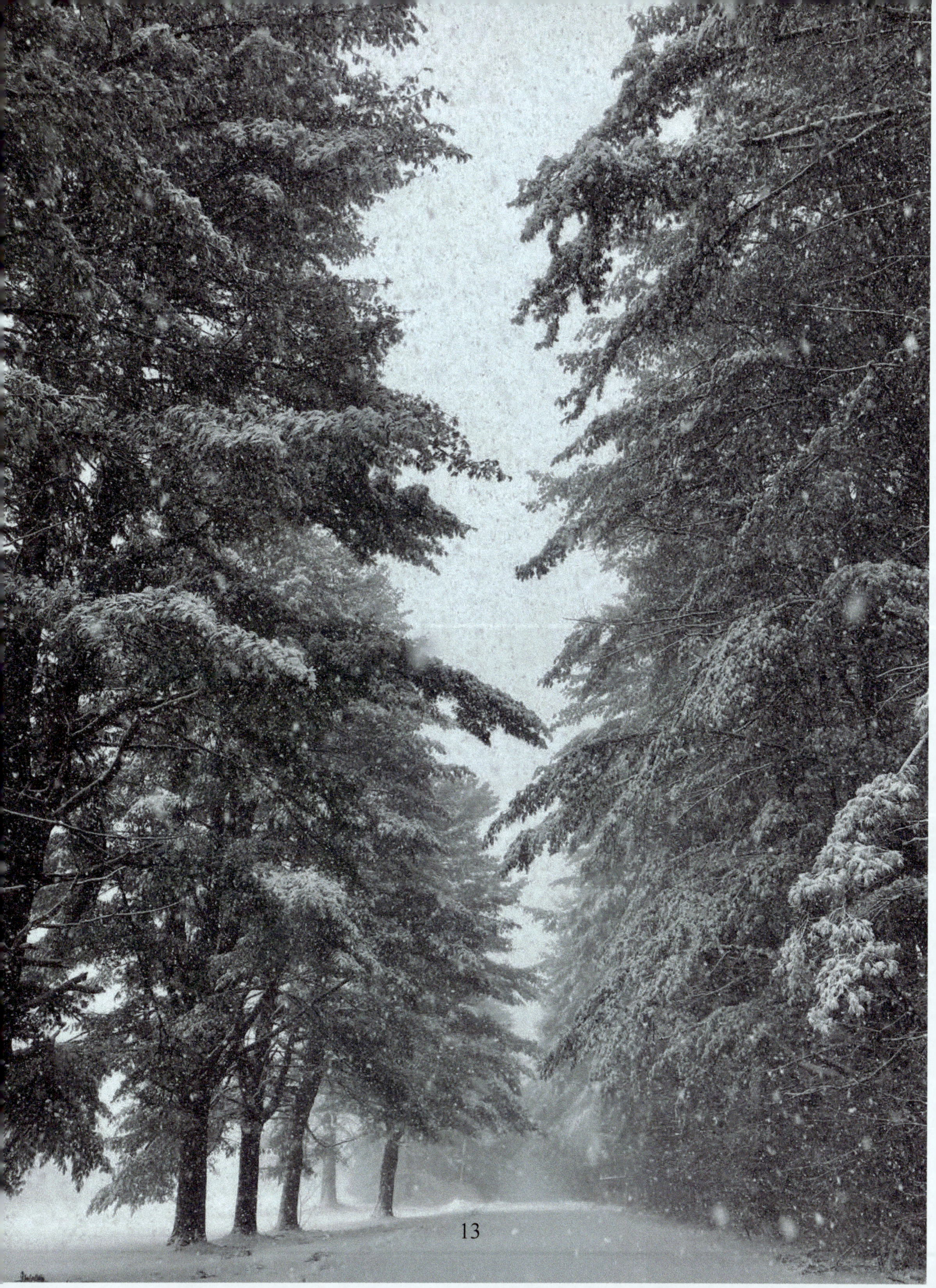

"Nature is painting for us, day after day, pictures of infinite beauty."

John Ruskin

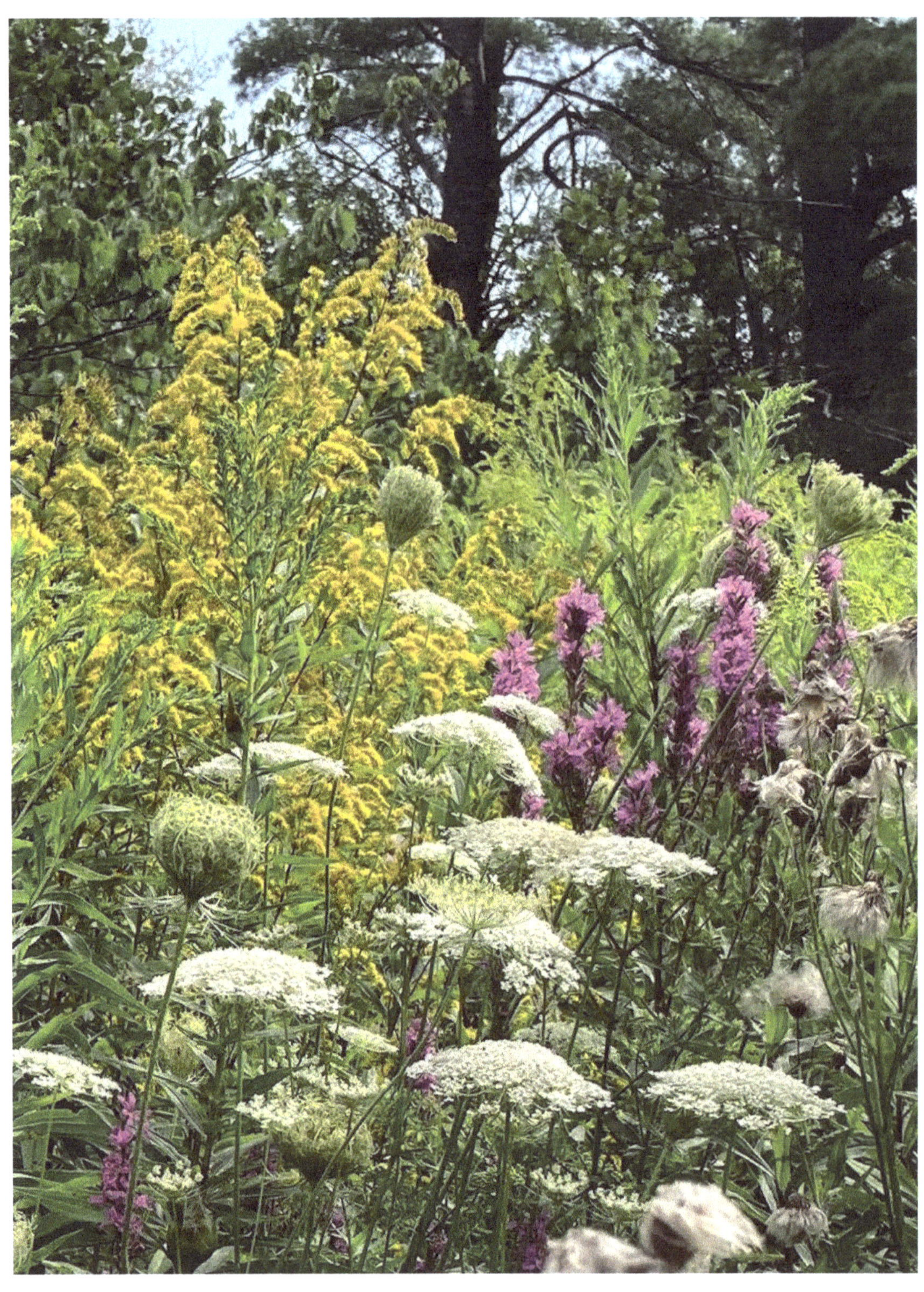

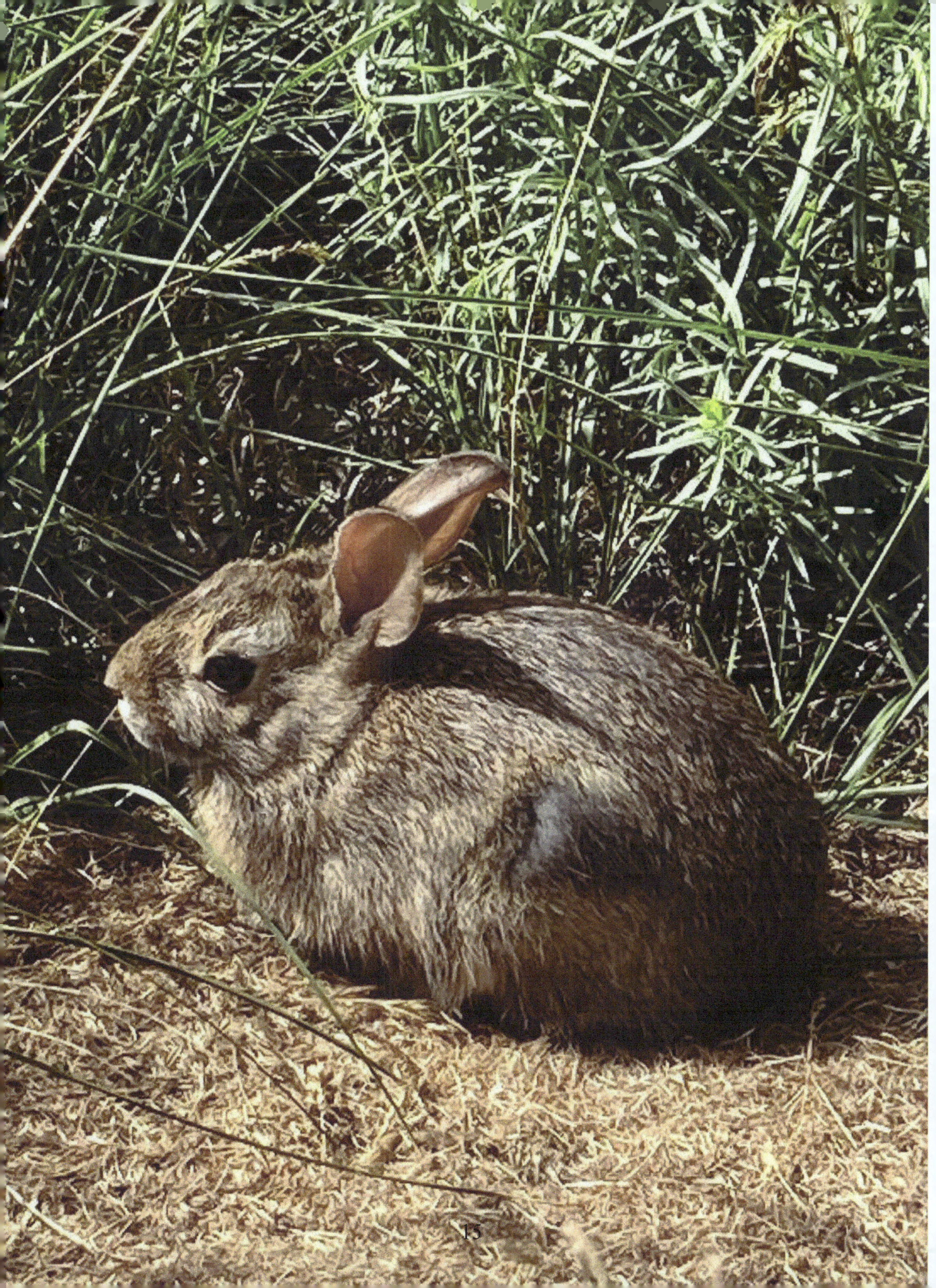

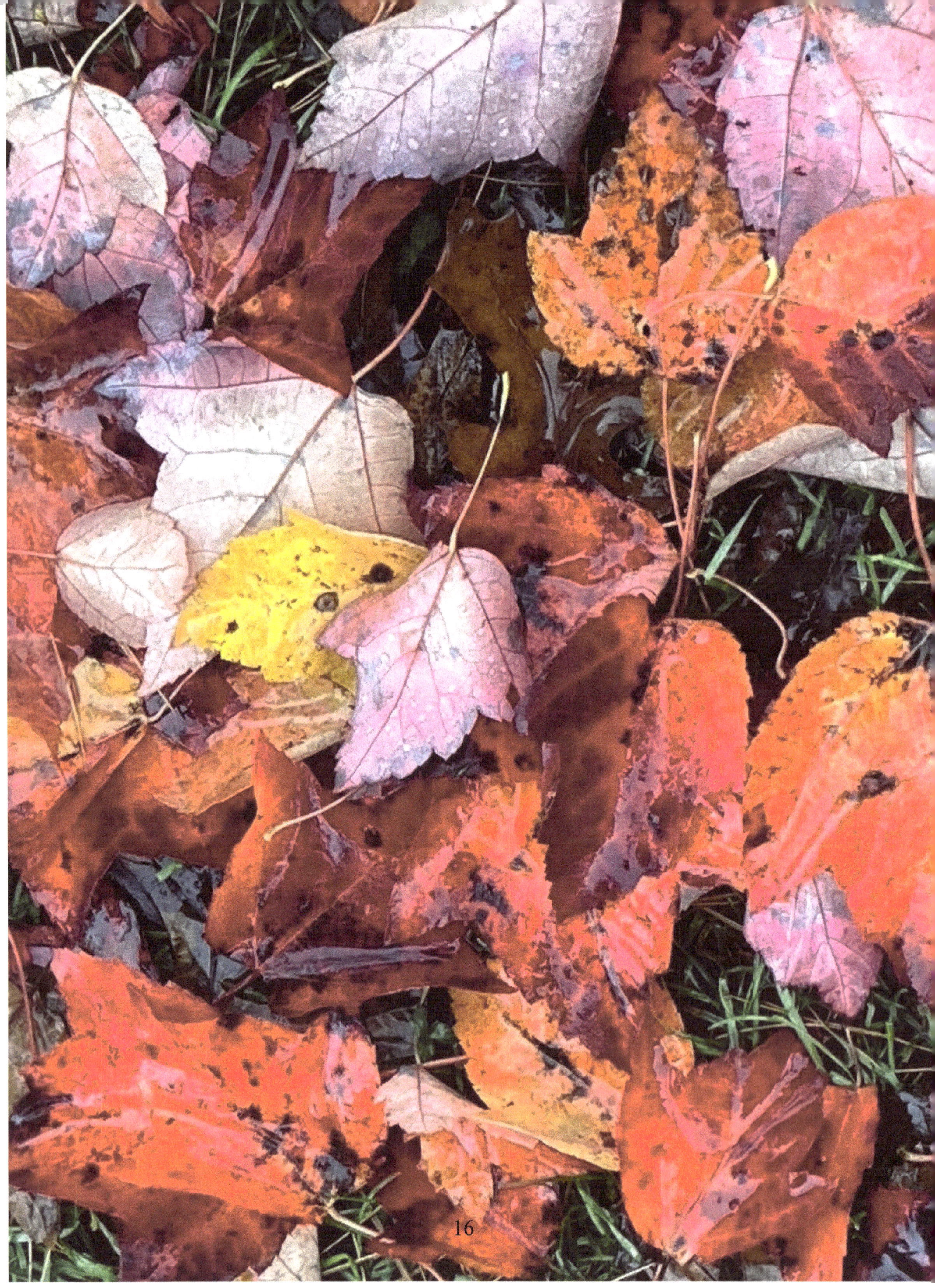

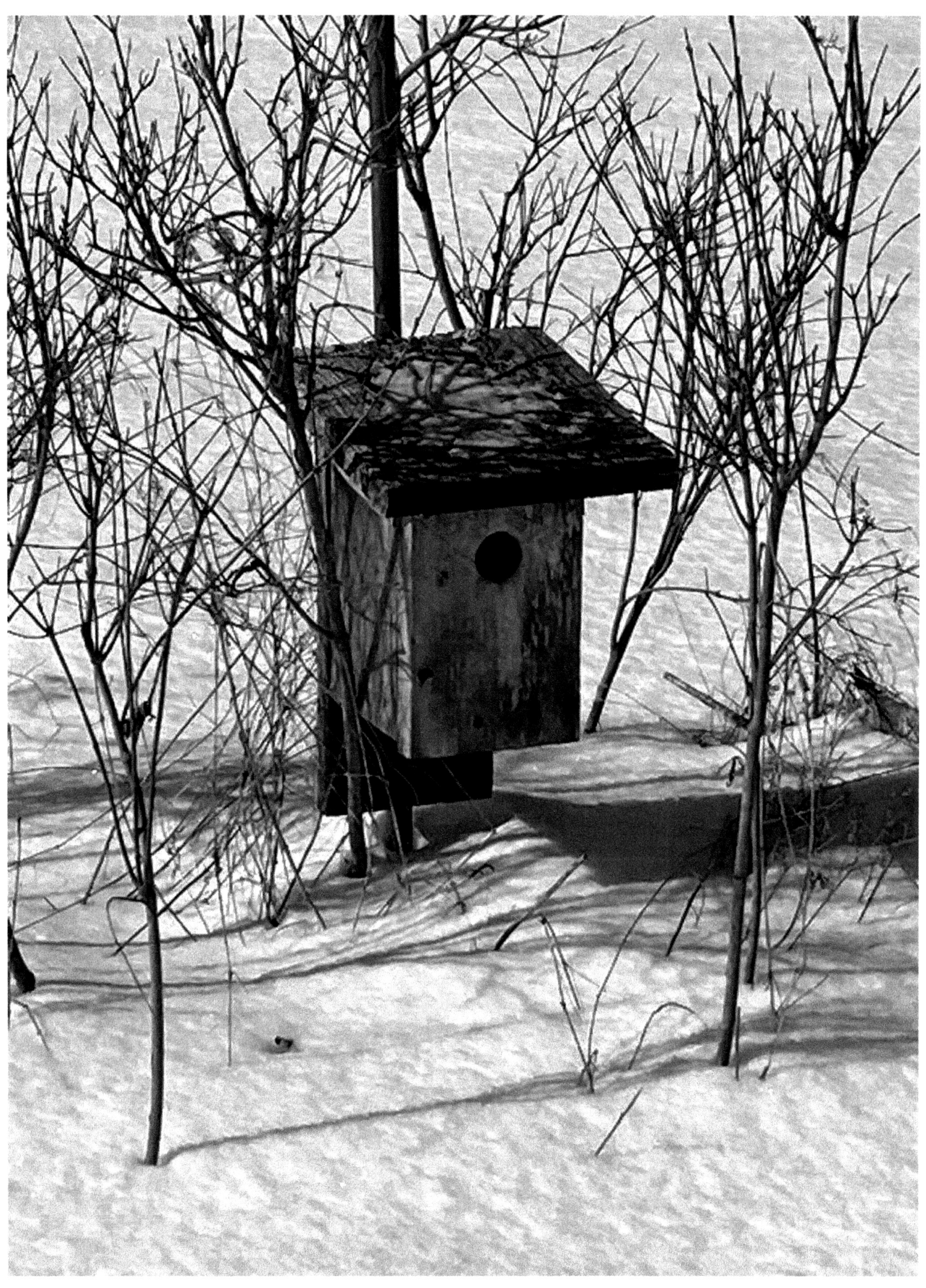

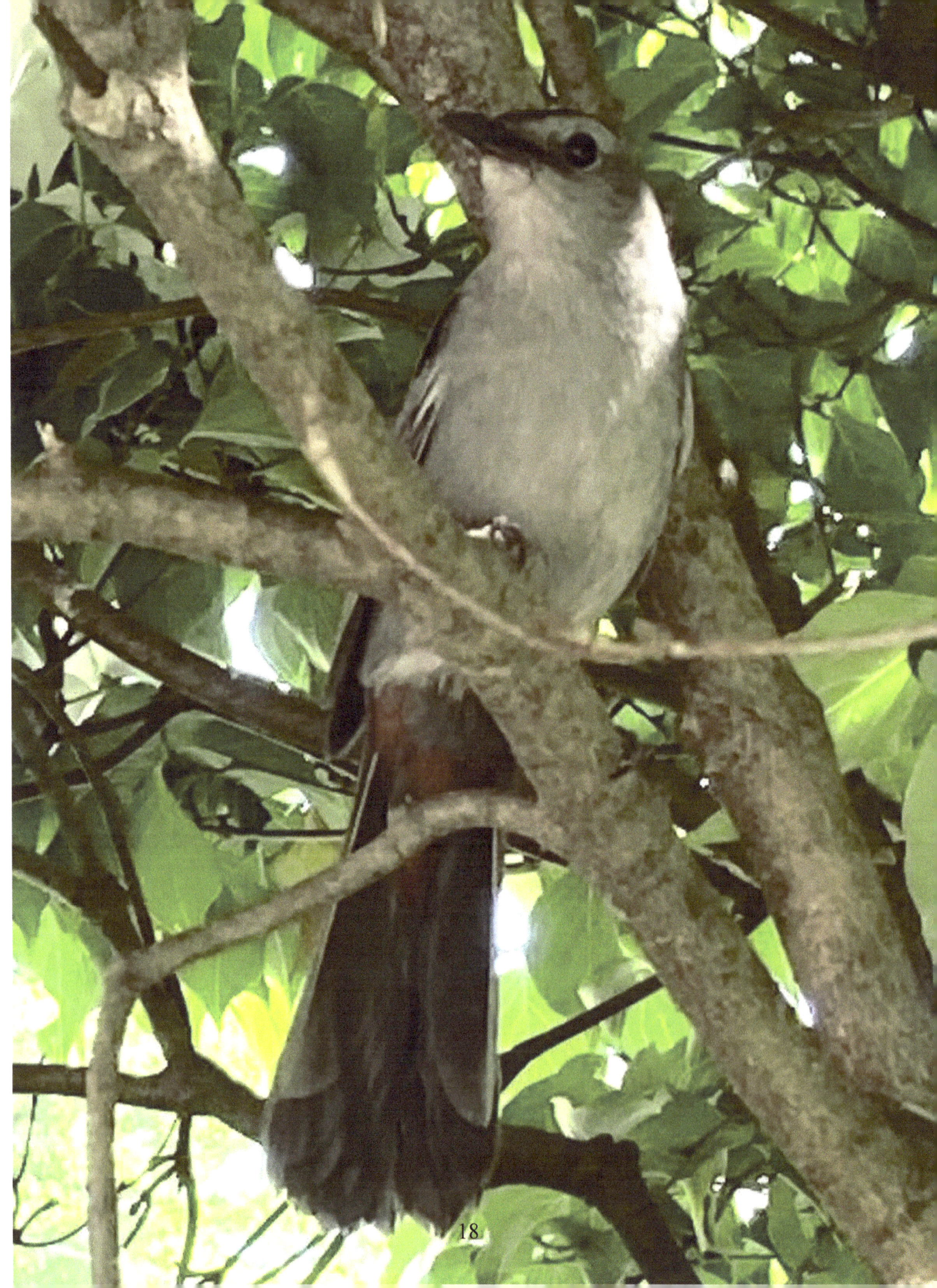

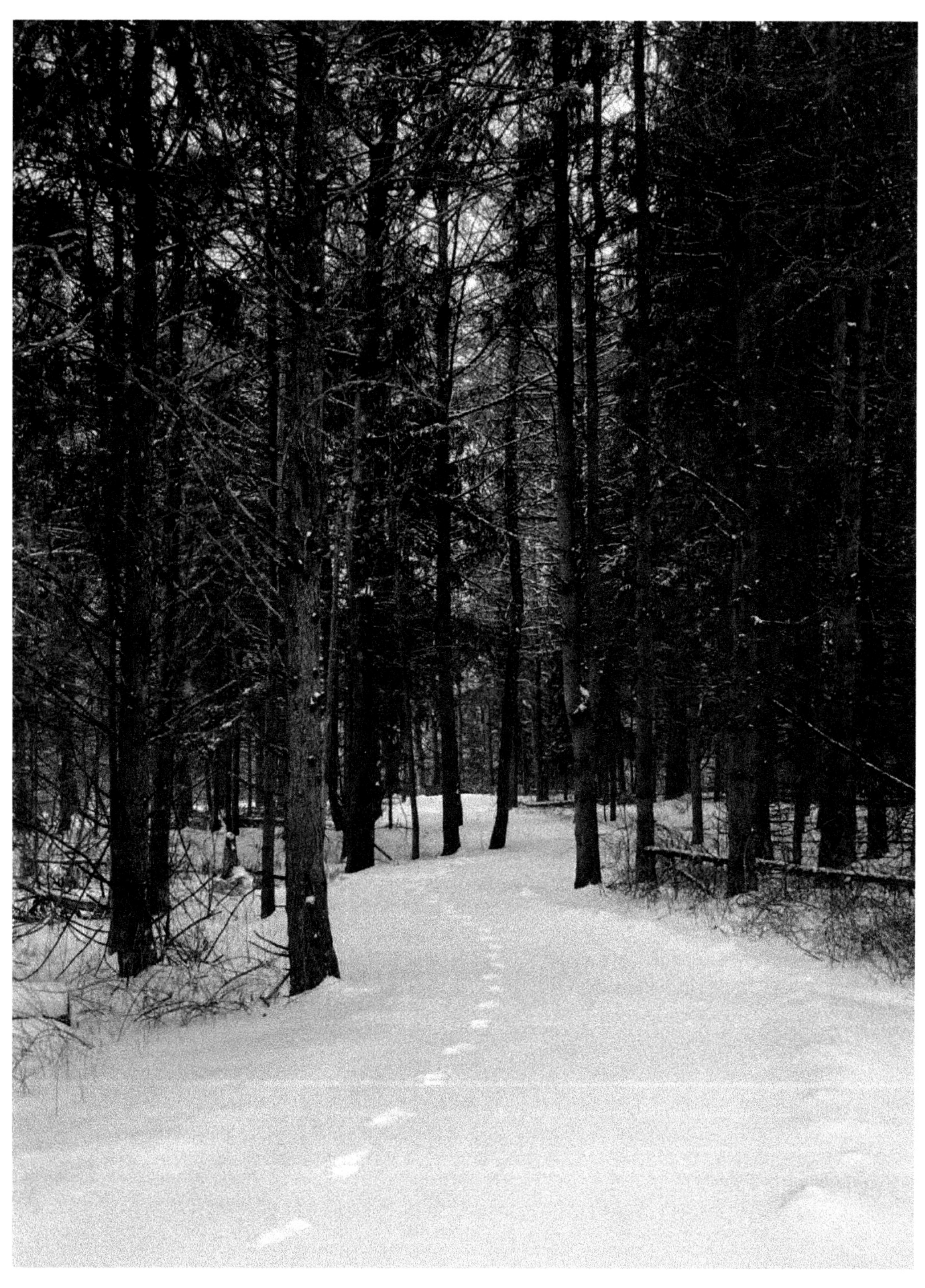

"And into the forest I go, to lose my mind and find my soul."

John Muir

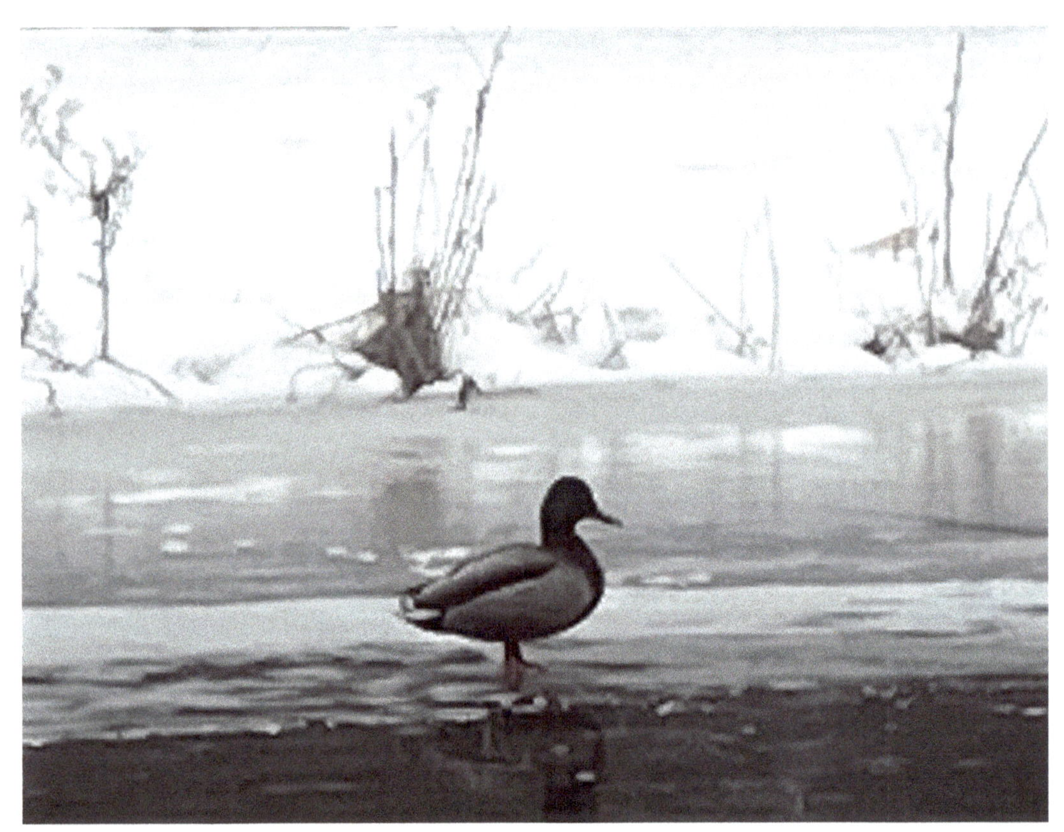

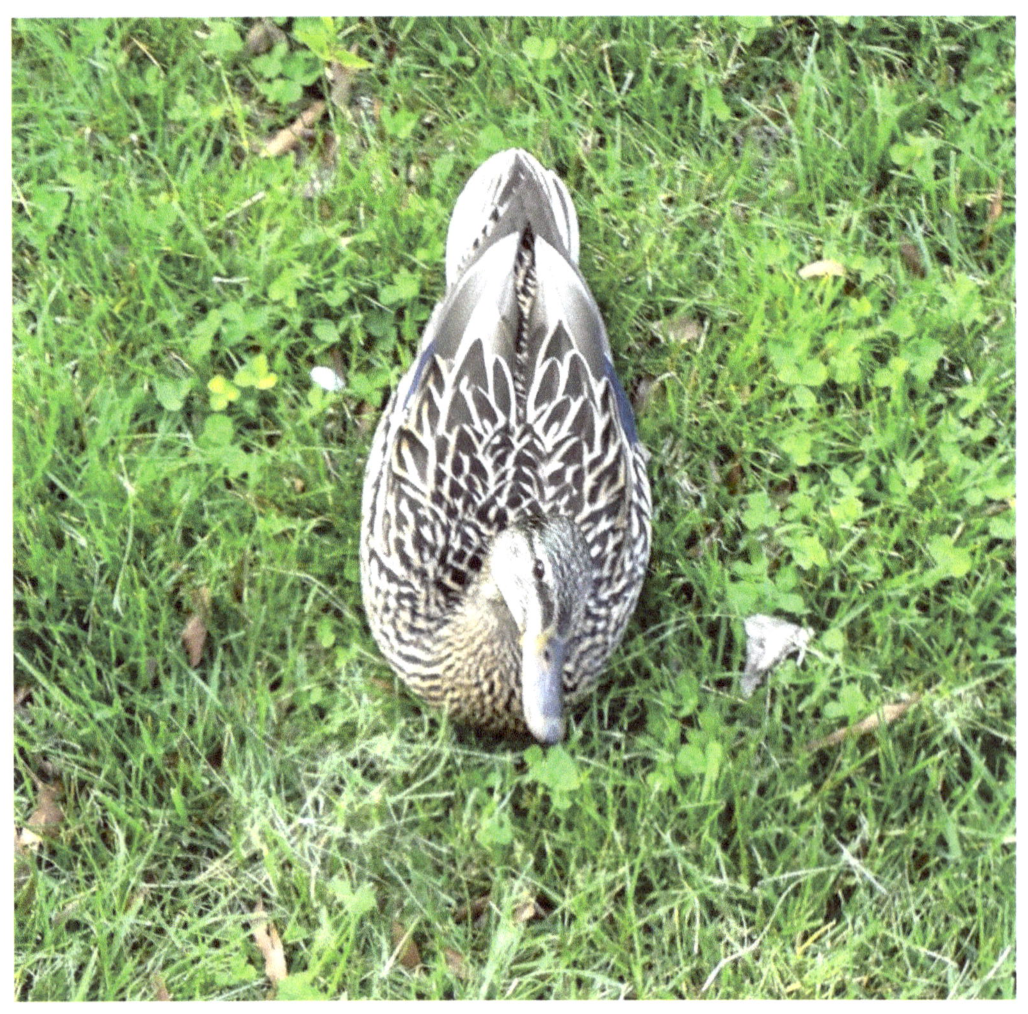

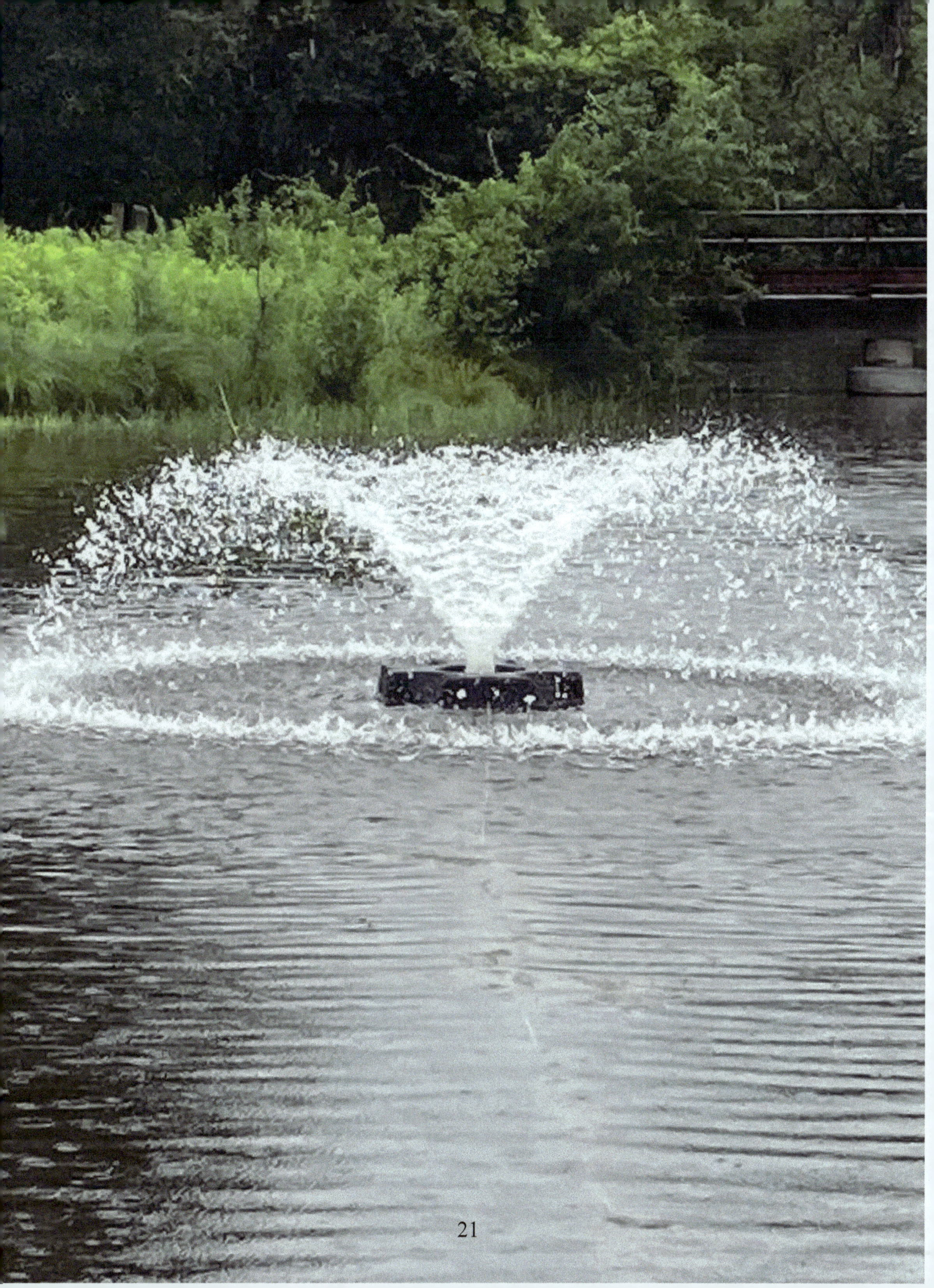

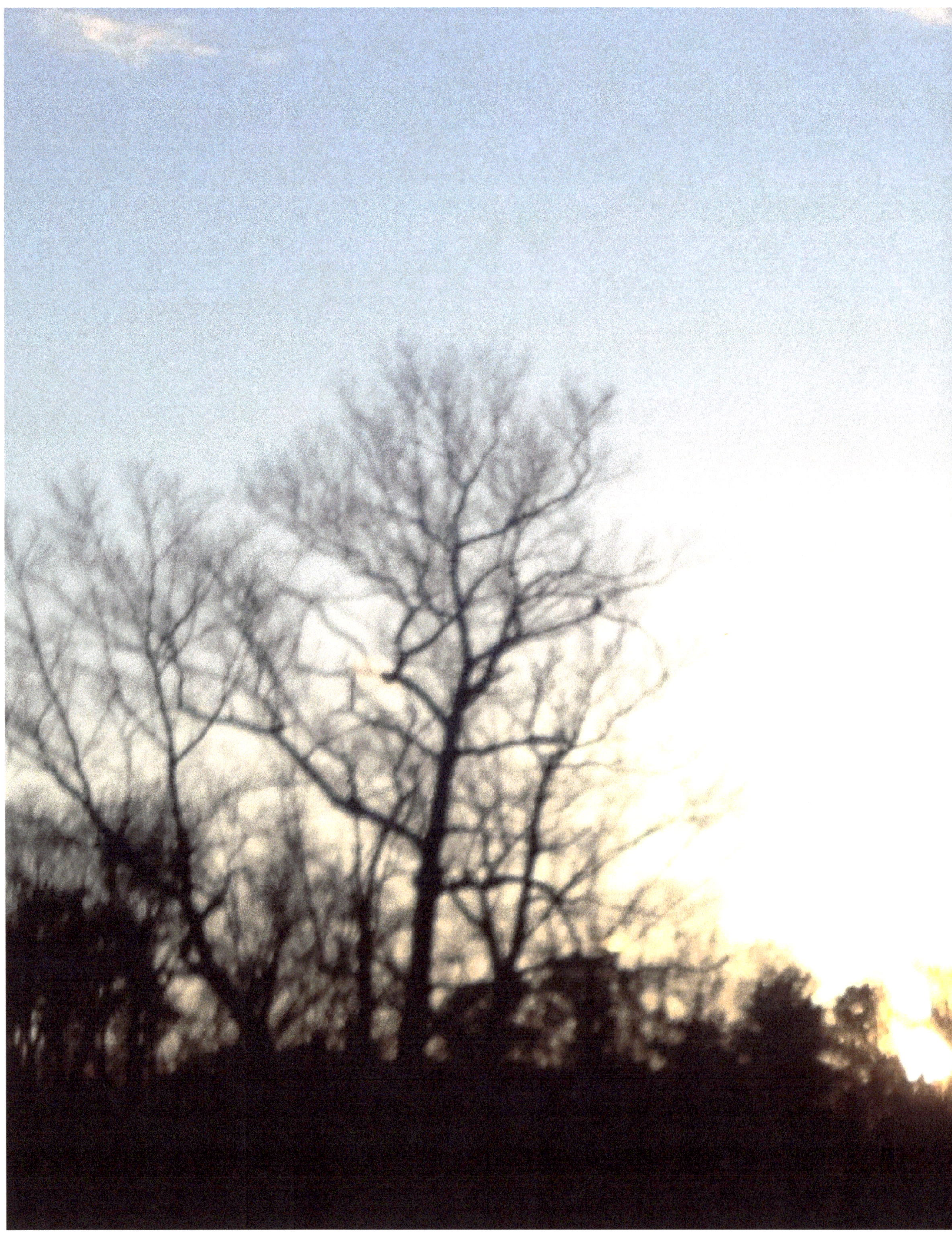

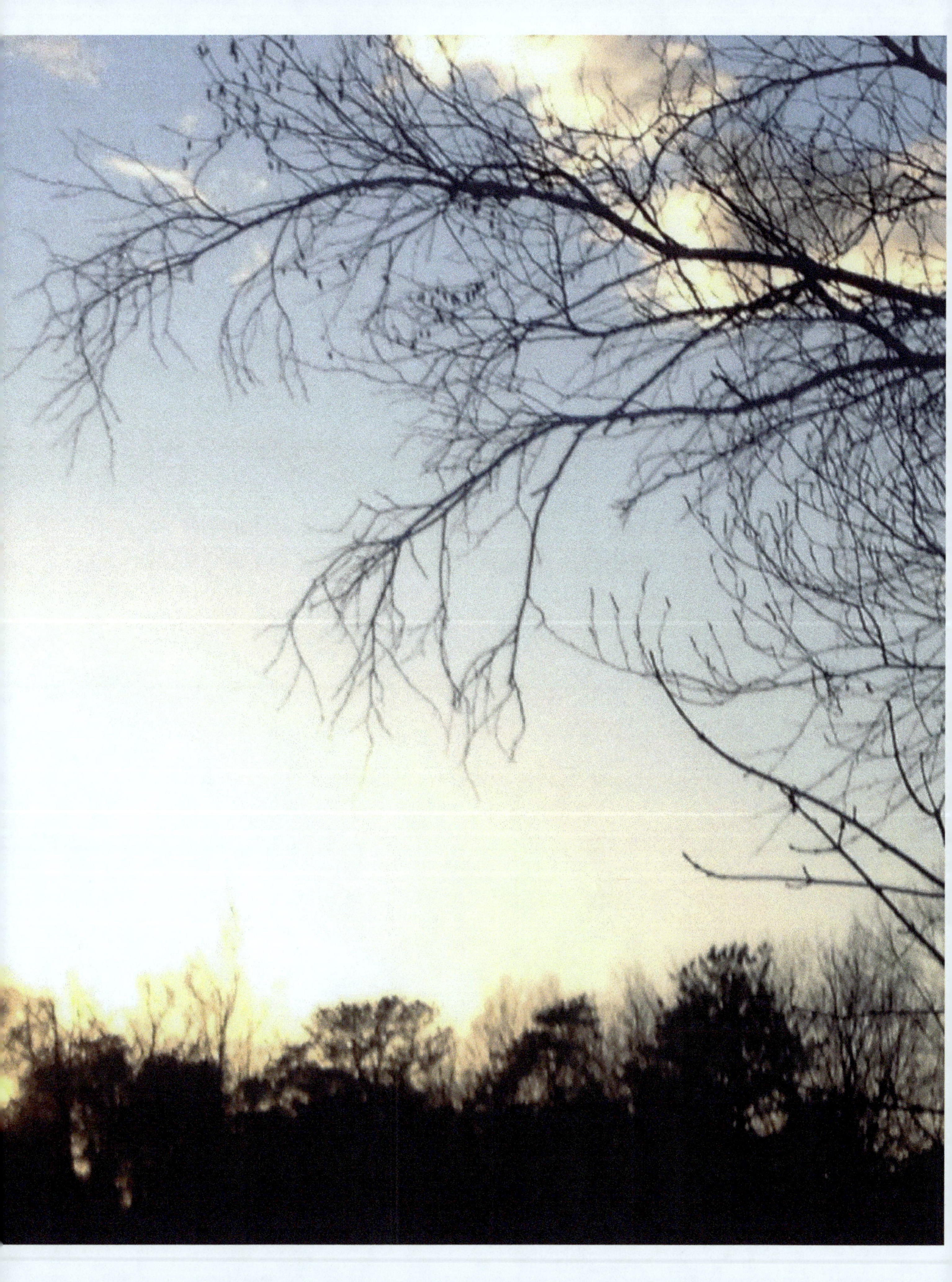

Gorgeous flowers in the sunlight shining,
Blossoms flaunting in the eye of day,
Tremulous leaves, with soft and silver lining,
Buds that open only to decay.

Henry Wadsworth Longfellow

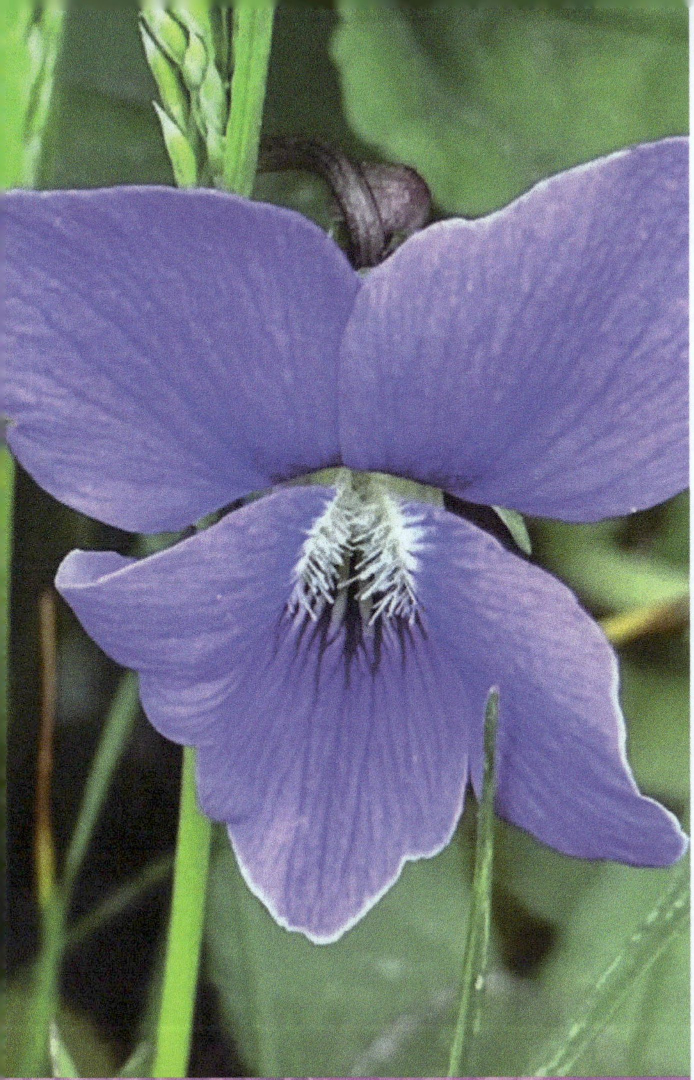

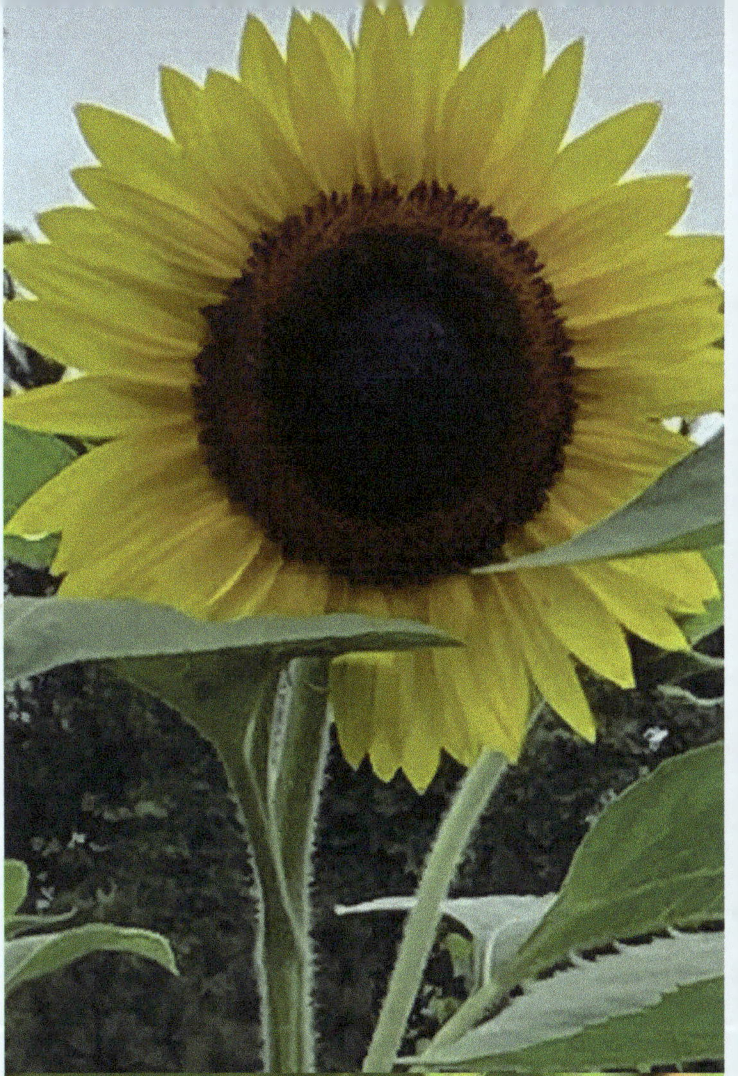

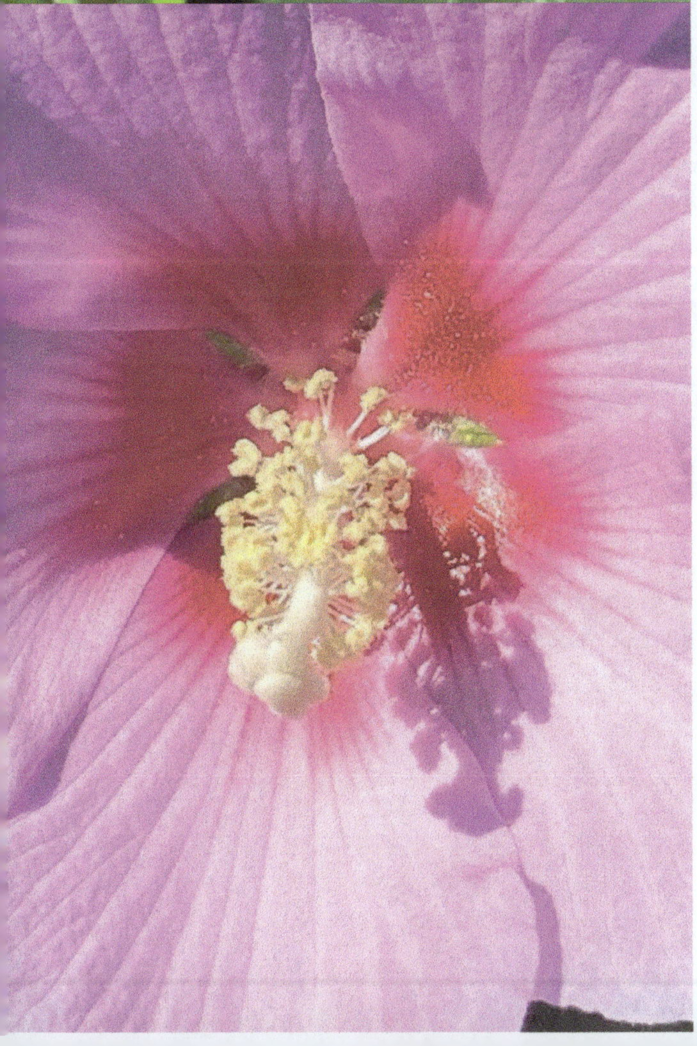

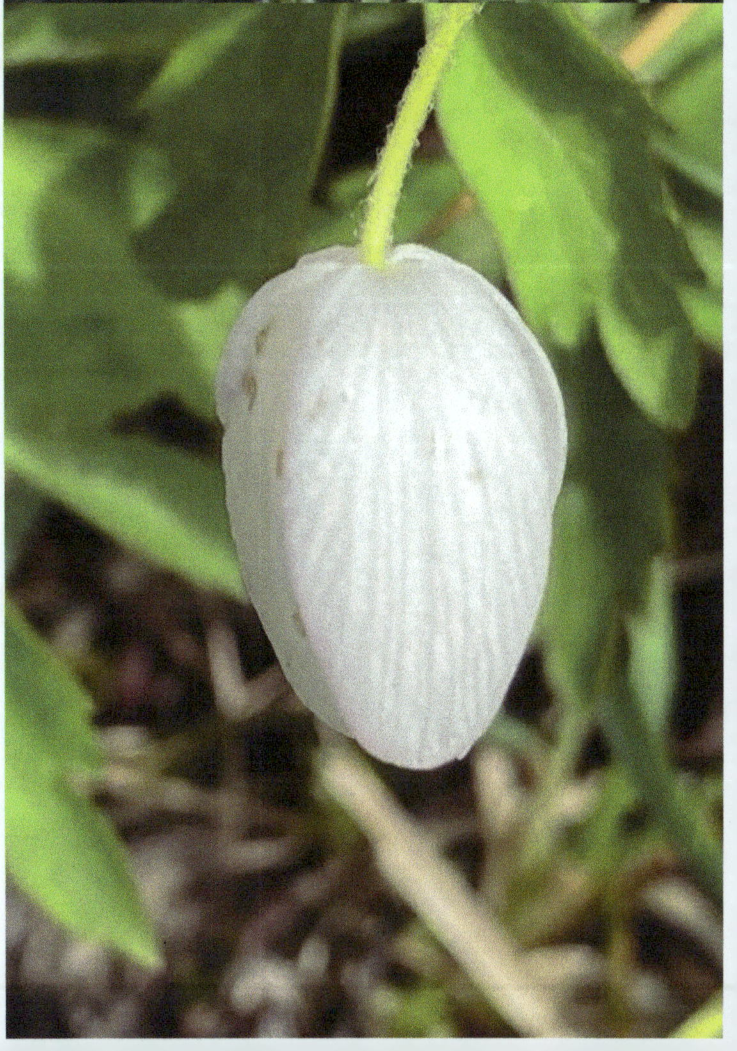

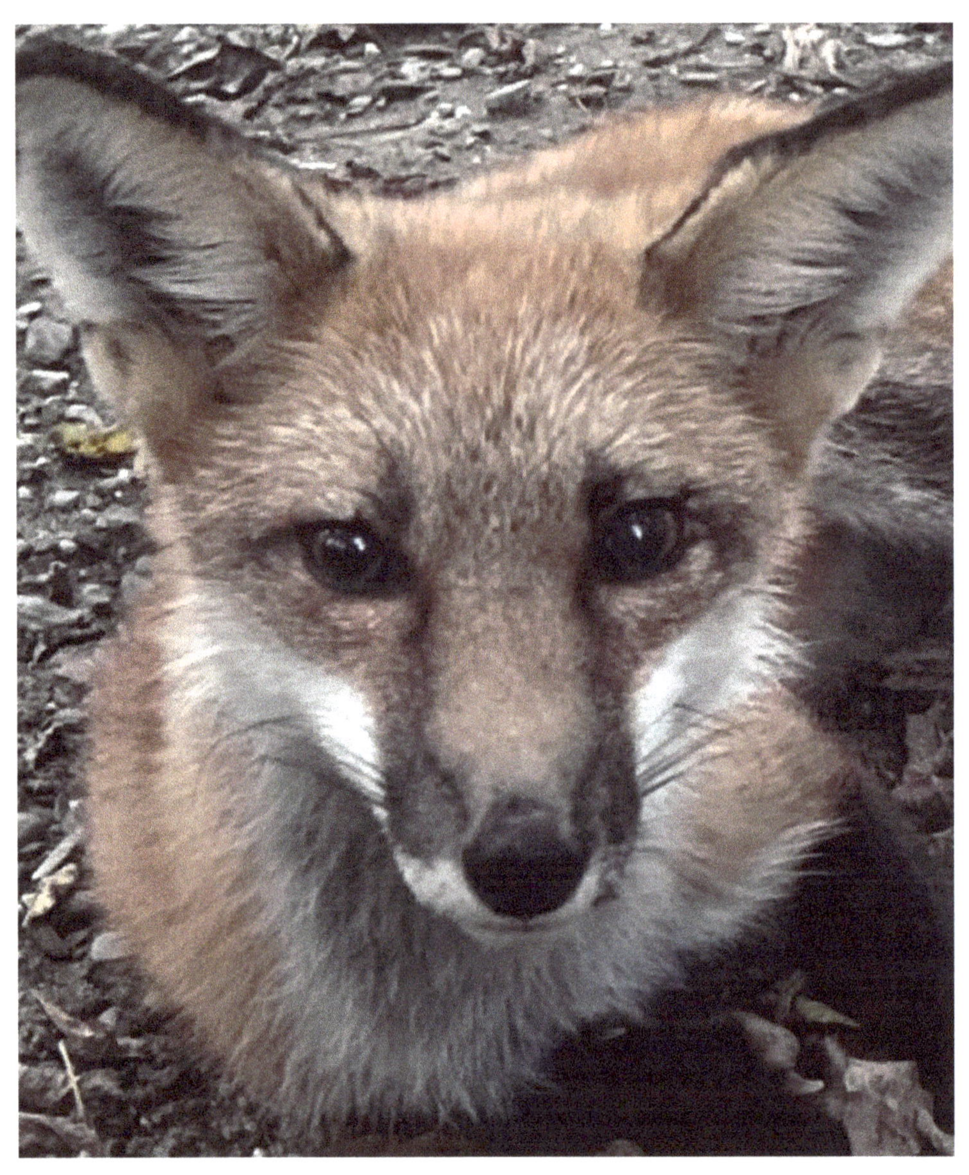

Colonel William F. Fox Memorial Saratoga Tree Nursery

Nature is life . . .
No beginning, no end.

Nature is strong within us.
It confronts you . . .

Nature gets you out of
Your head and into your body.

Jakusho Kwong

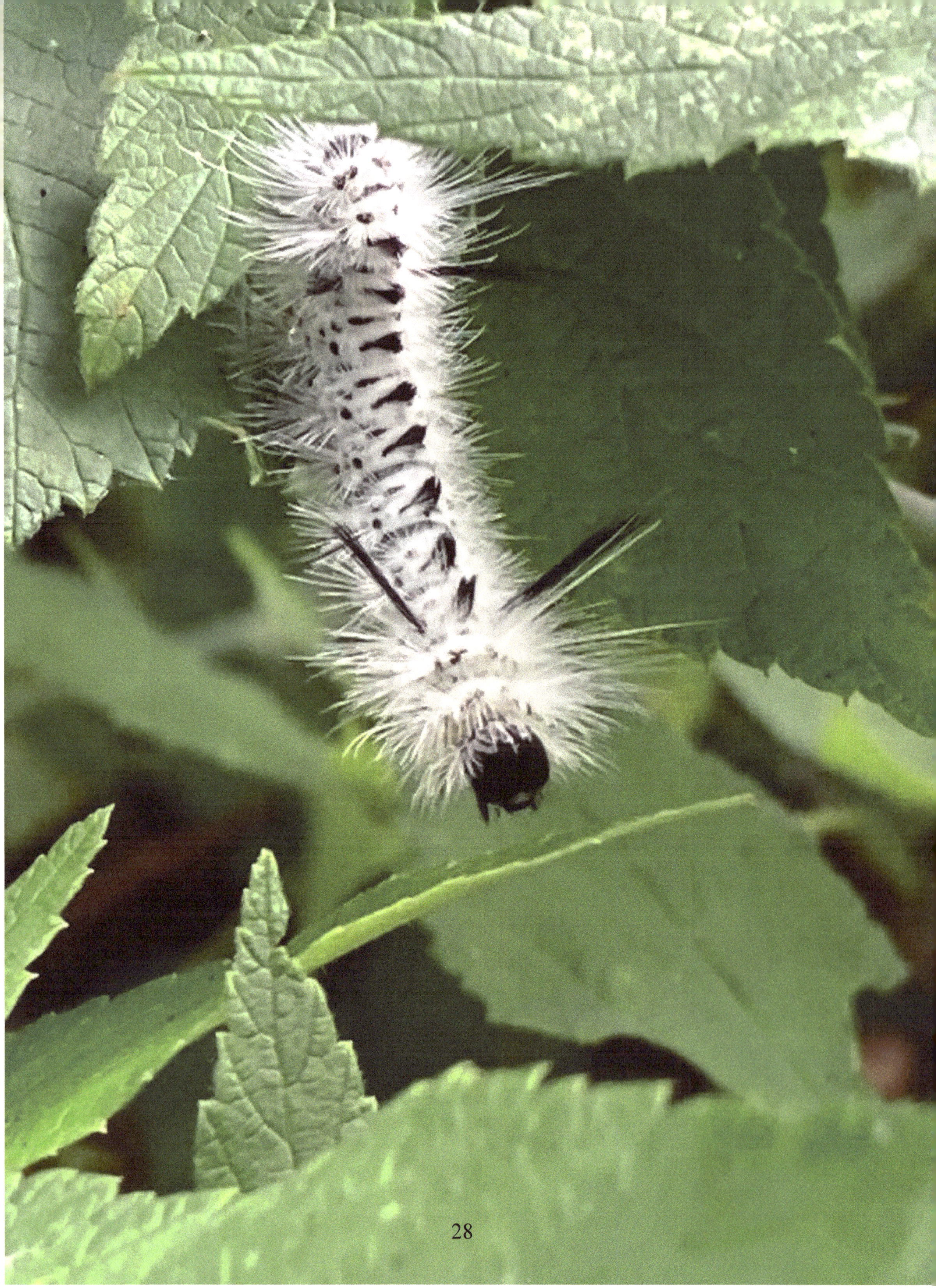

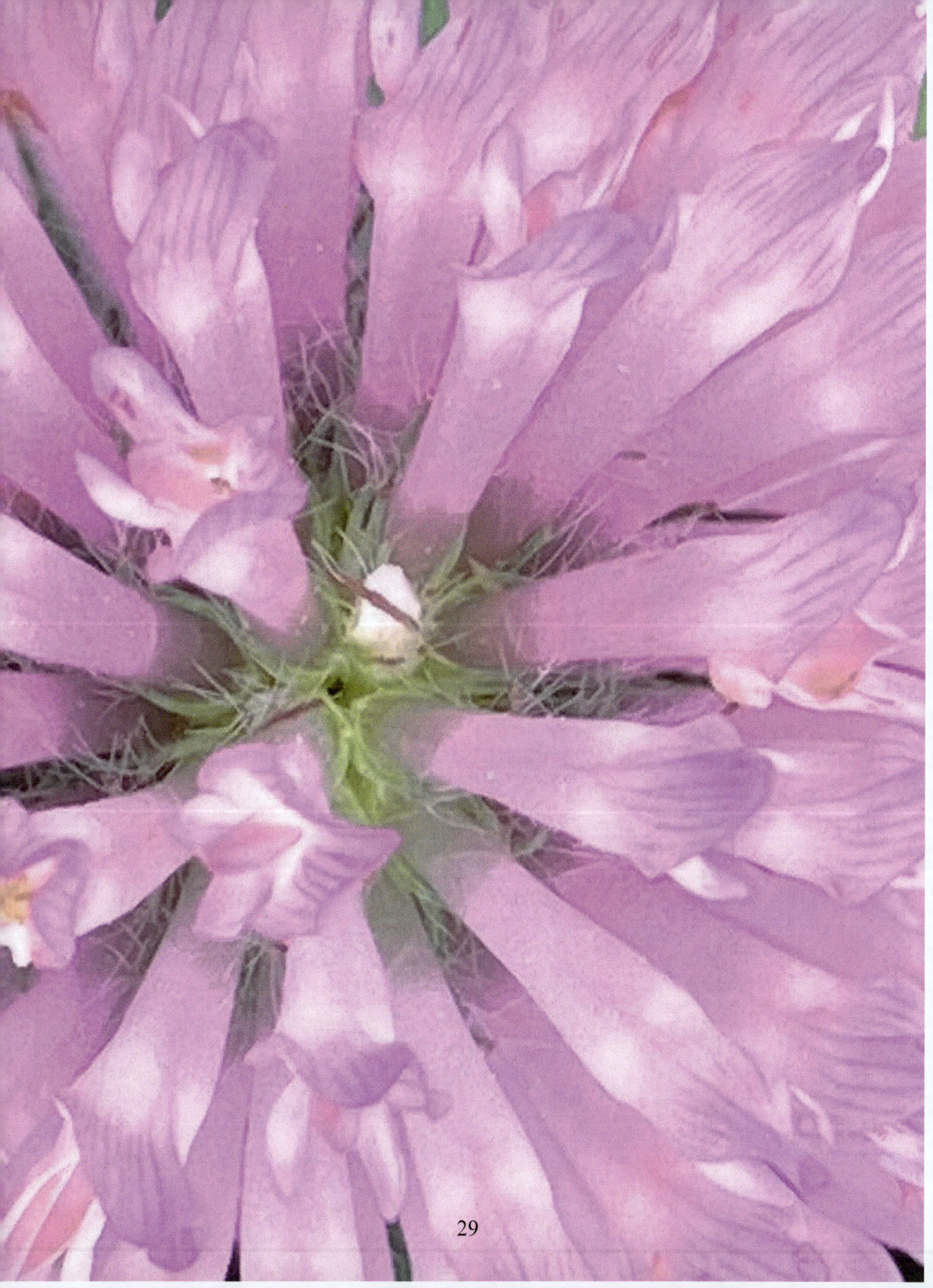

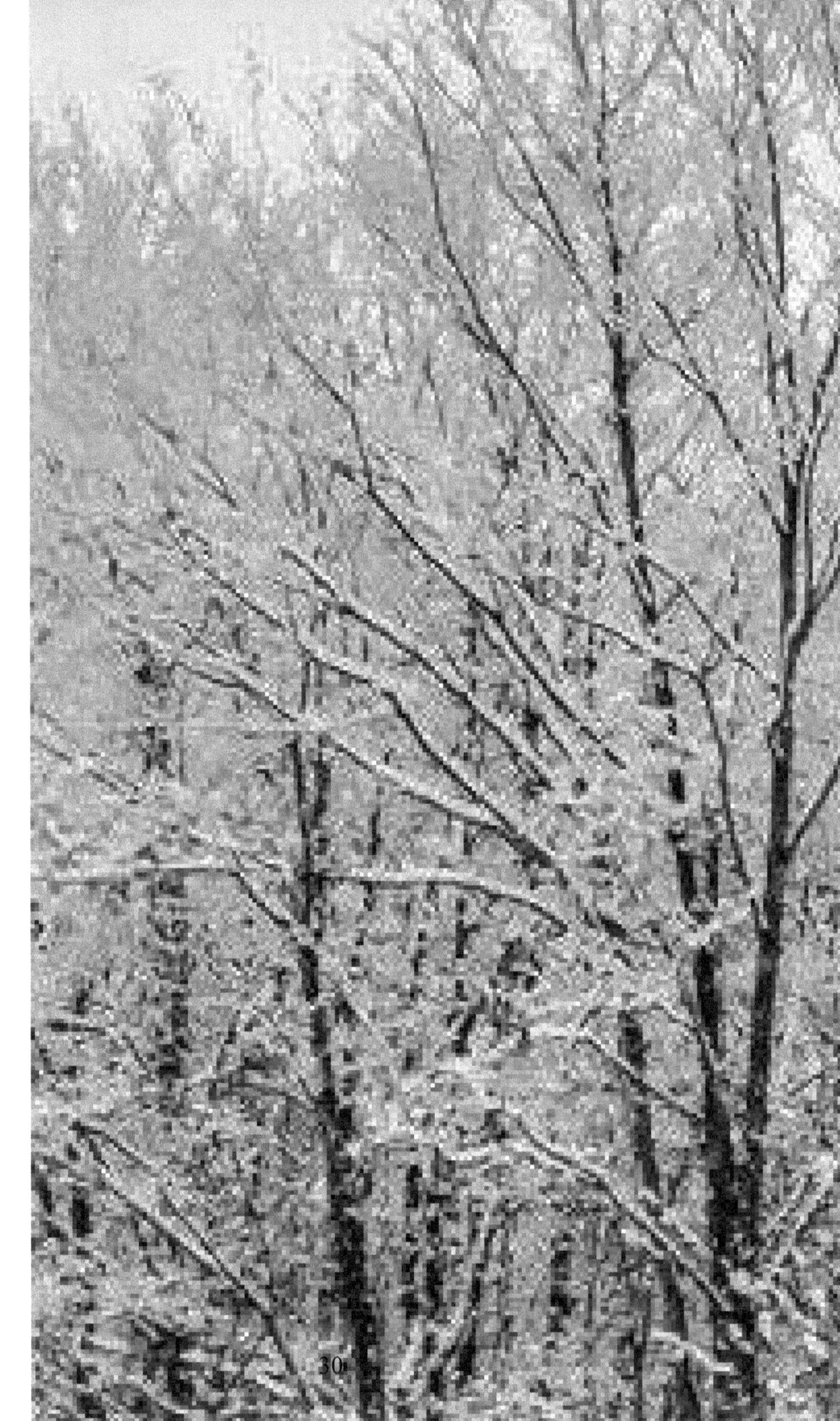

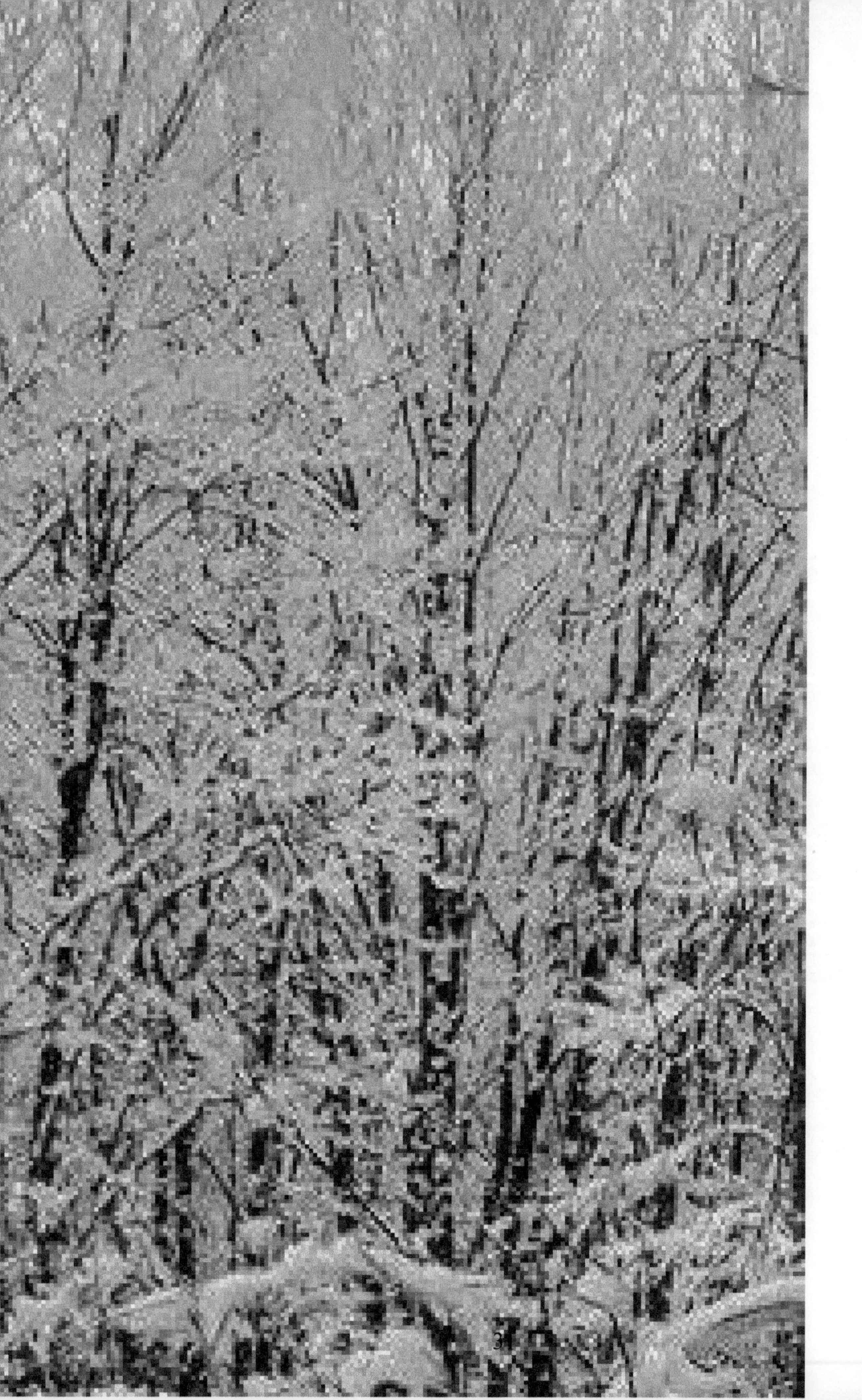

"Look deep into Nature, and then you will understand everything better. "

Albert Einstein

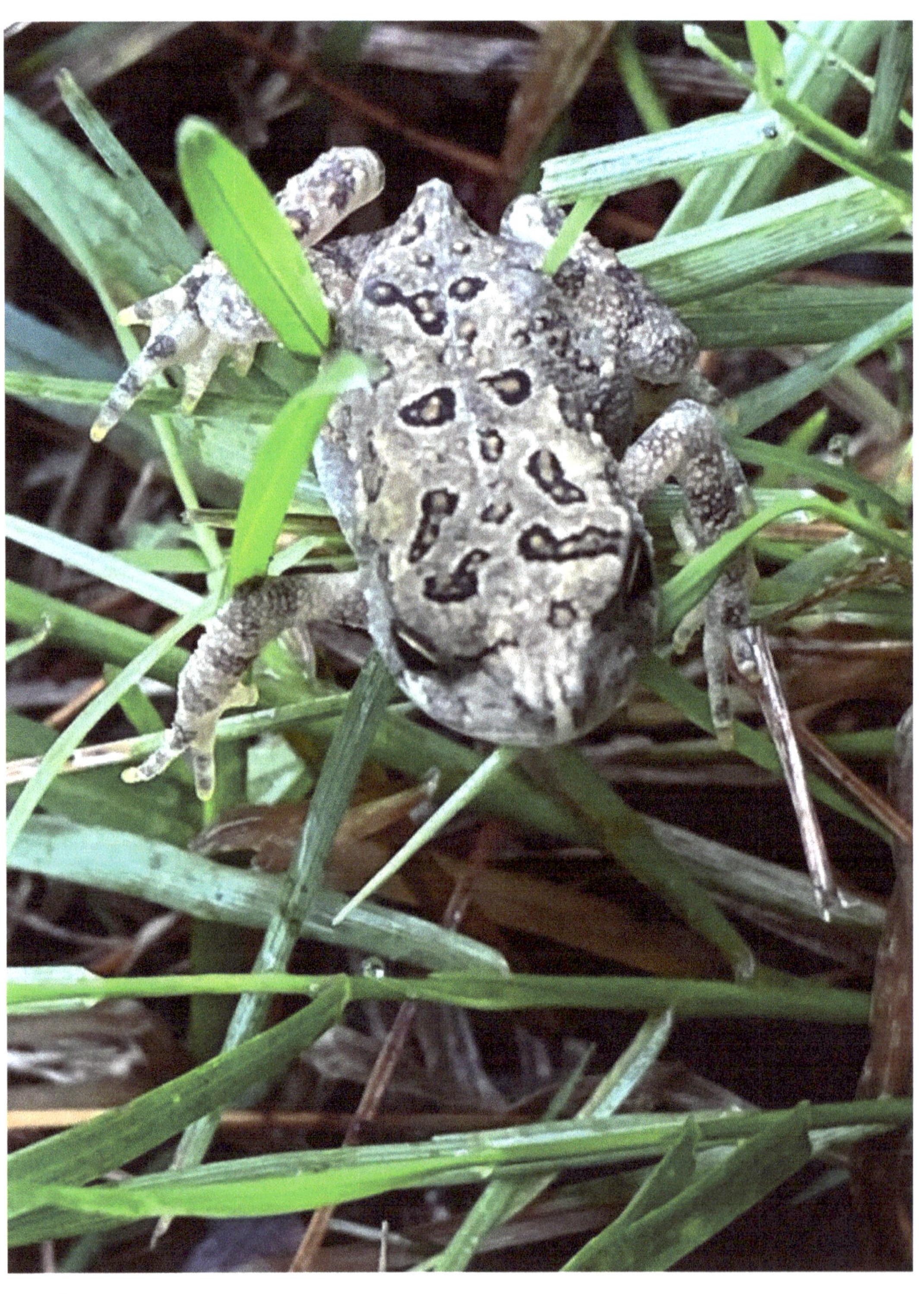

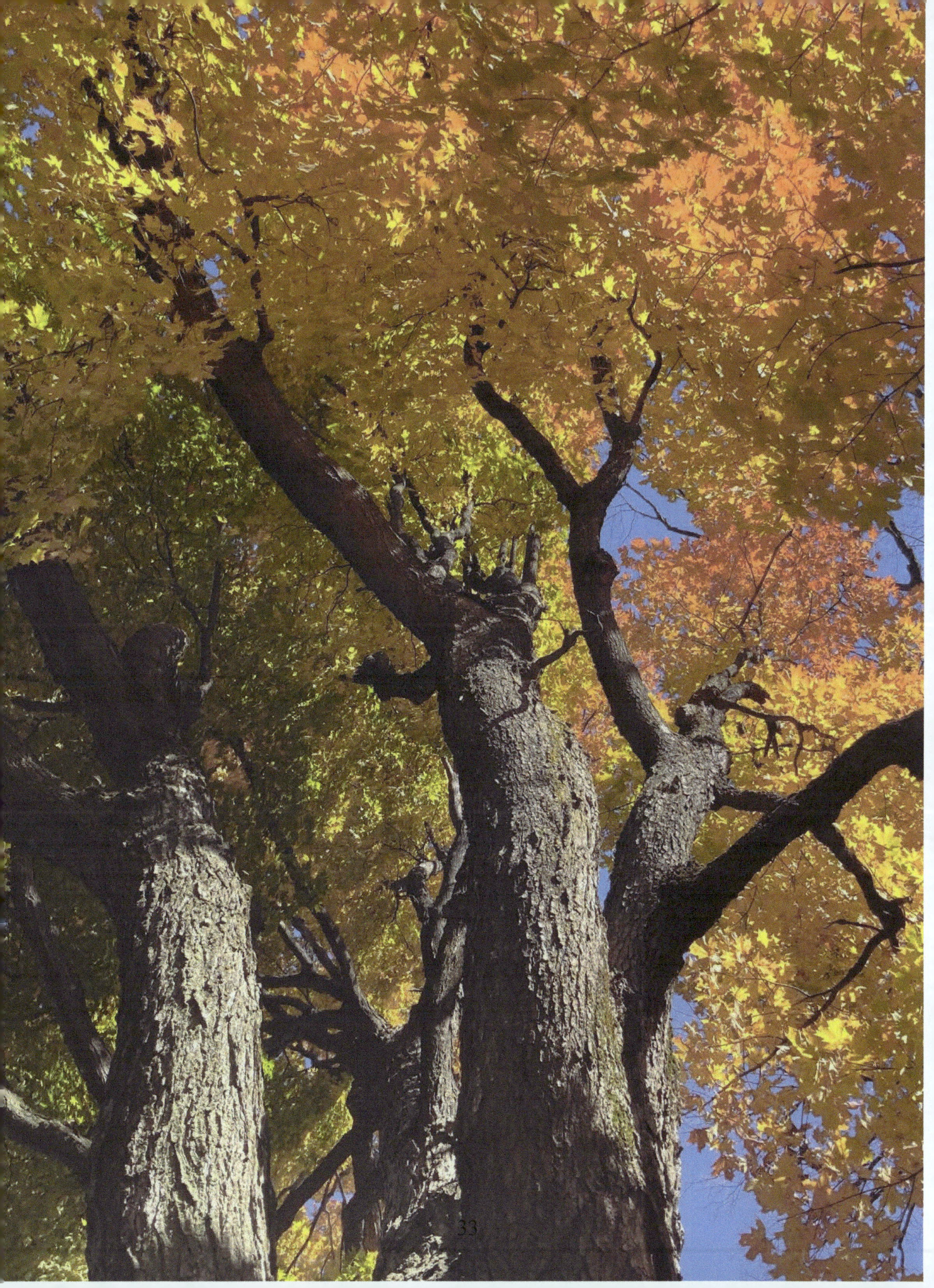

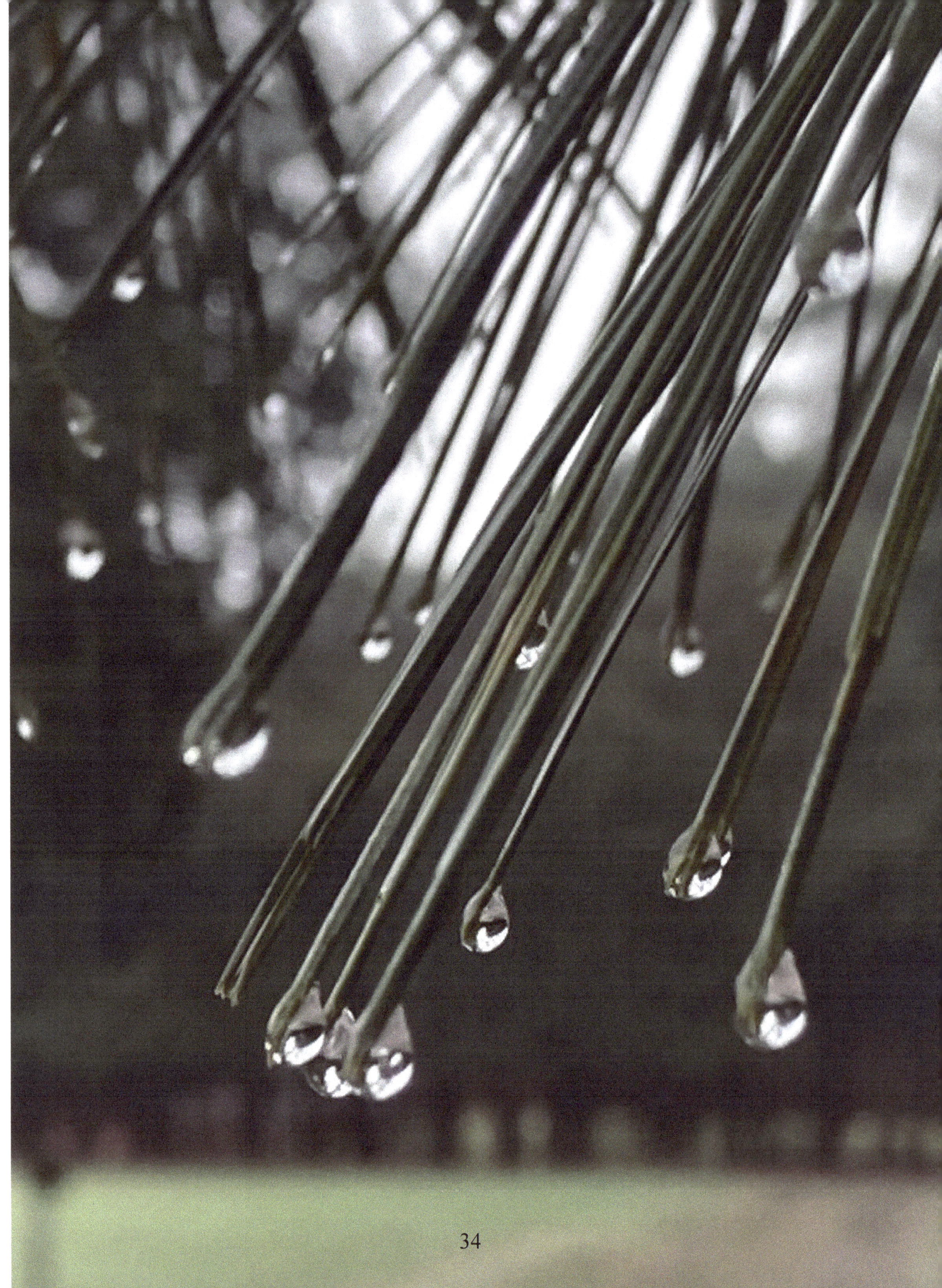

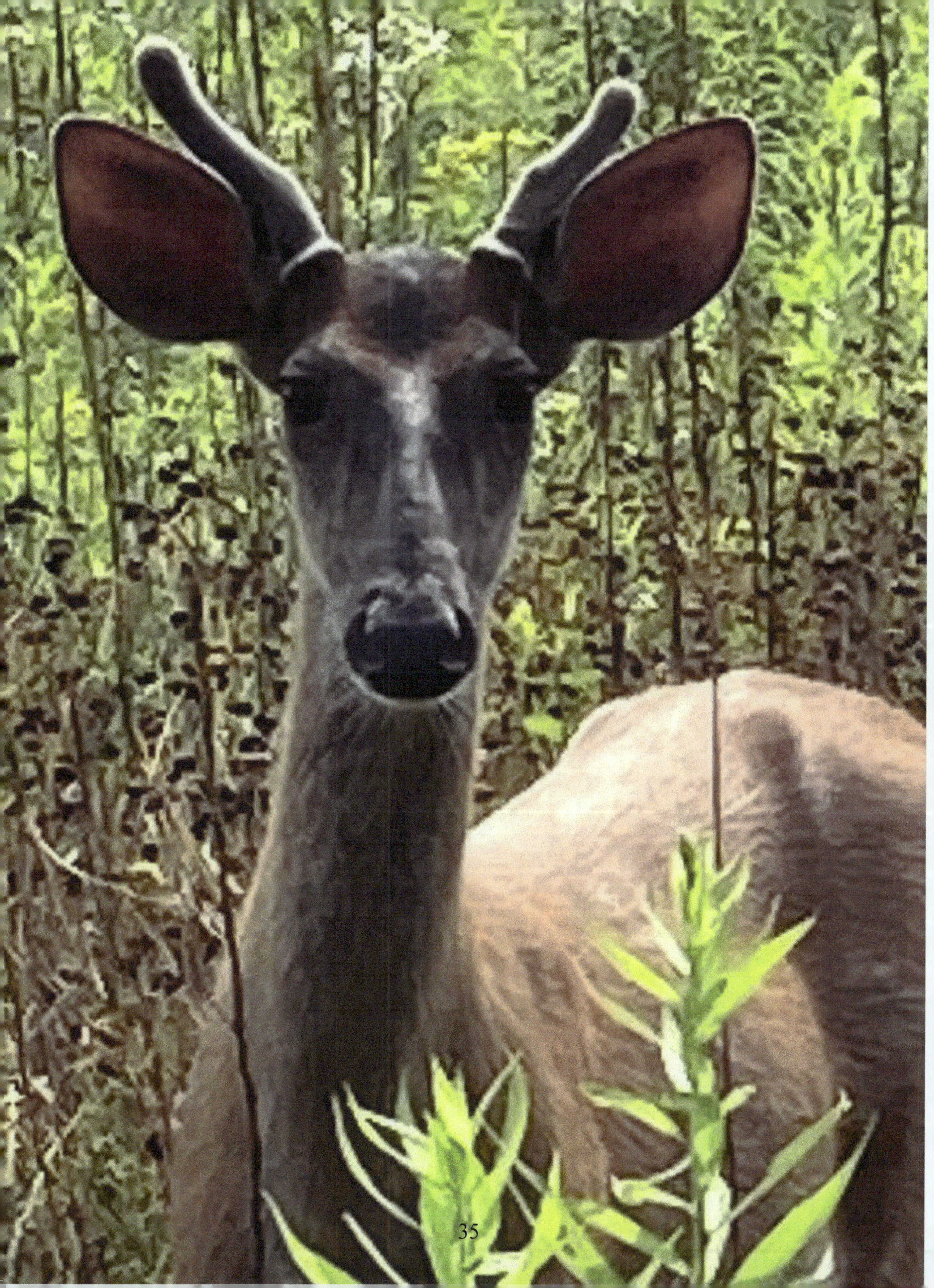

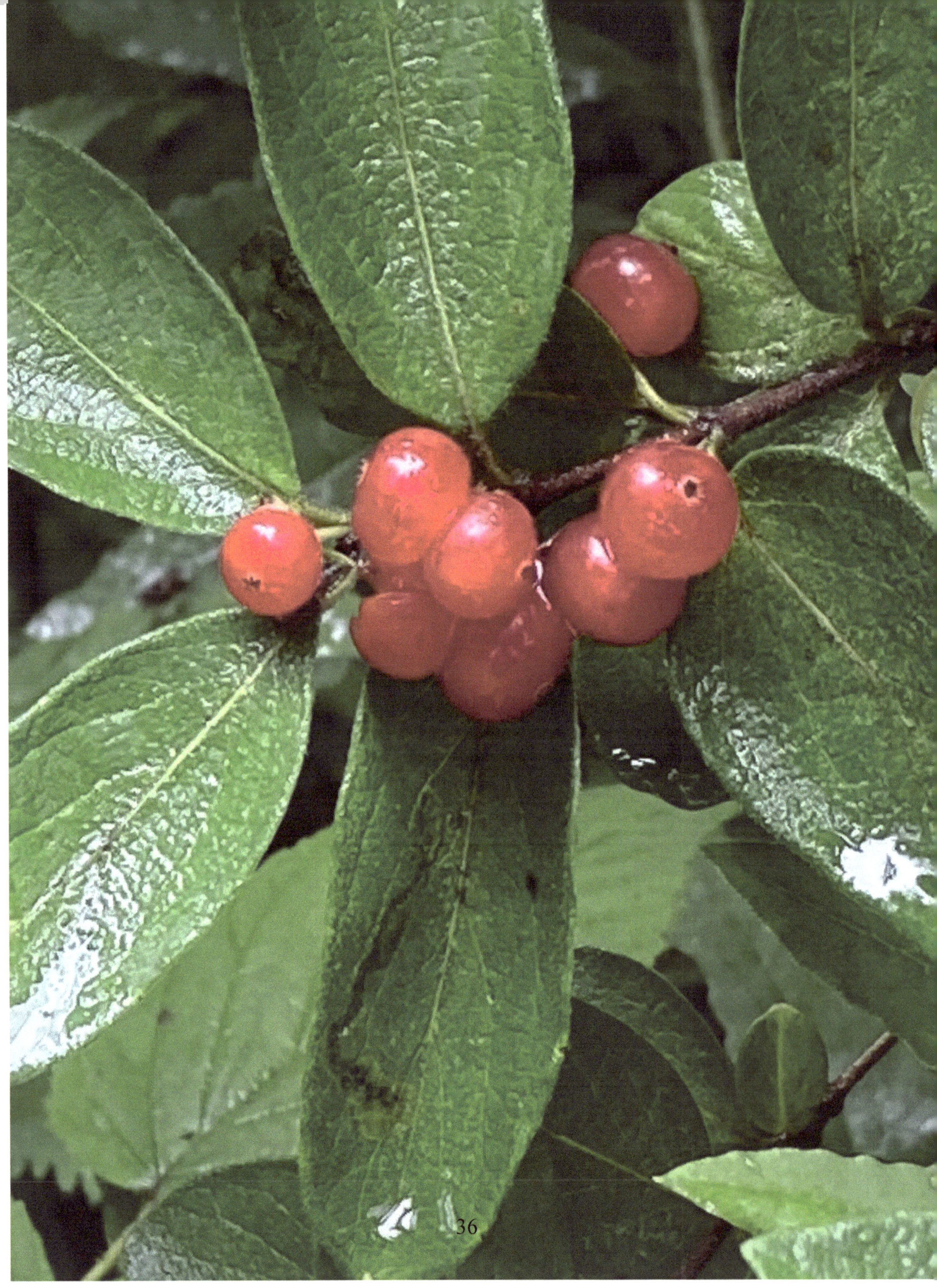

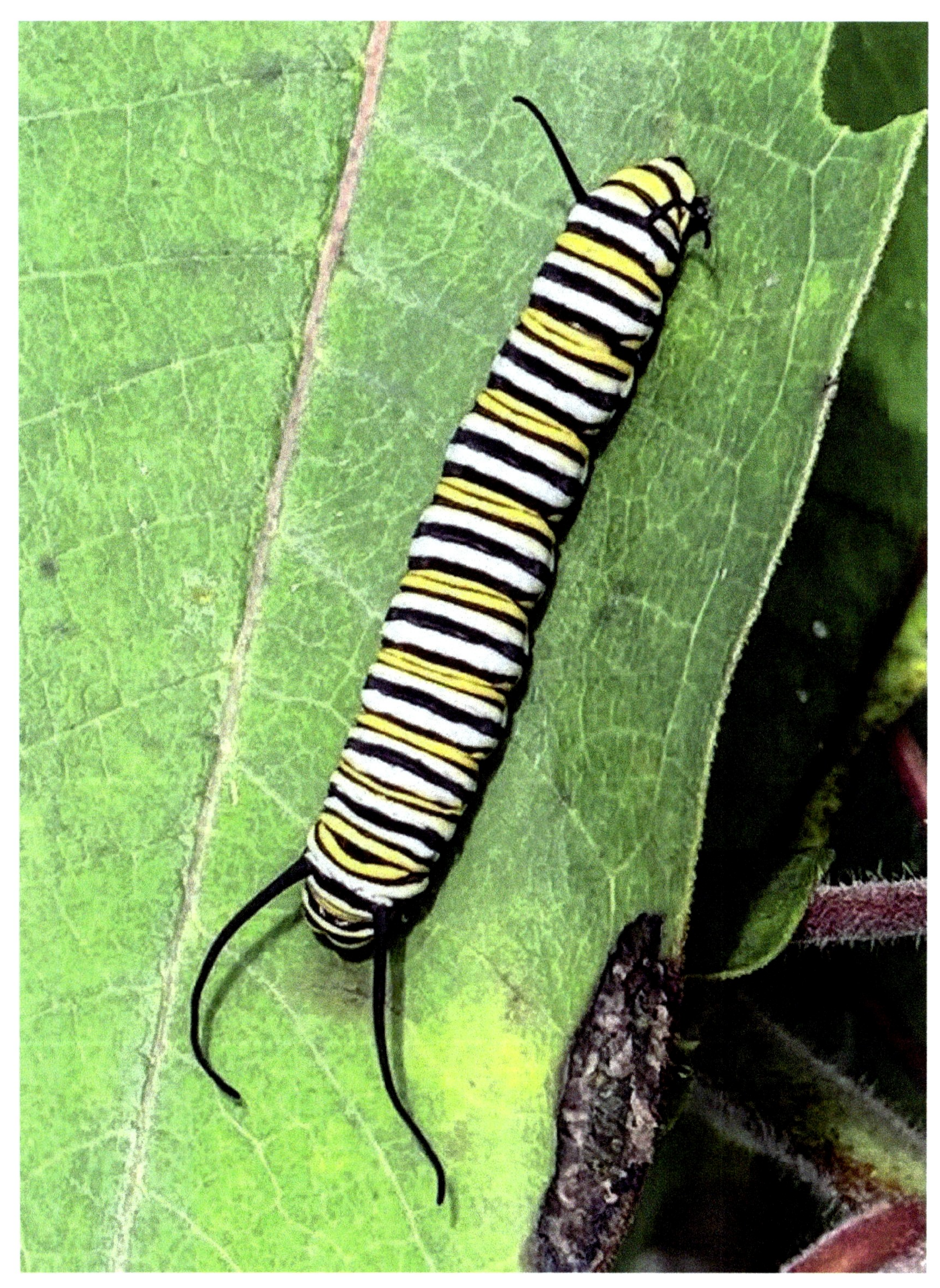

"Nature does not hurry yet everything is accomplished."

Lau Tzu

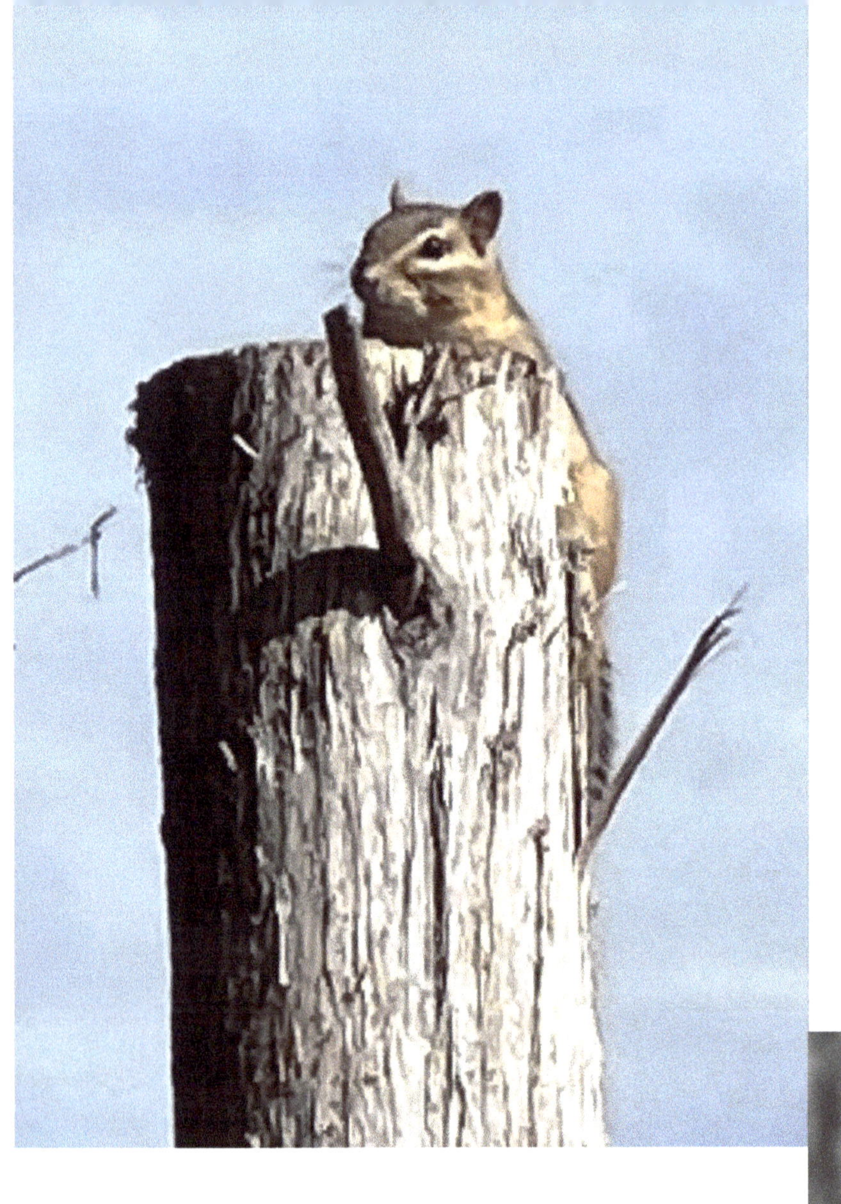

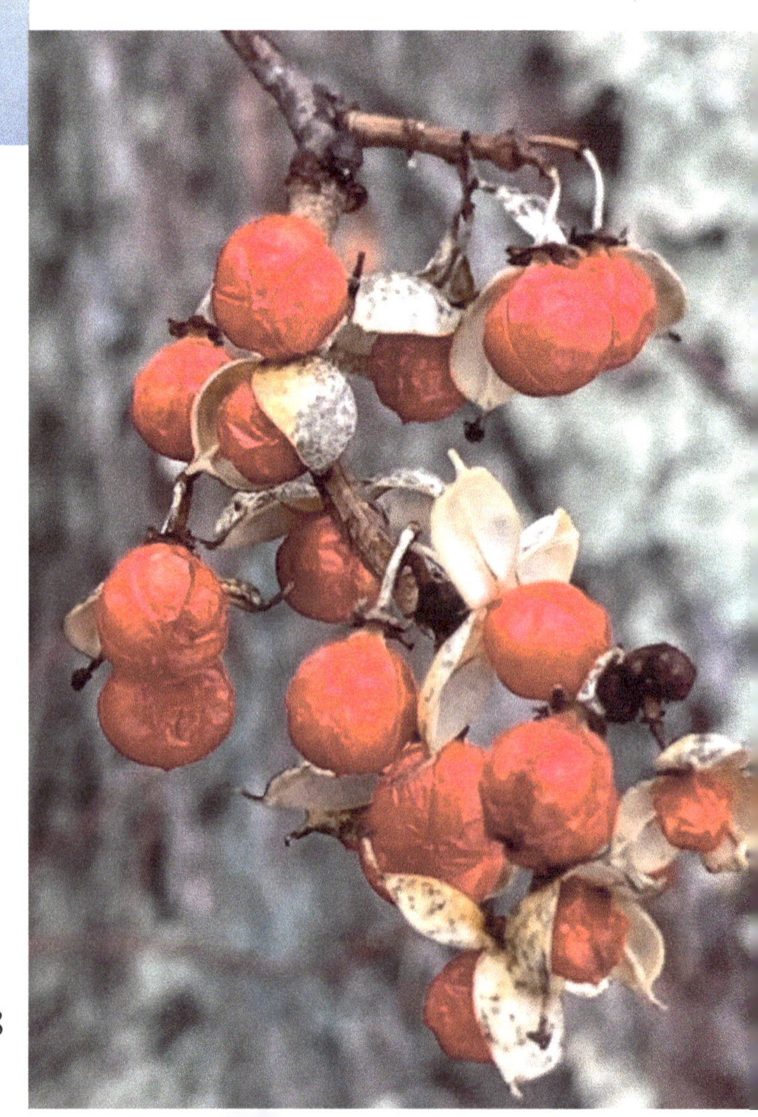

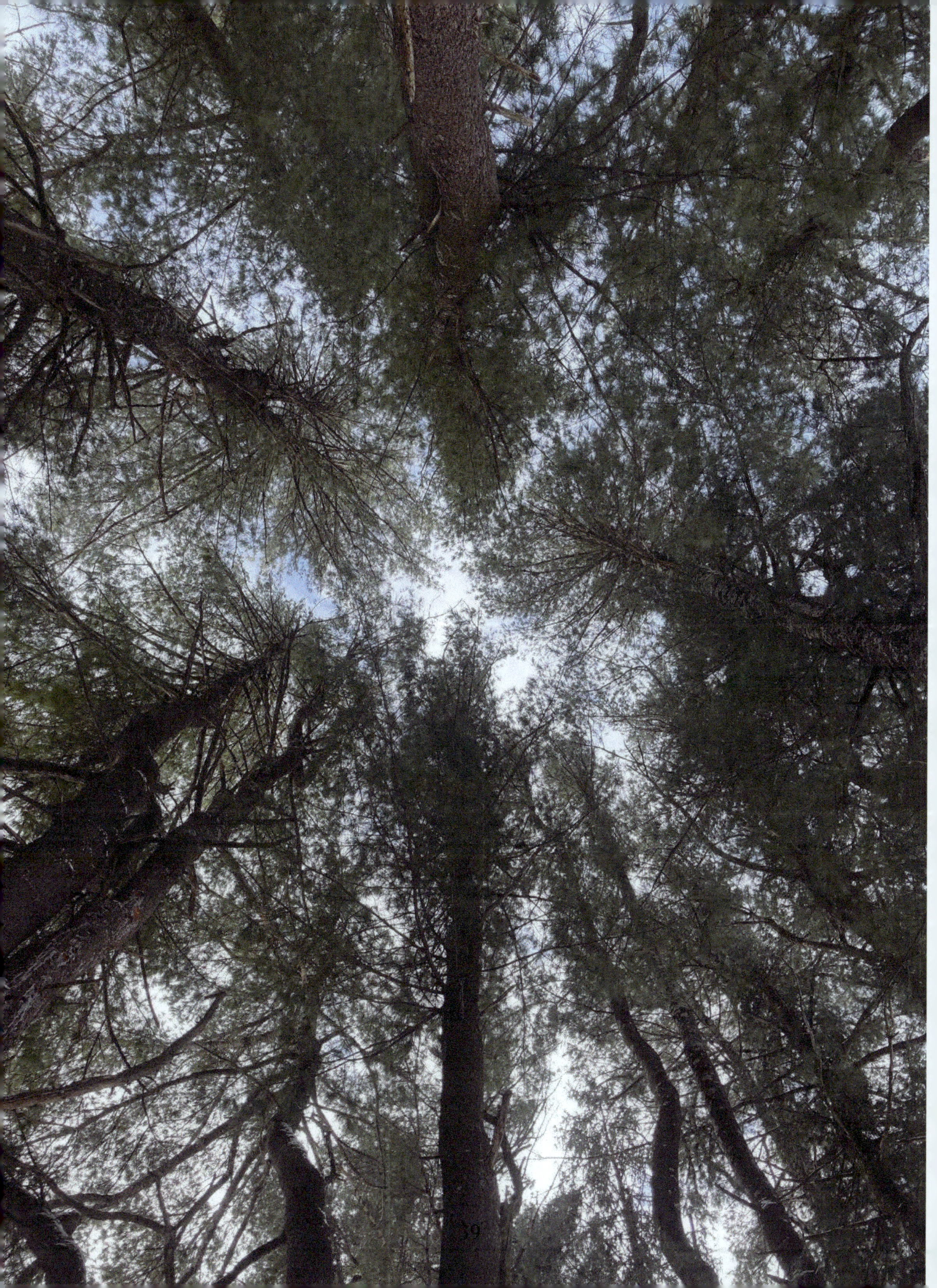

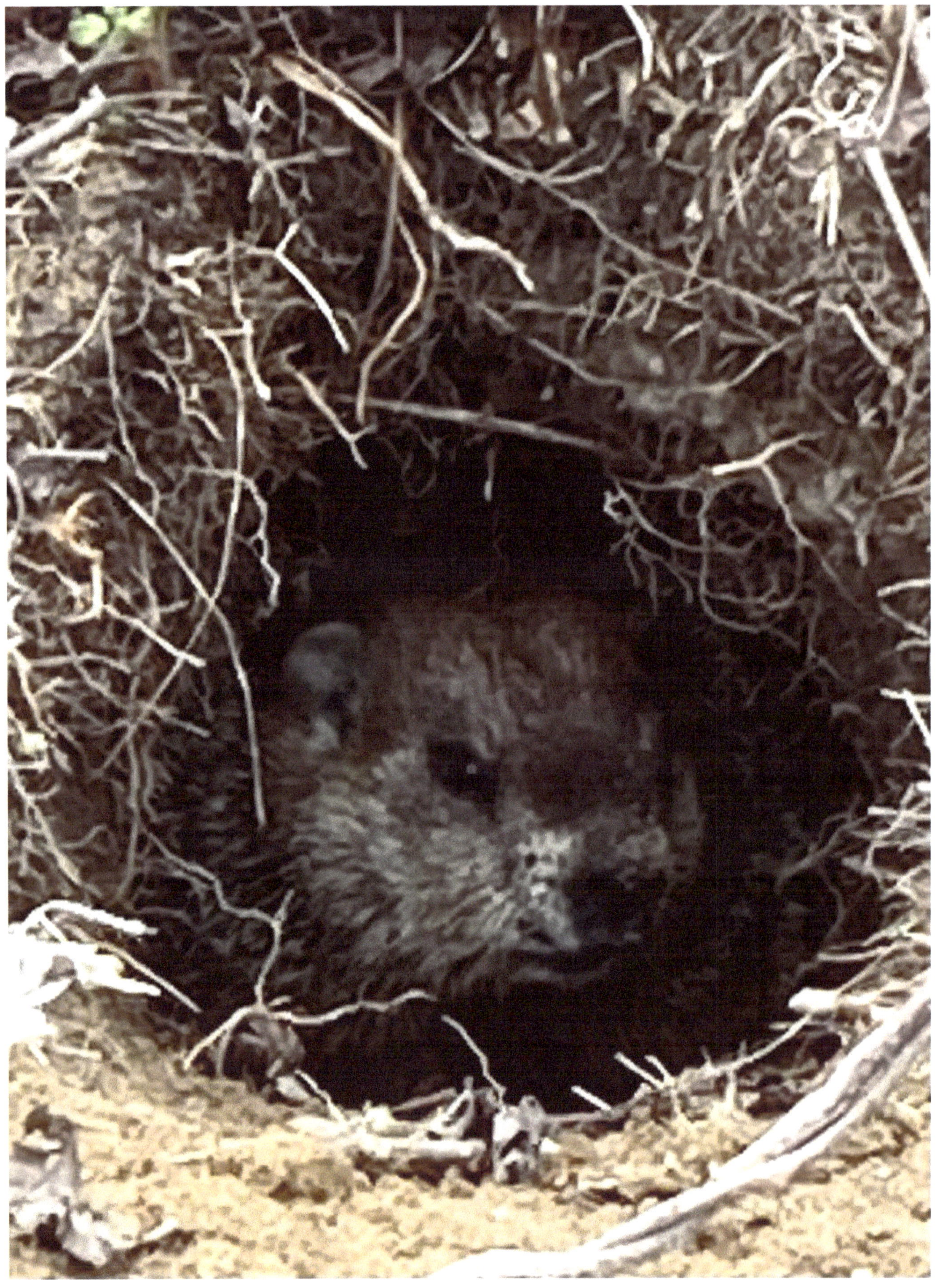

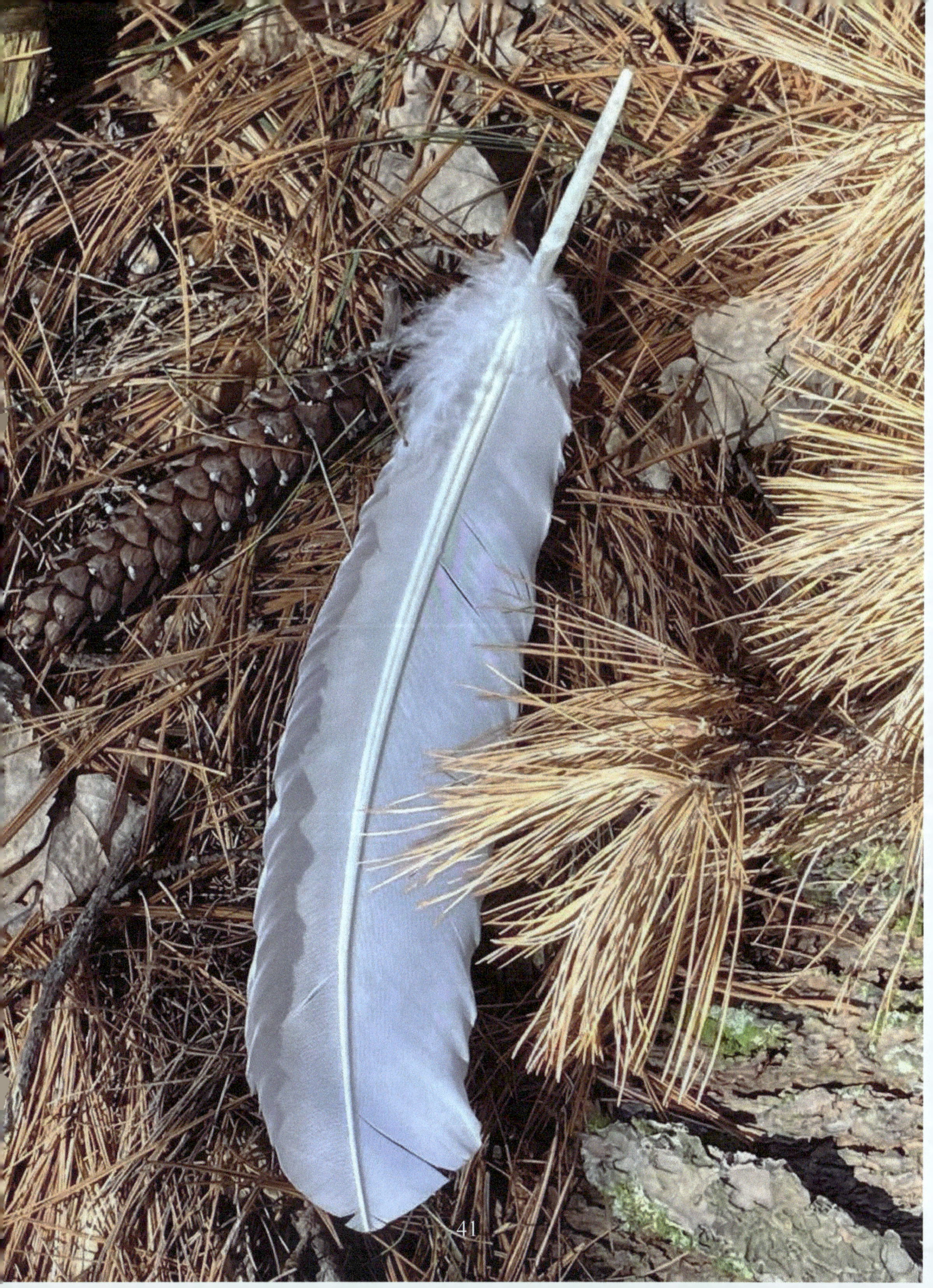

"Look at a tree, a flower, a plant. Let your awareness rest upon it.
How still they are, how deeply rooted in Being. Allow Nature
to teach you stillness."

Eckart Tolle

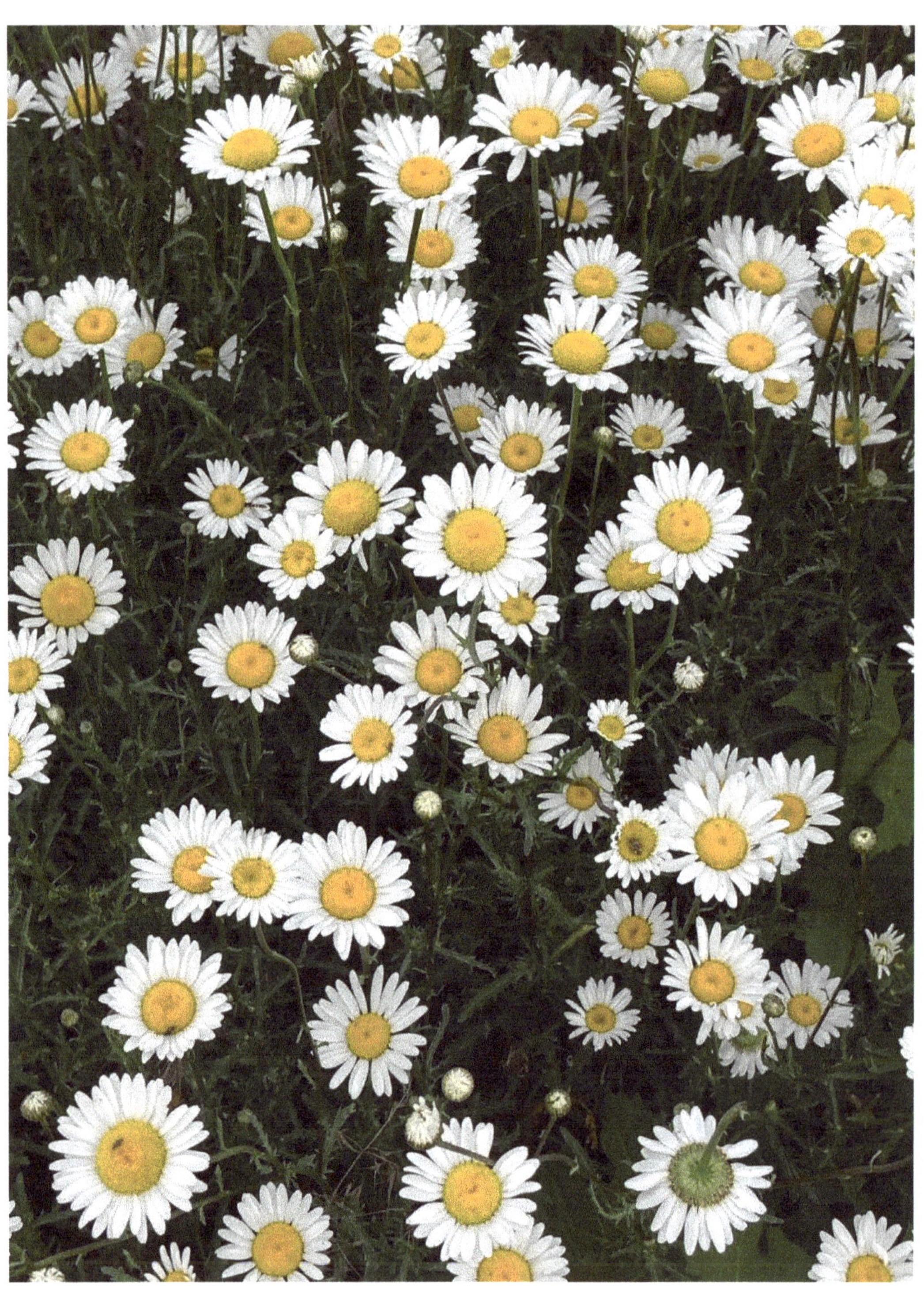

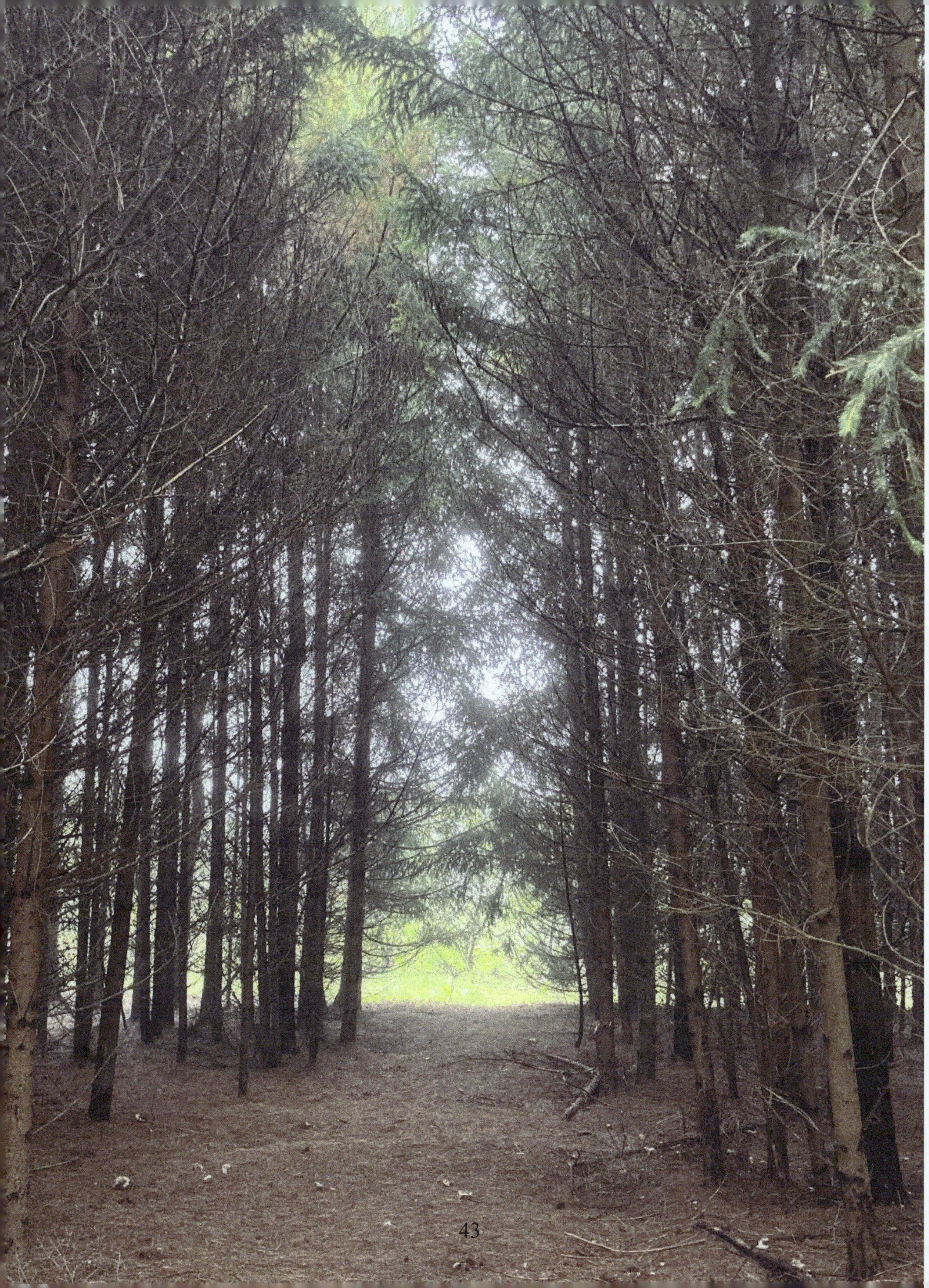

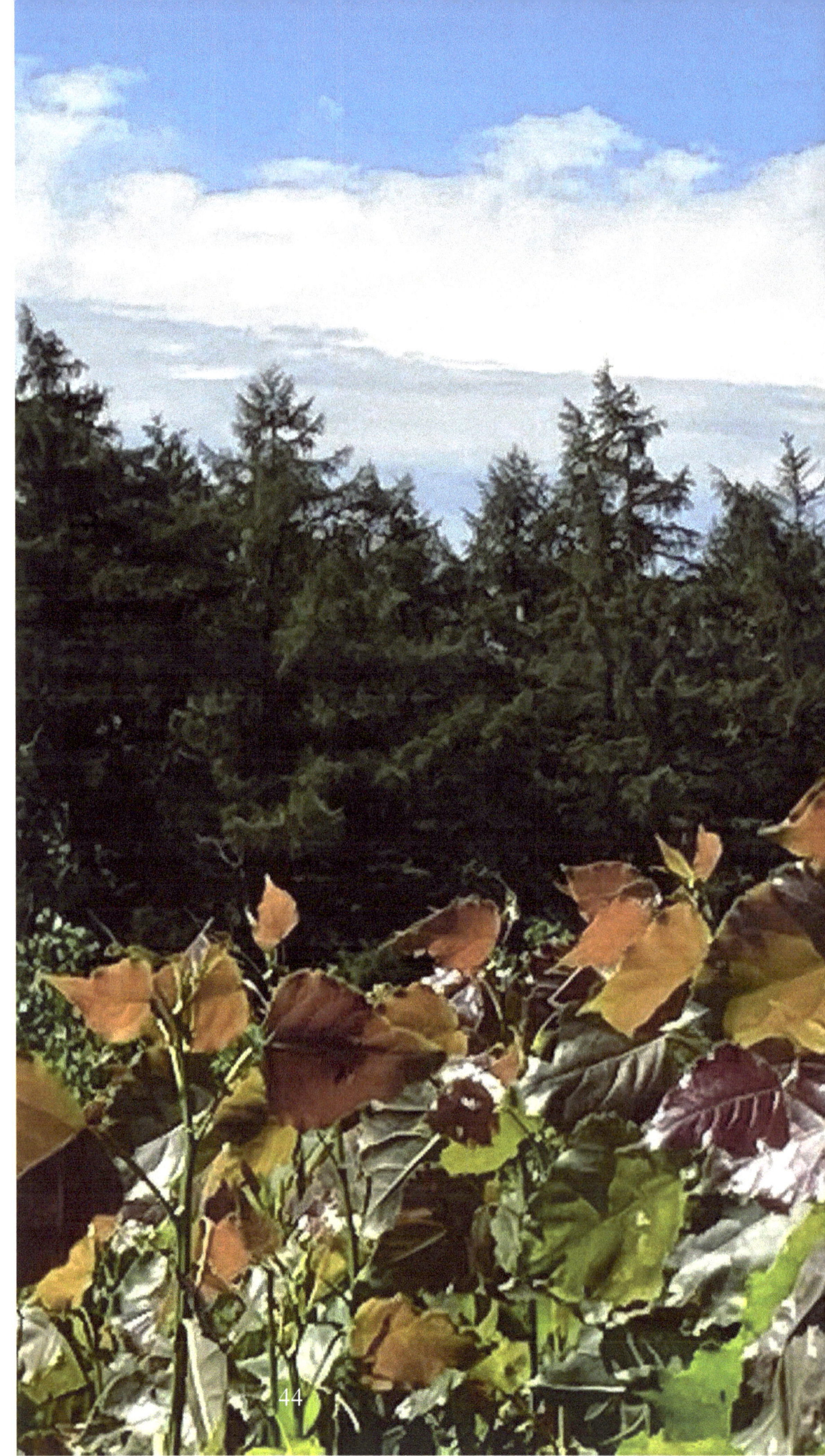

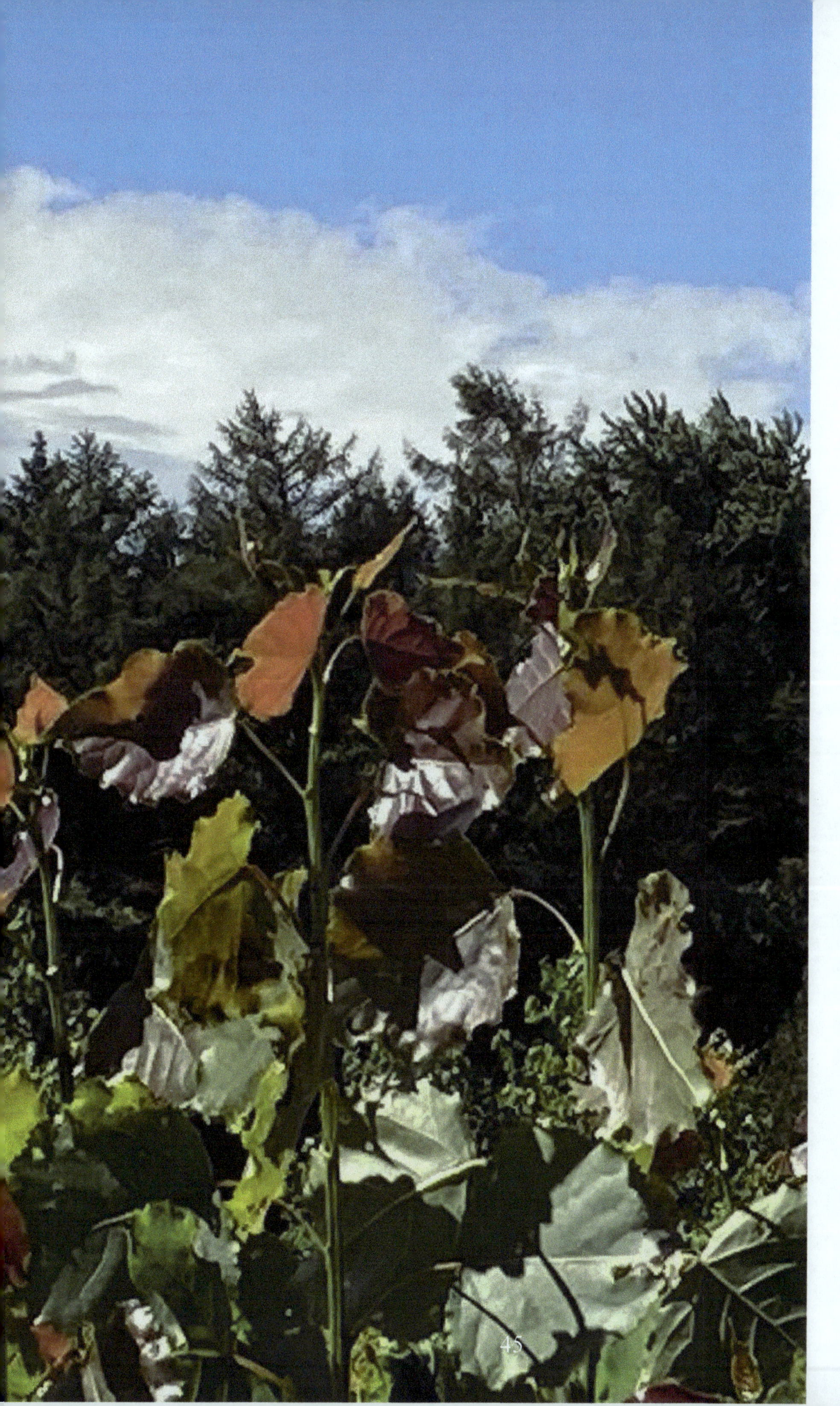

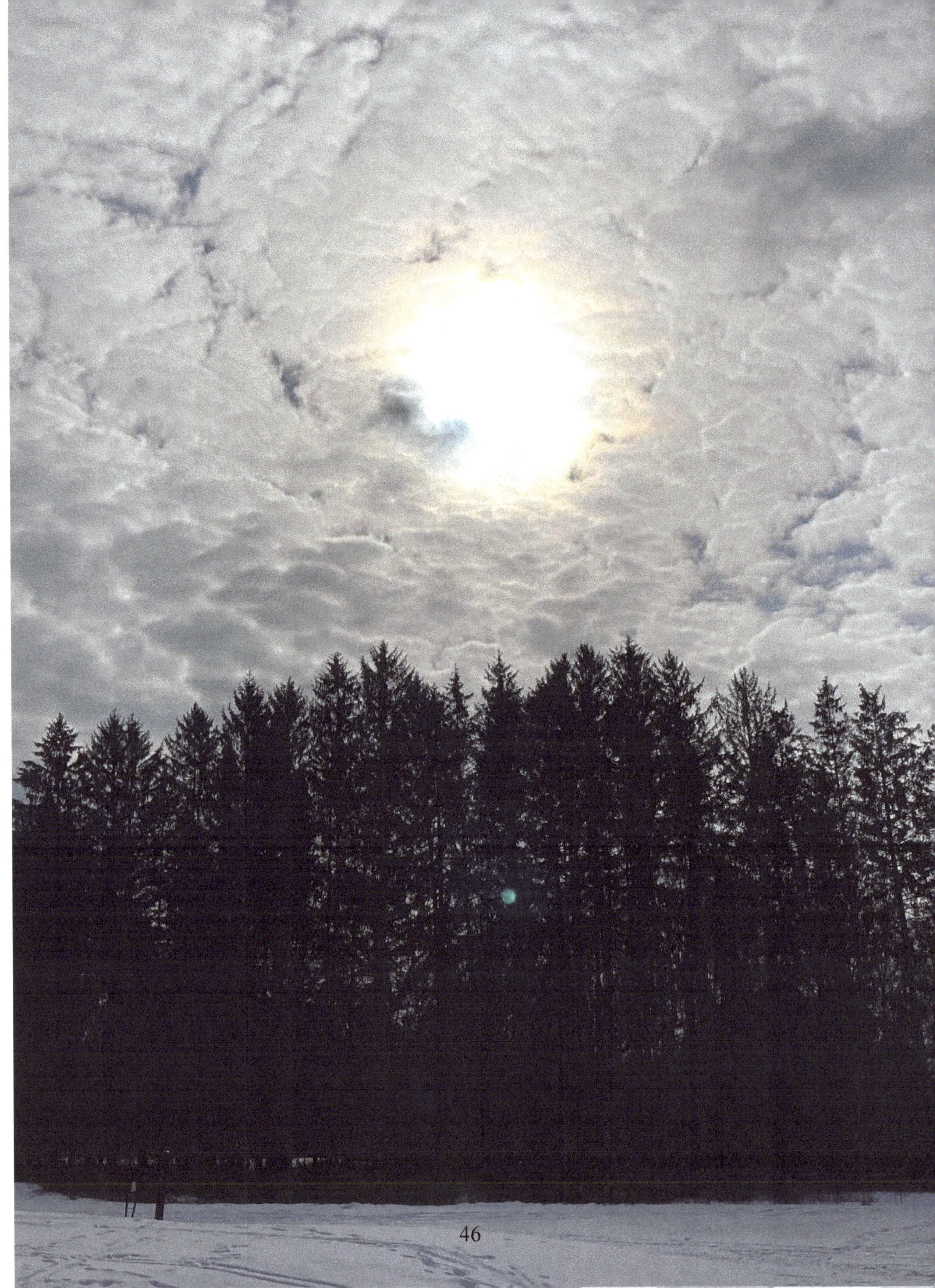

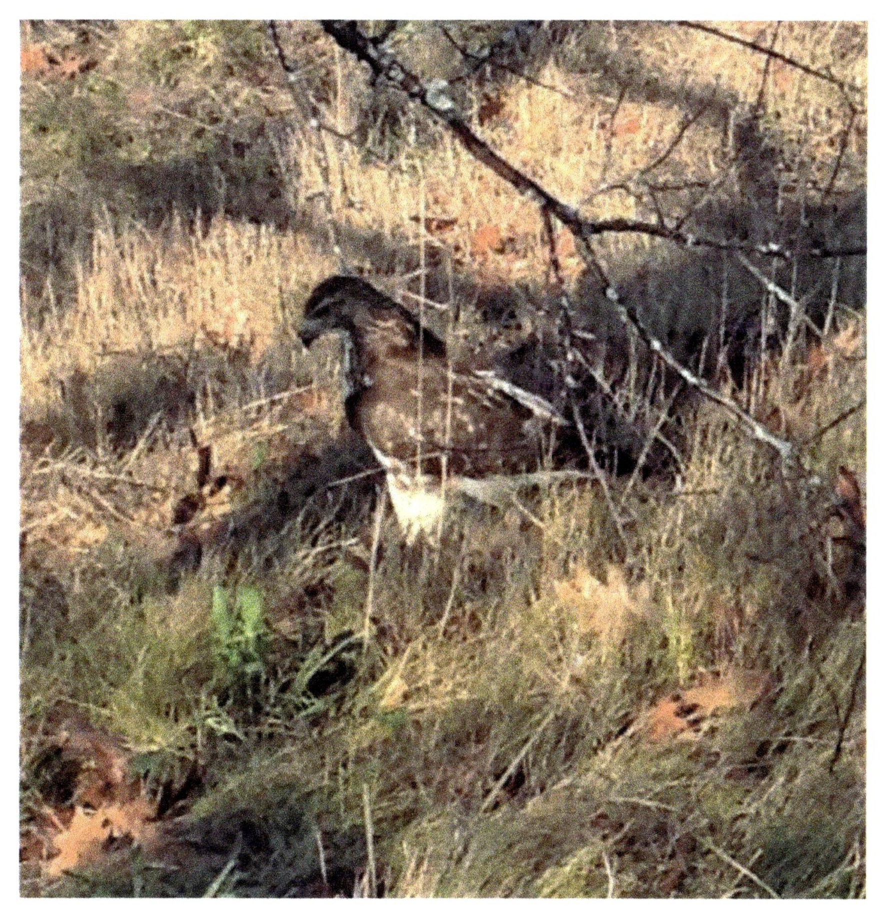

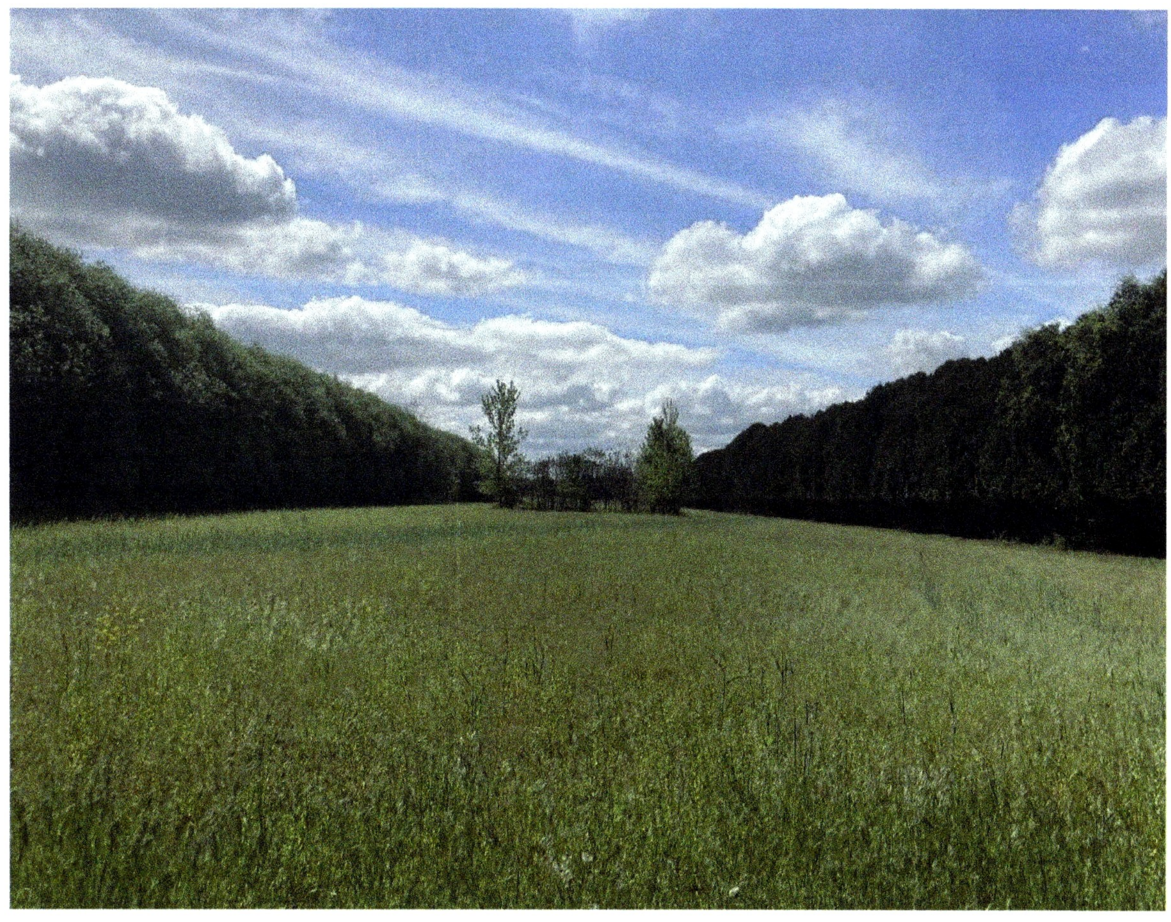

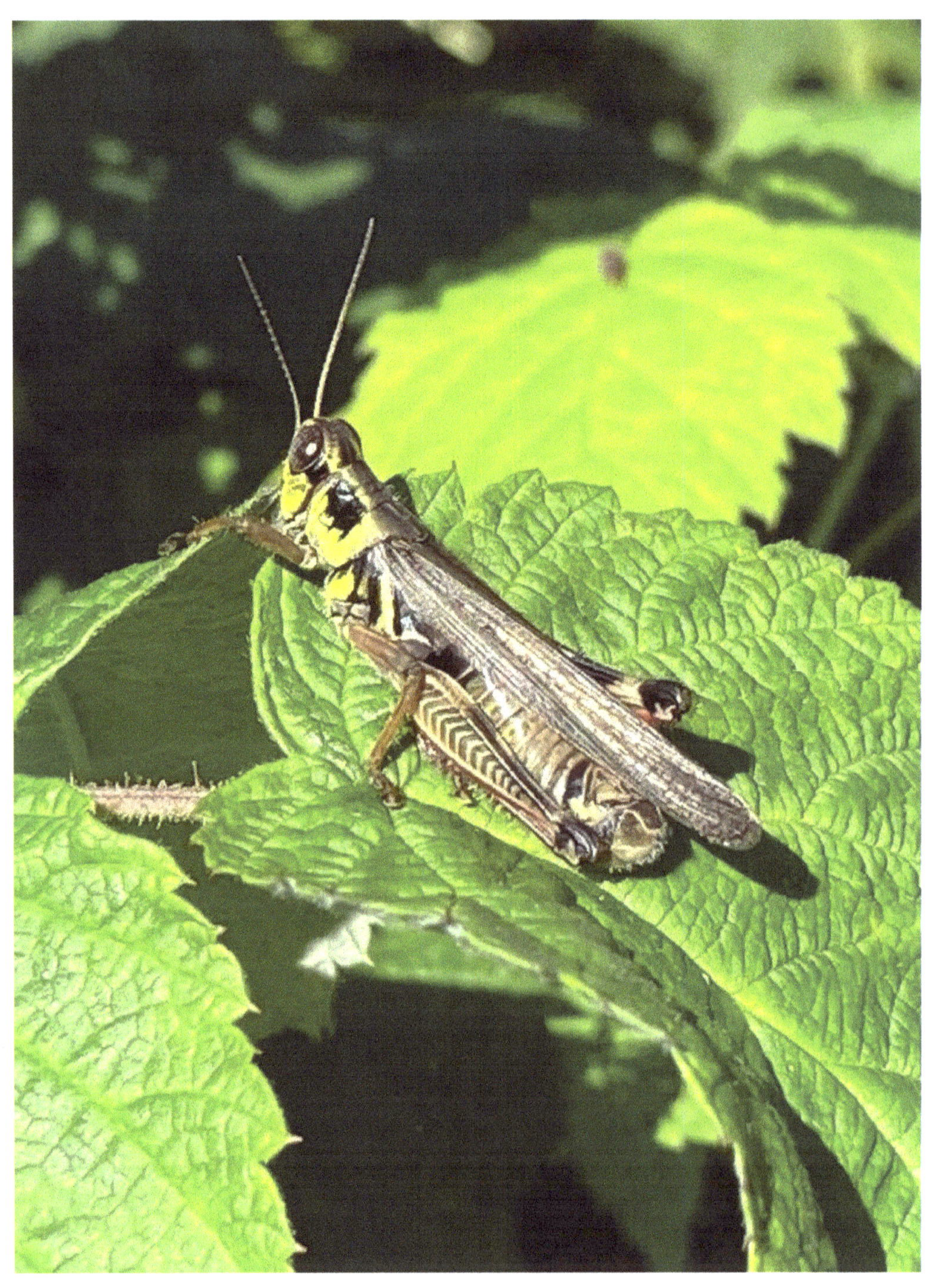

"I firmly believe that Nature brings solace in all troubles."

Anne Frank

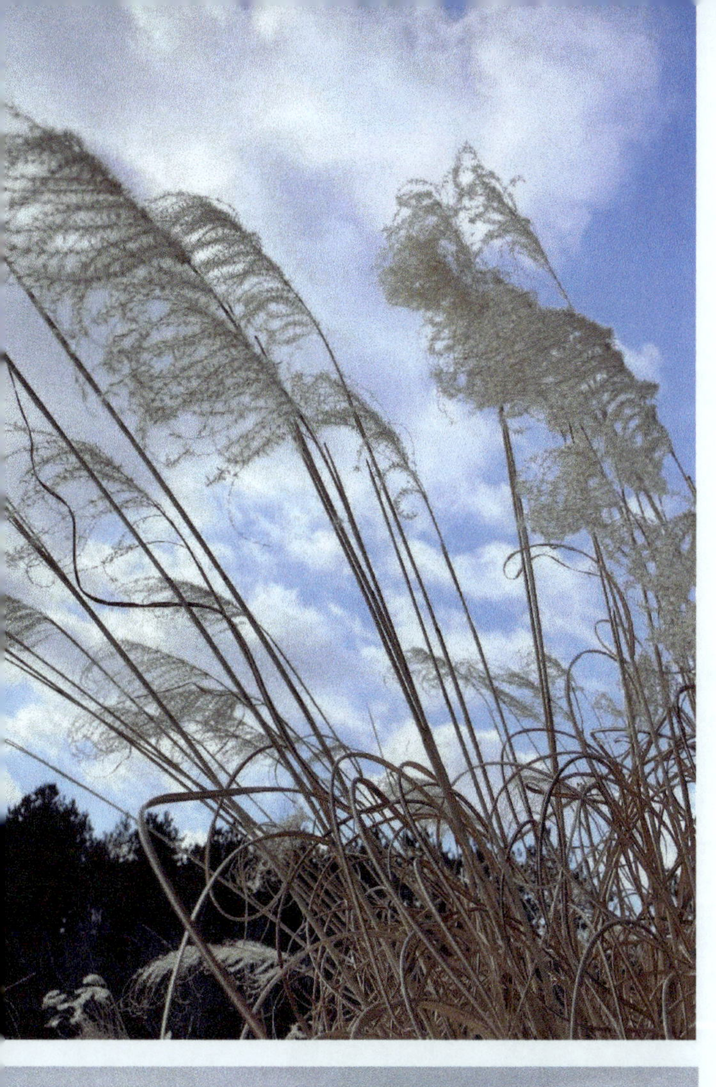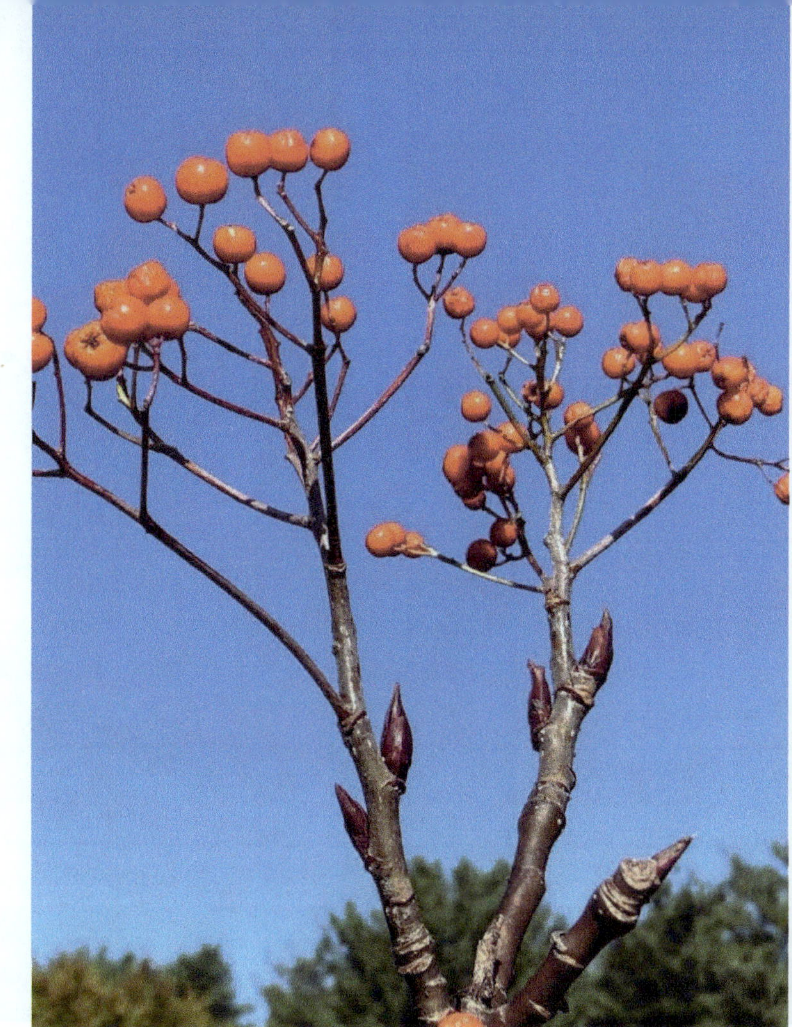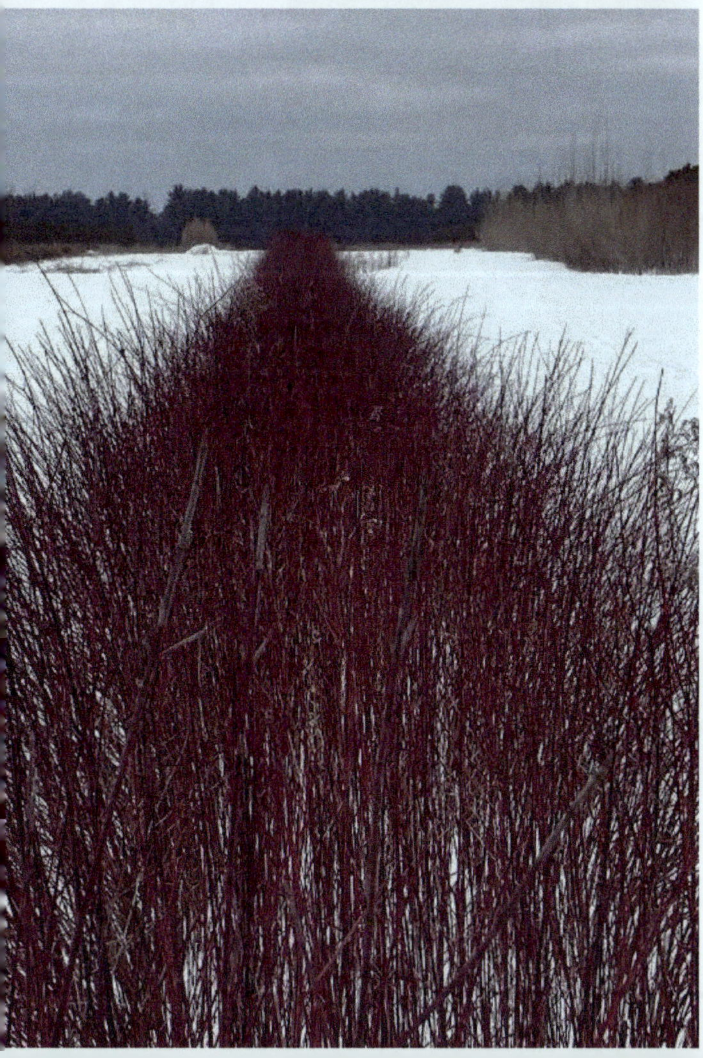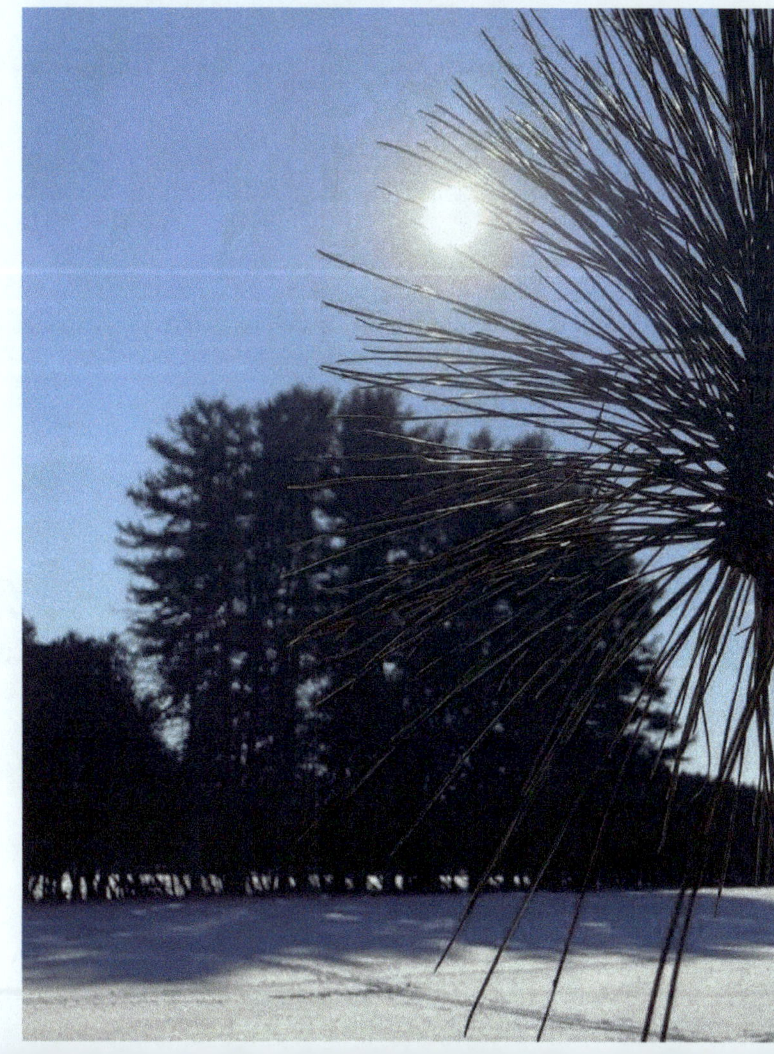

Geyser Creek Trail

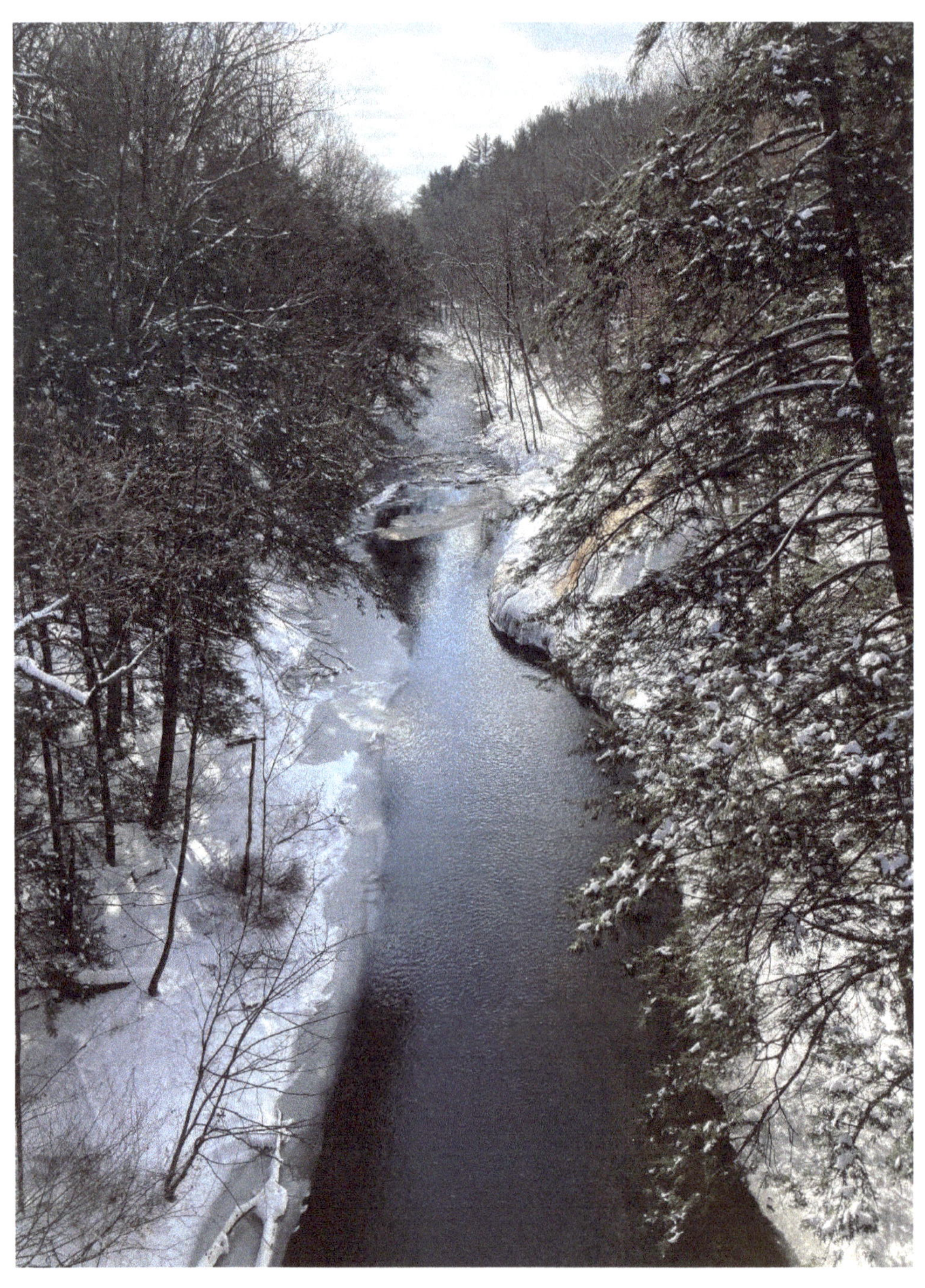

The night is darkening round me.
The wild winds coldly blow;
But a tyrant spell has bound me
And I cannot, cannot go.

The giant trees are bending.
Their bare boughs weighed with snow.
And the storm is fast descending.
And yet I cannot go.

Clouds beyond clouds above me.
Waters beyond waters below me:
Nothing dear can move me.
I will not, cannot go.

Emily Bronte

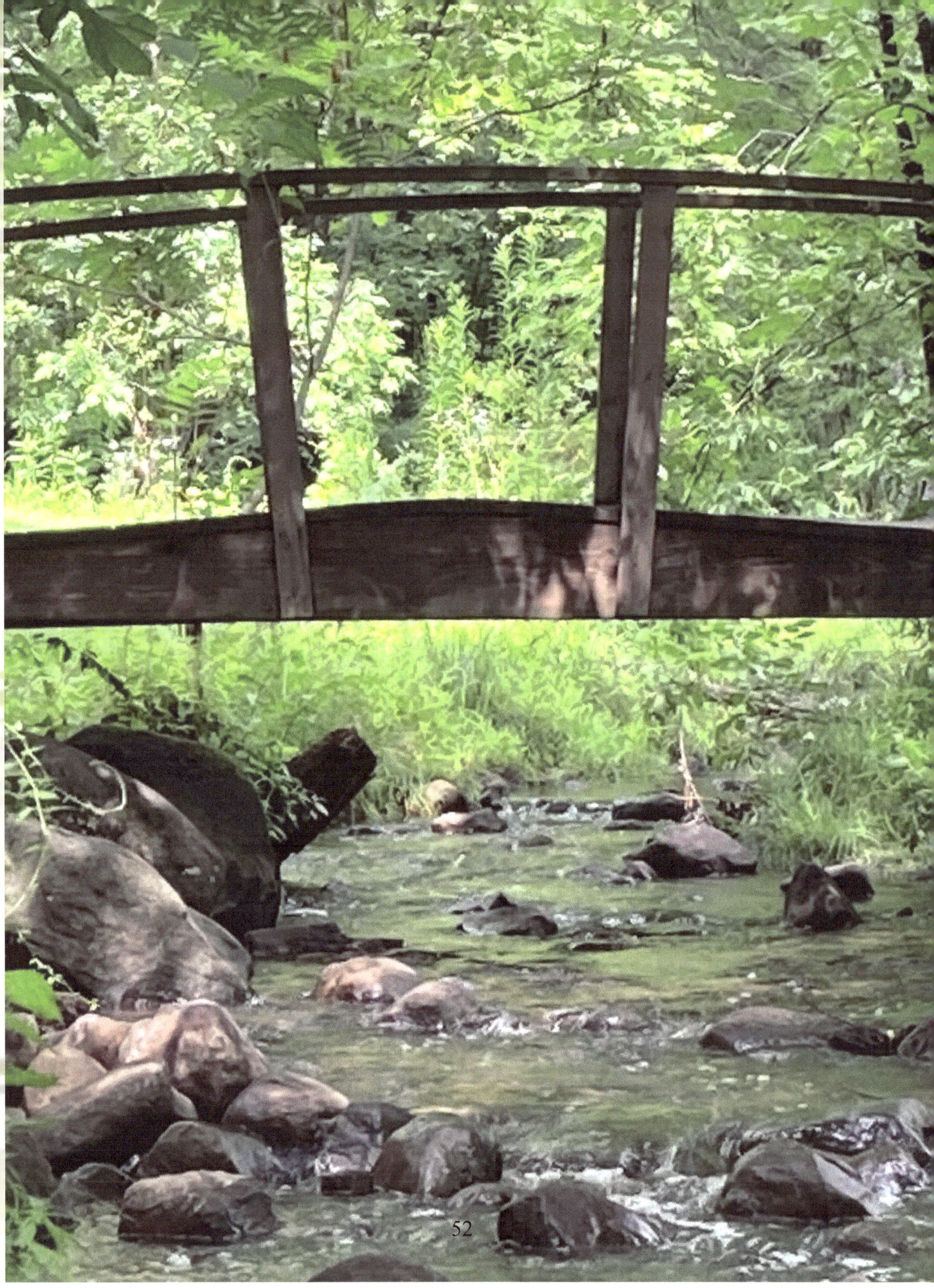

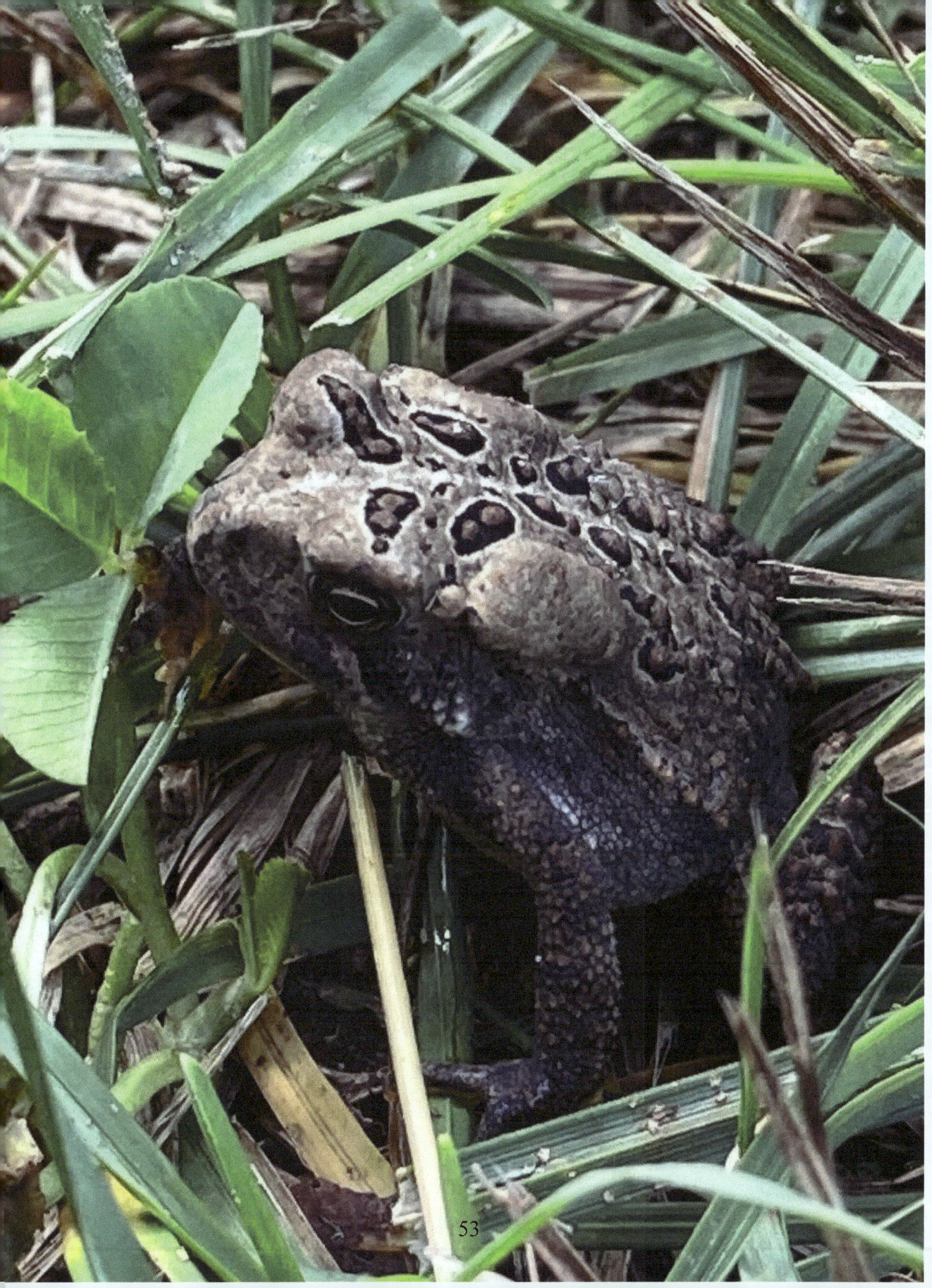

If you stay close to Nature,
To her simplicity,
To the small things hardly noticeable,
Those small things can unexpectedly
Become greater and immeasurable.

Rainer Maria Rilke

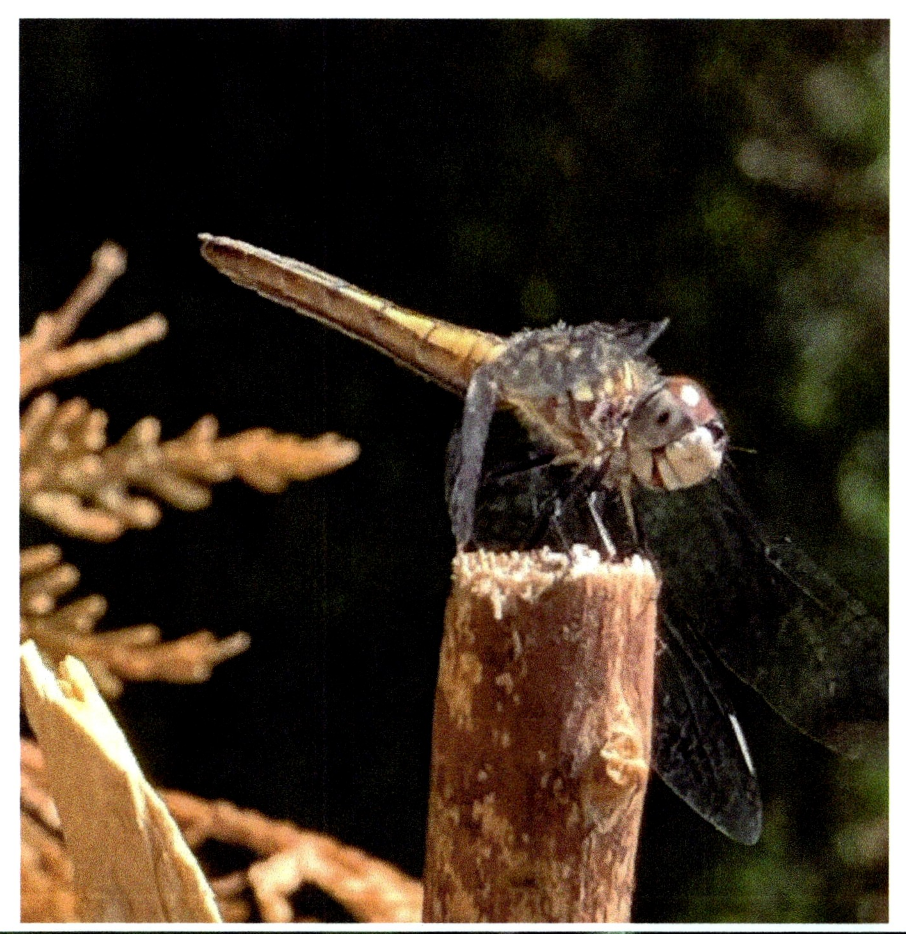

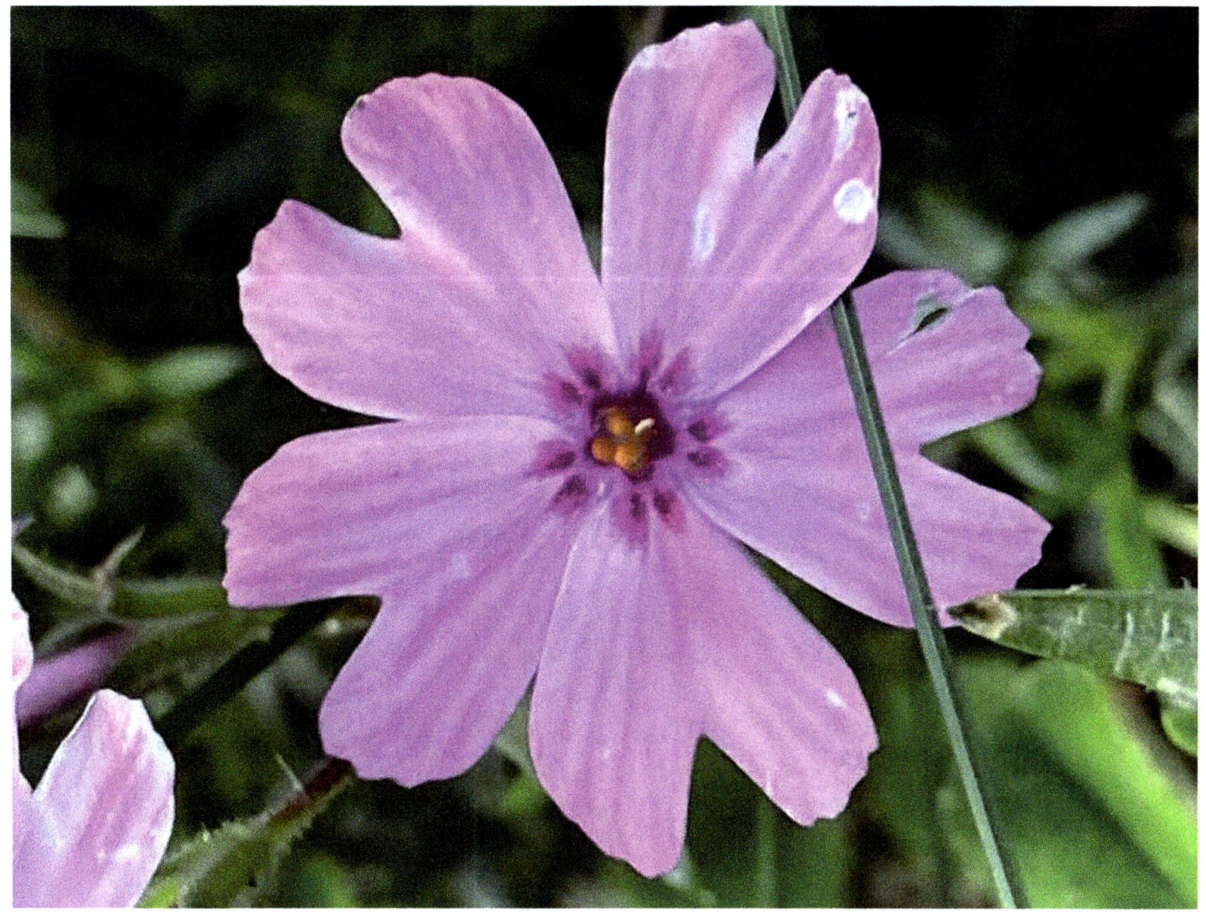

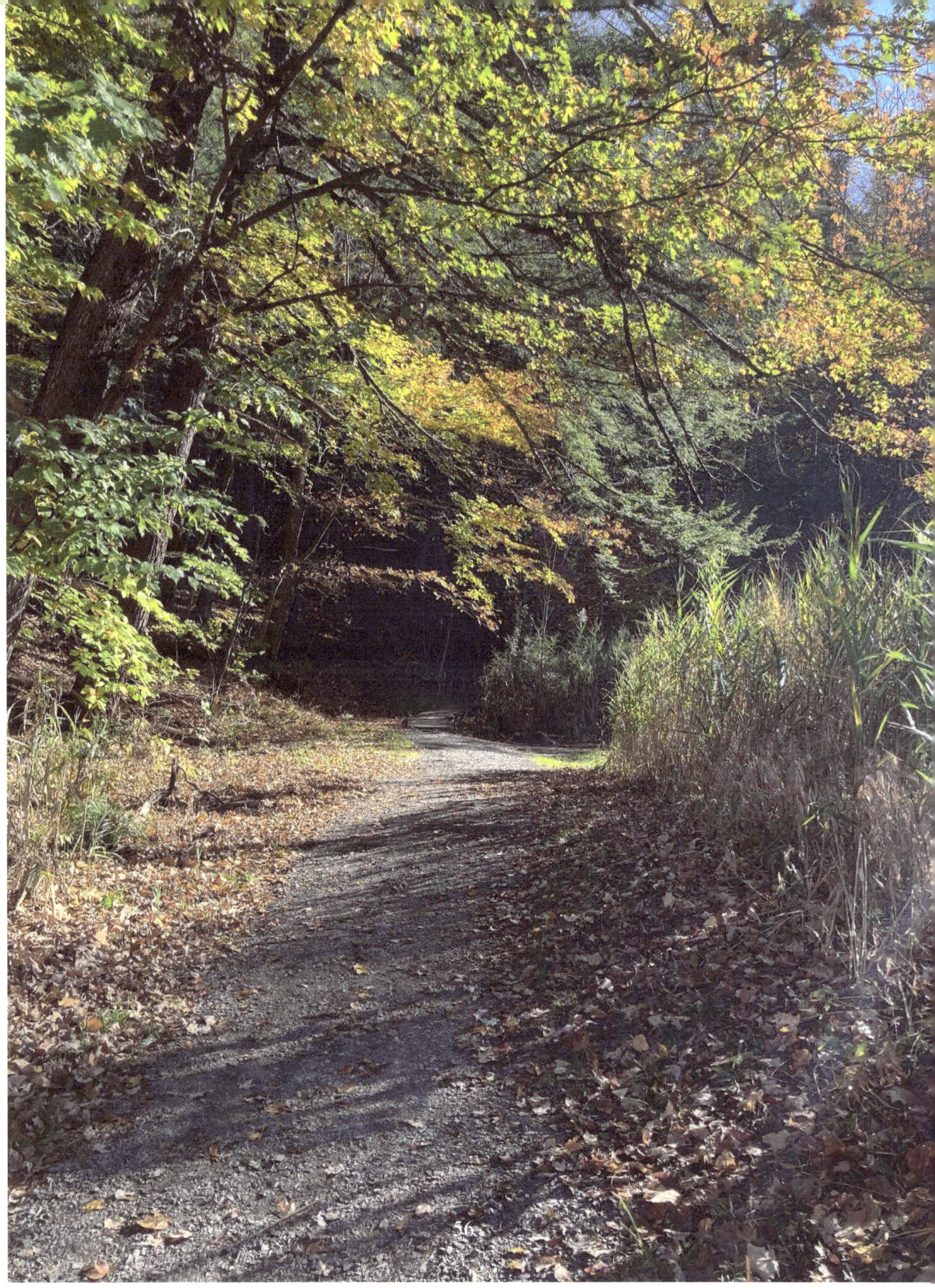

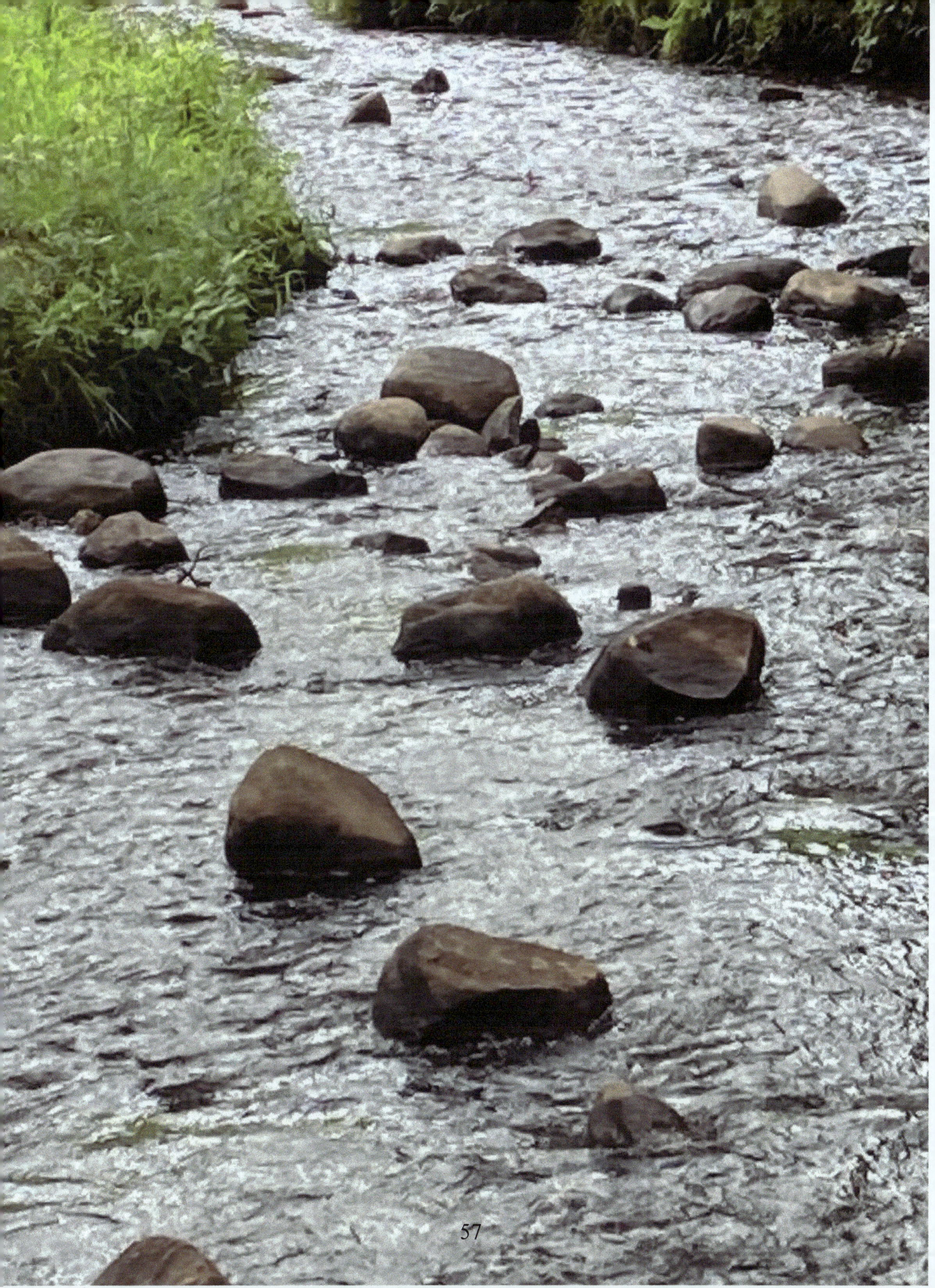

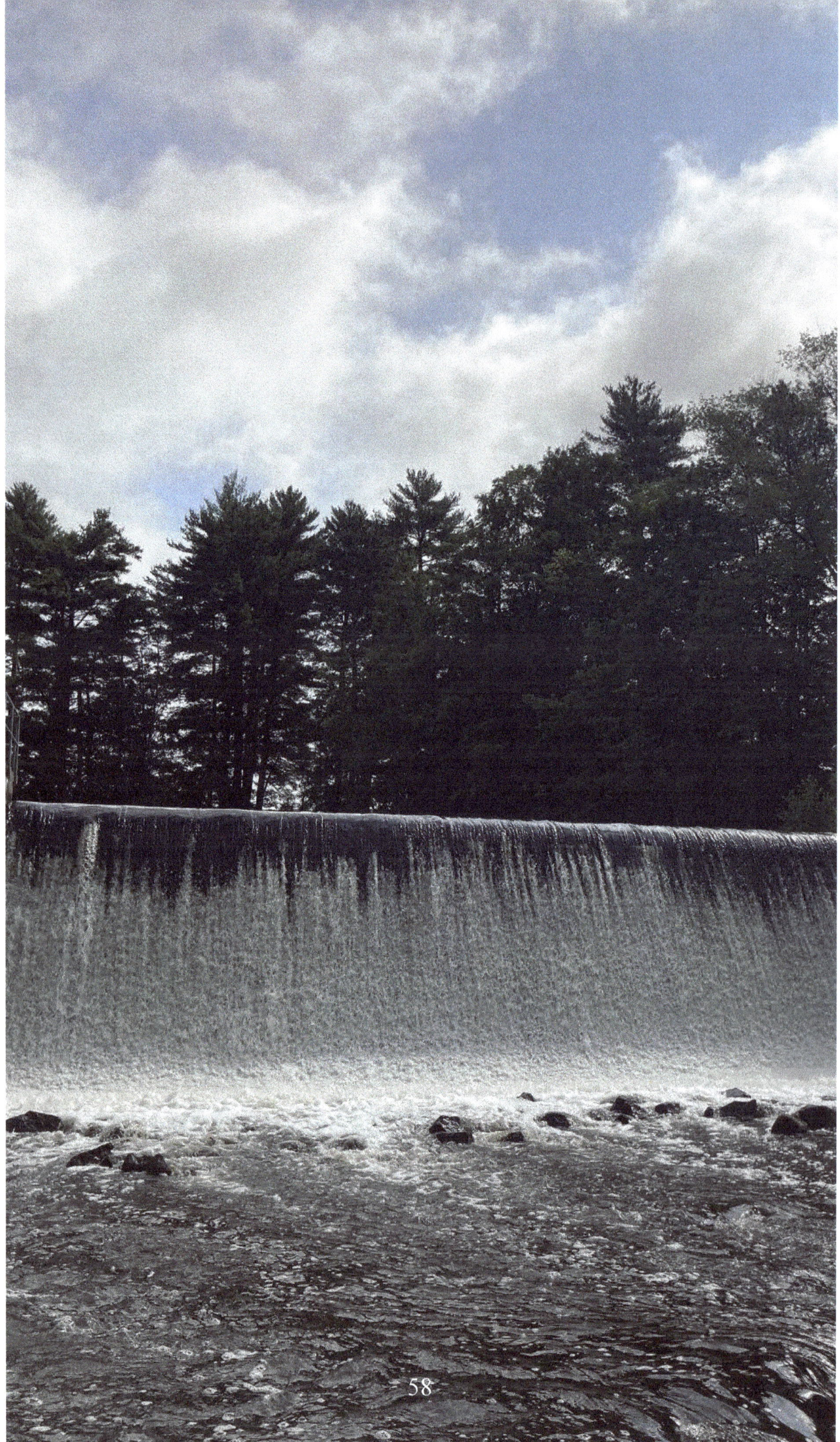

"Be kind to everything that lives."

Hanya Yanagihara

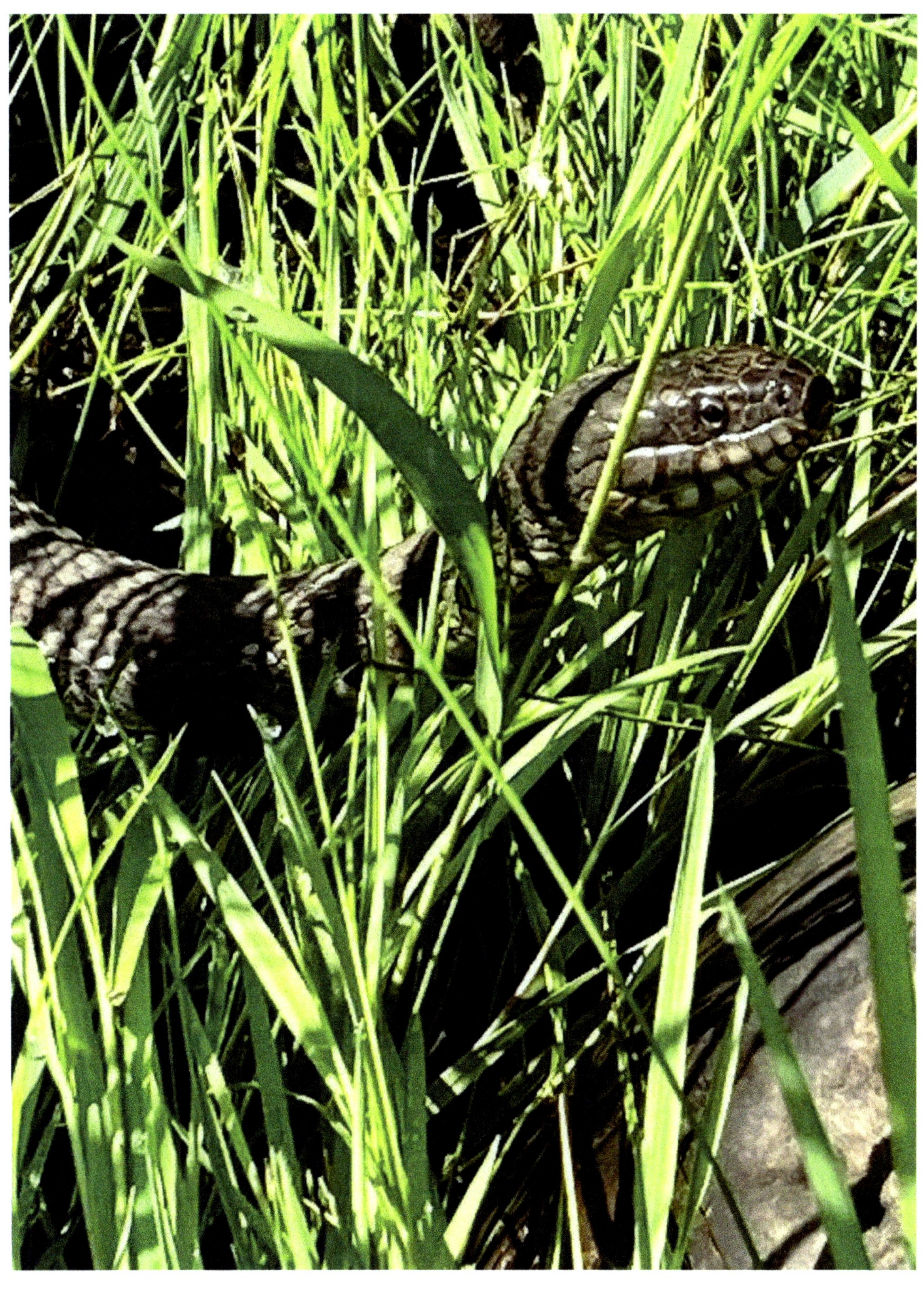

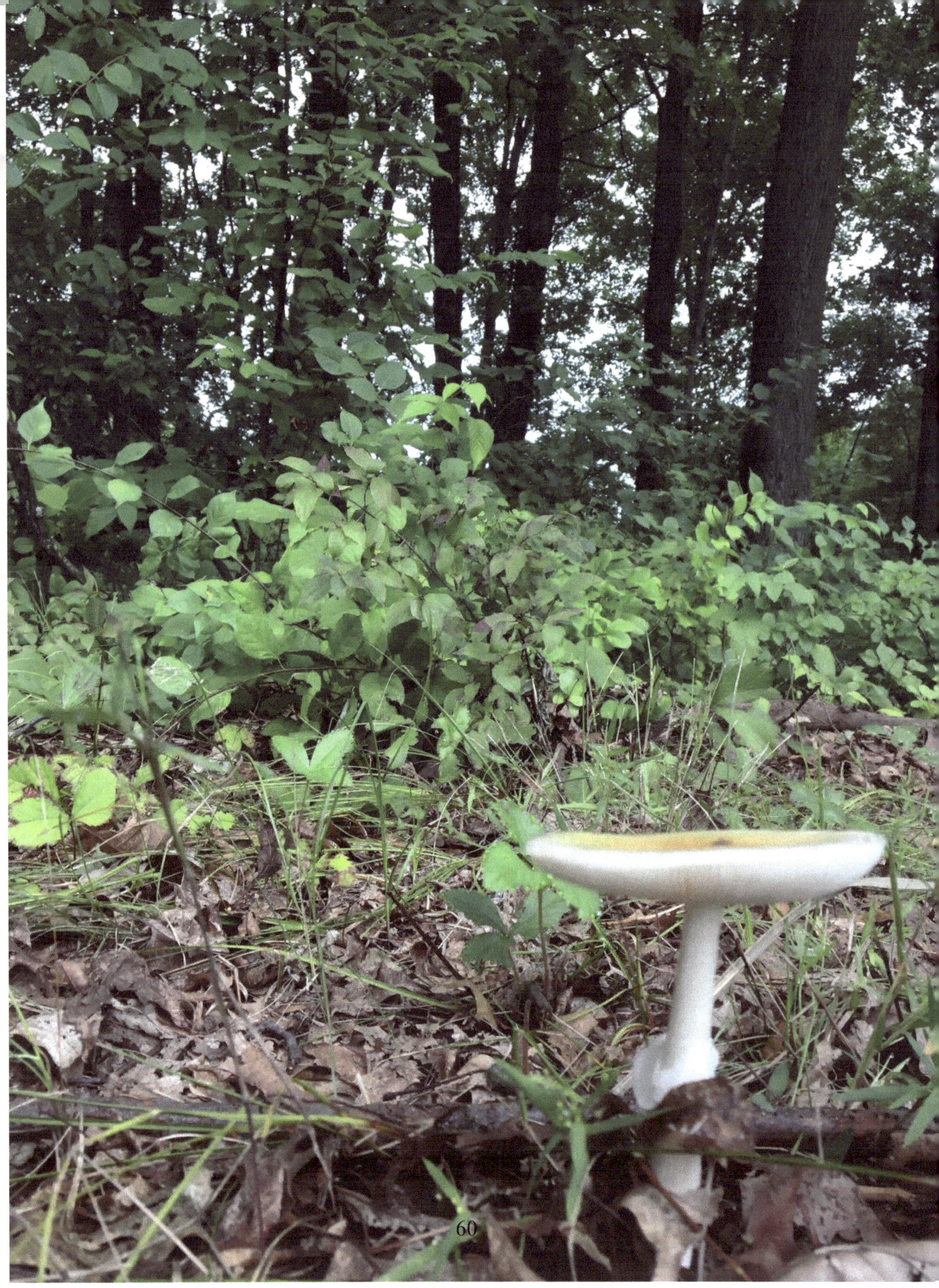

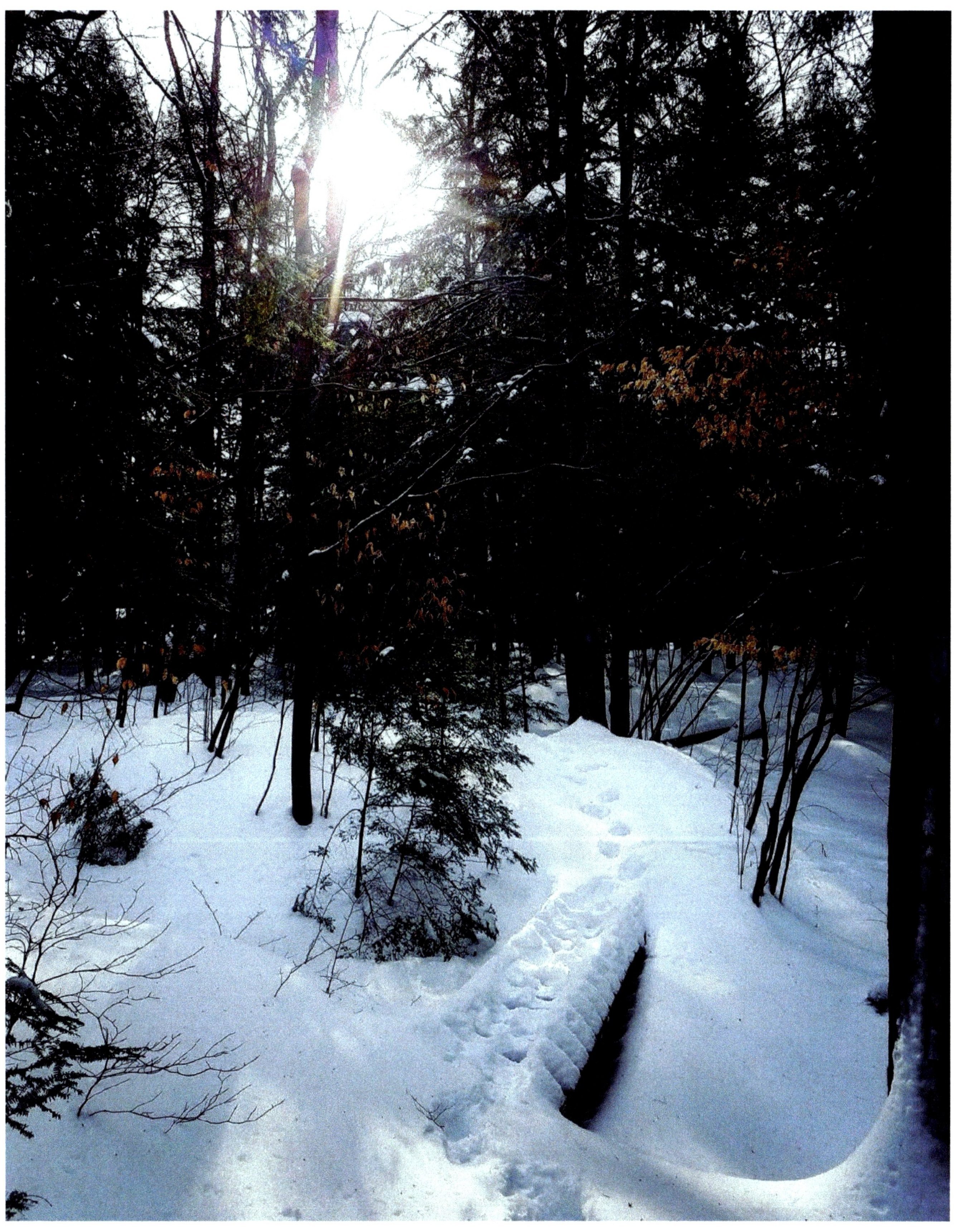

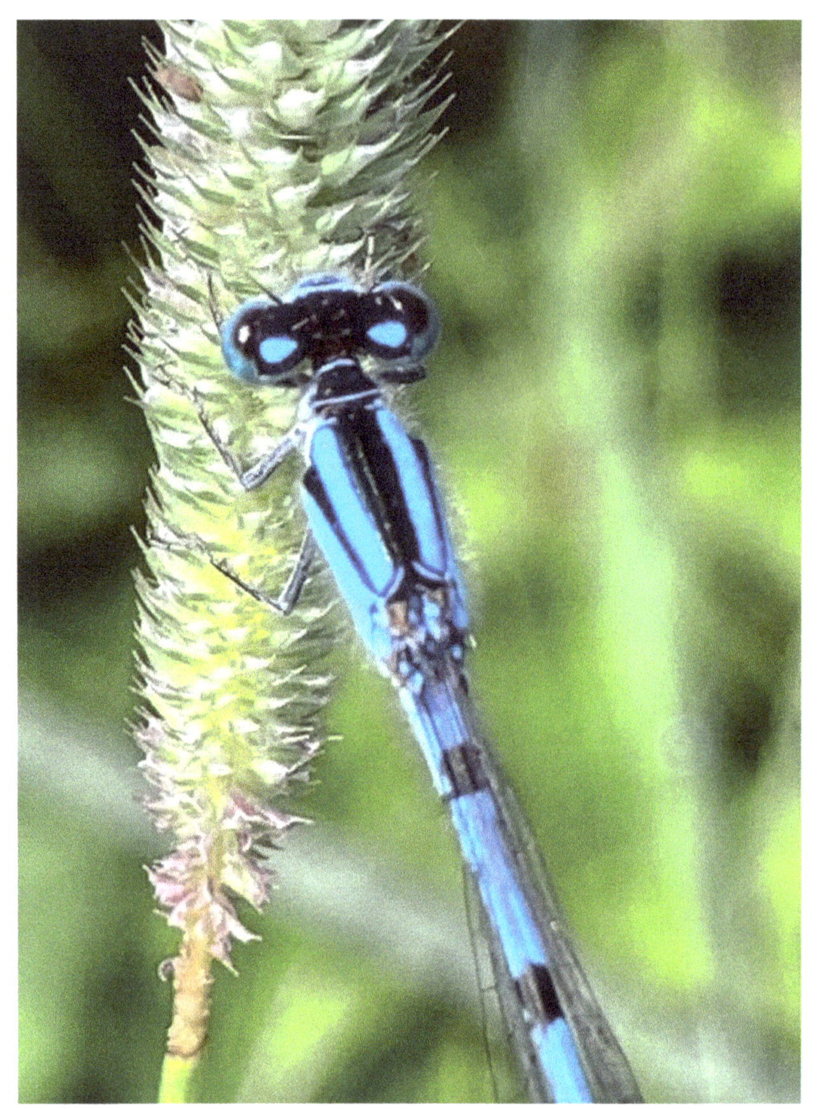

*"One of the first conditions of happiness is
That the link between man and Nature not be broken."*

Leo Tolstoy

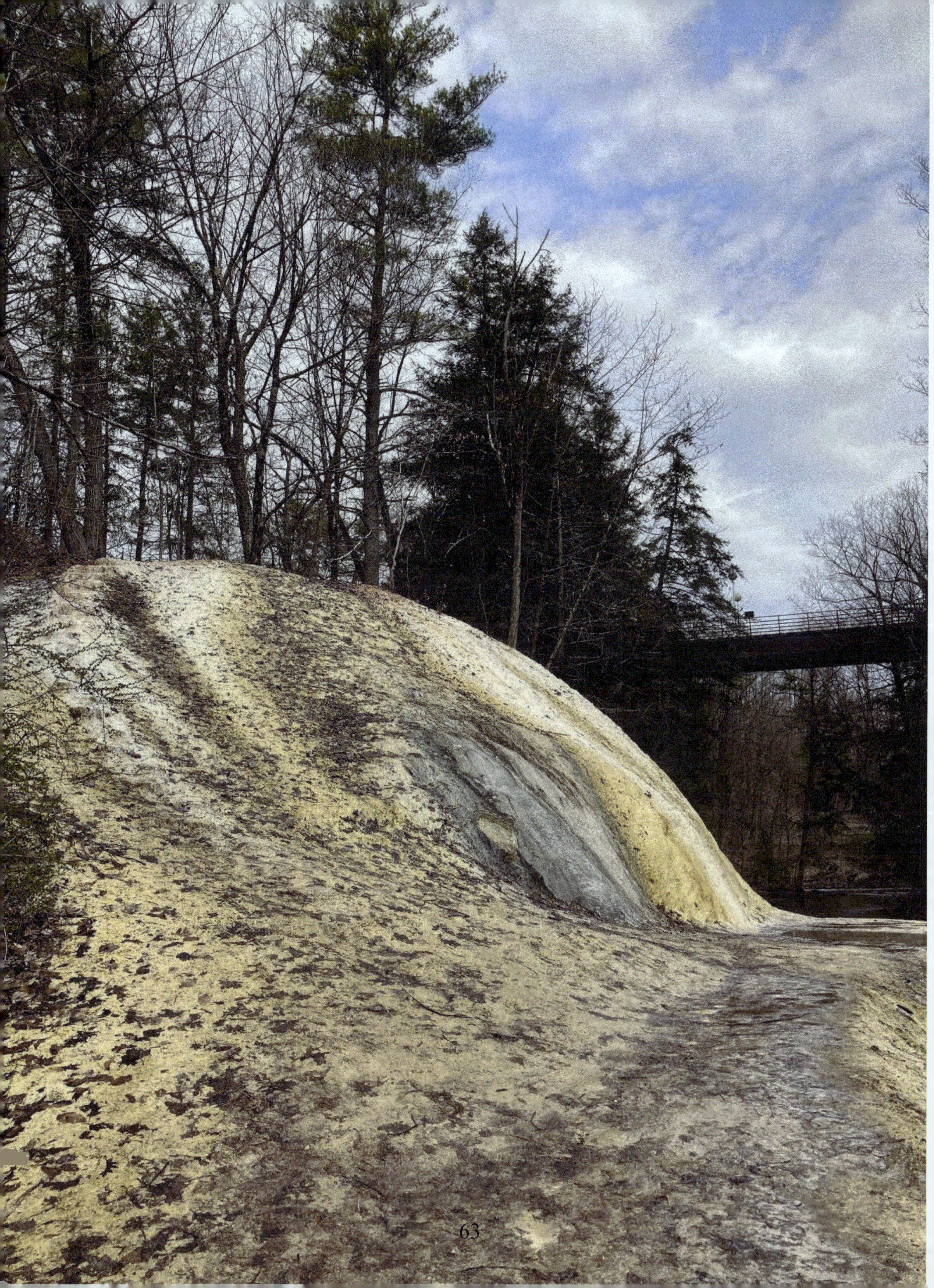

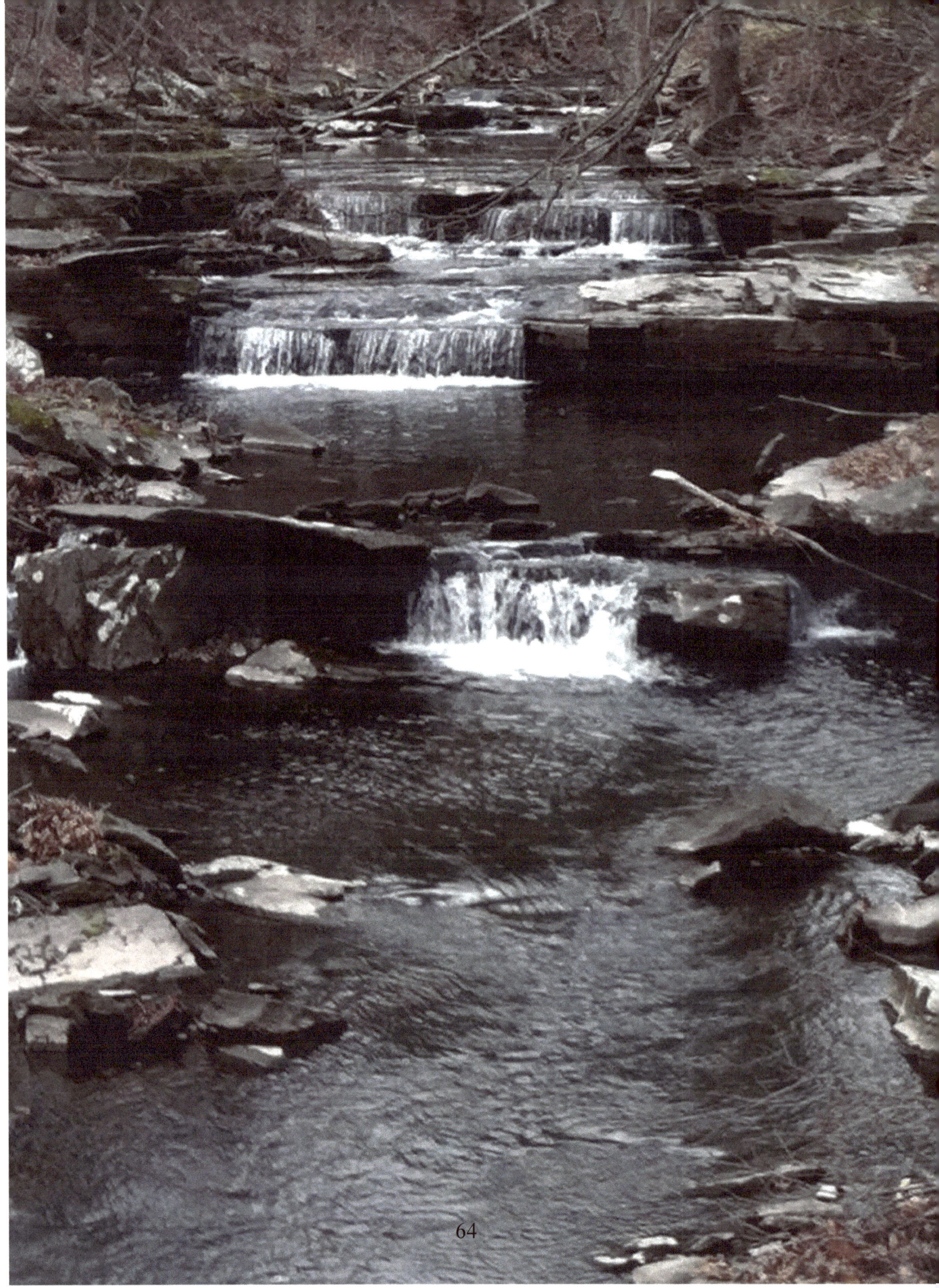

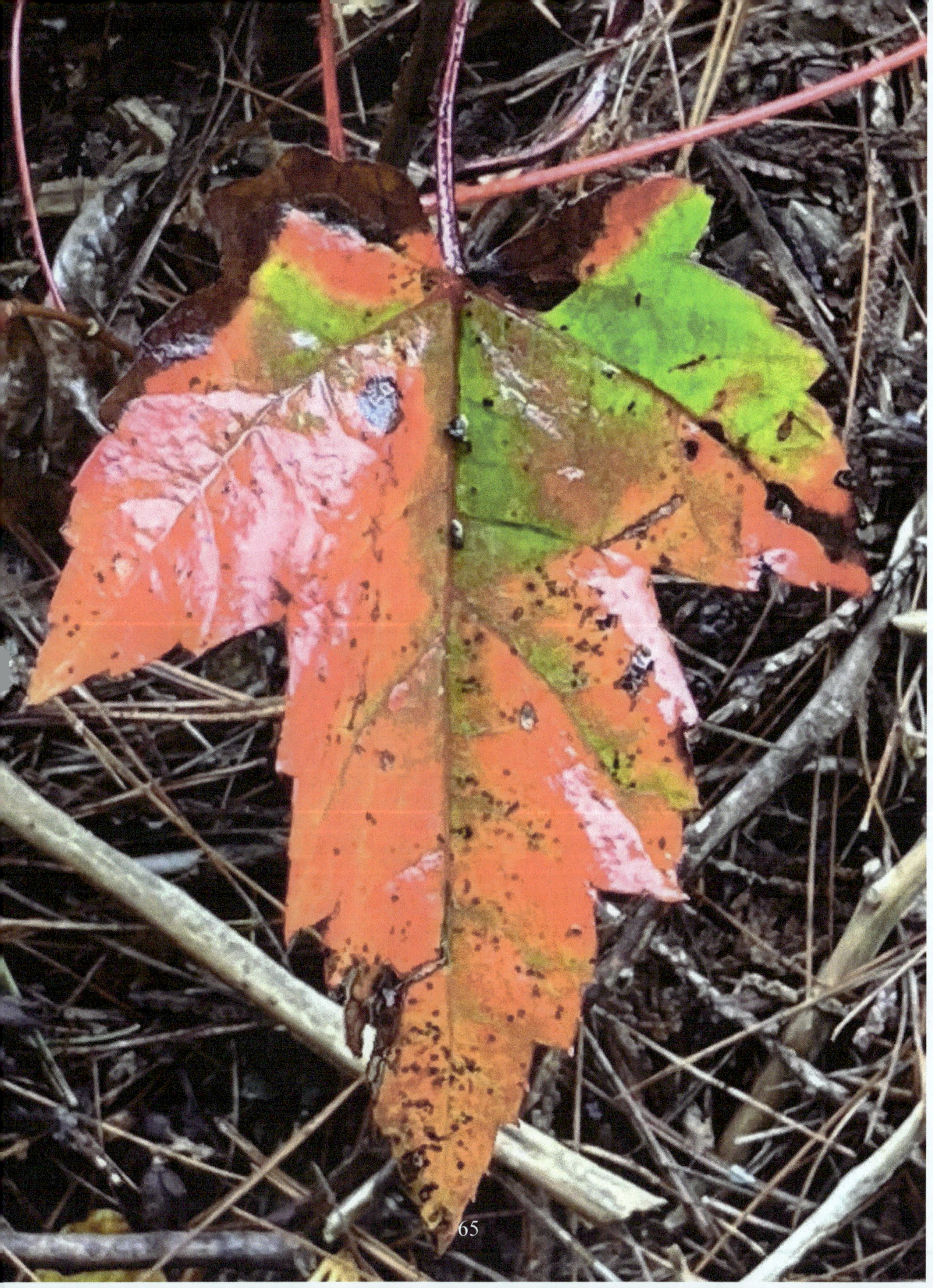

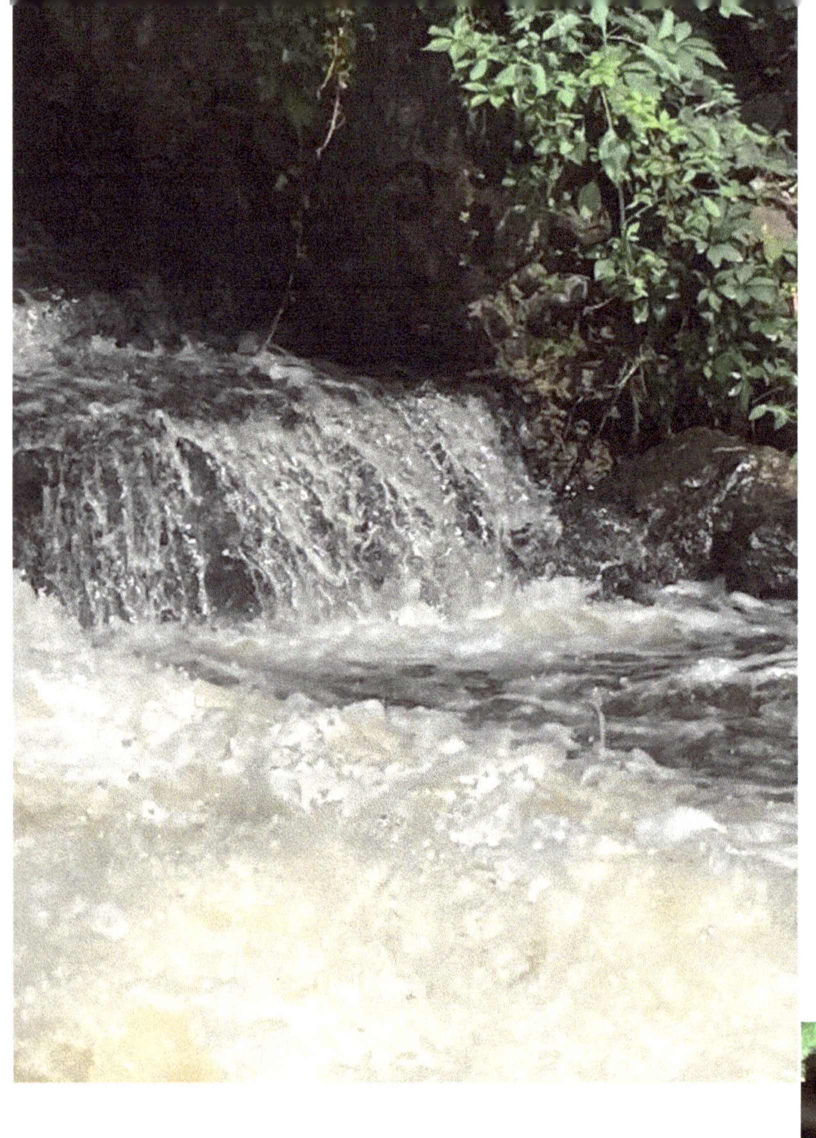

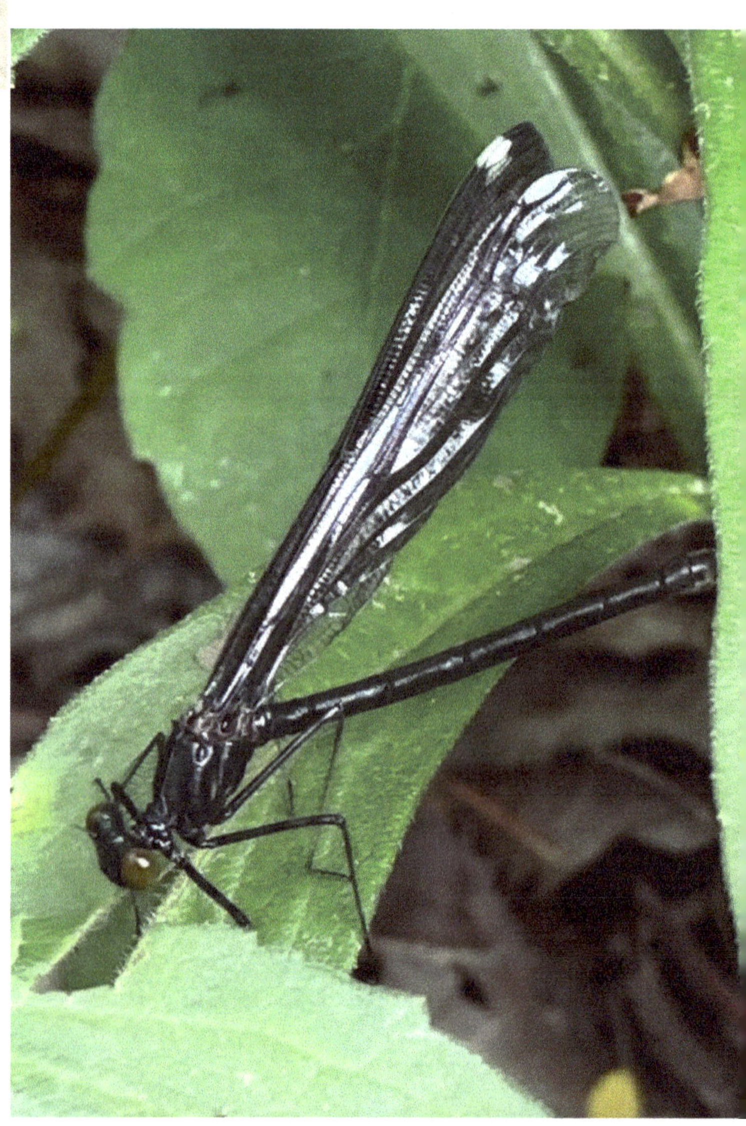

"I felt my lungs inflate with the onrush of scenery . . . air, mountains, trees, creatures. This is what it is to be happy."

Silvia Plath

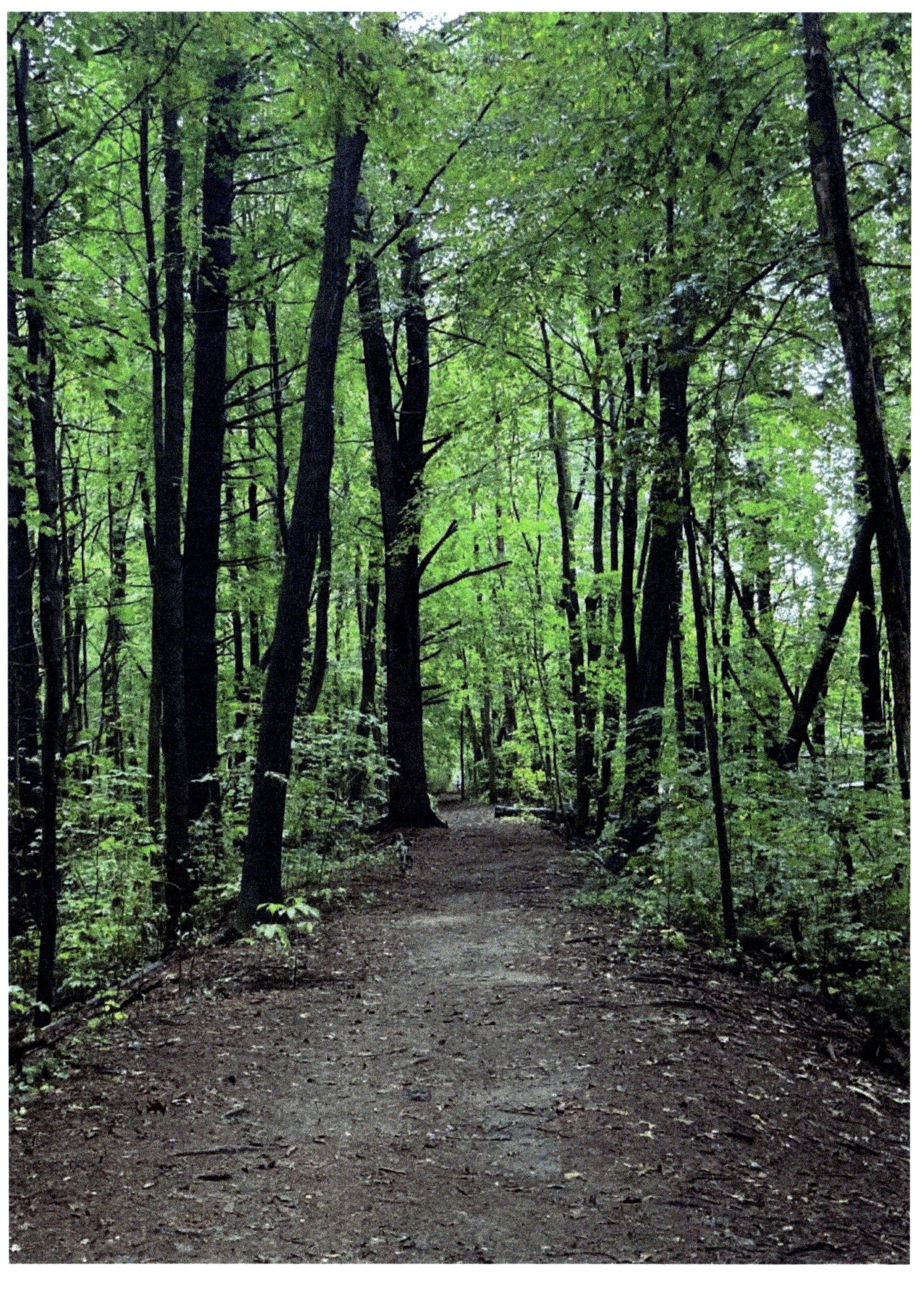

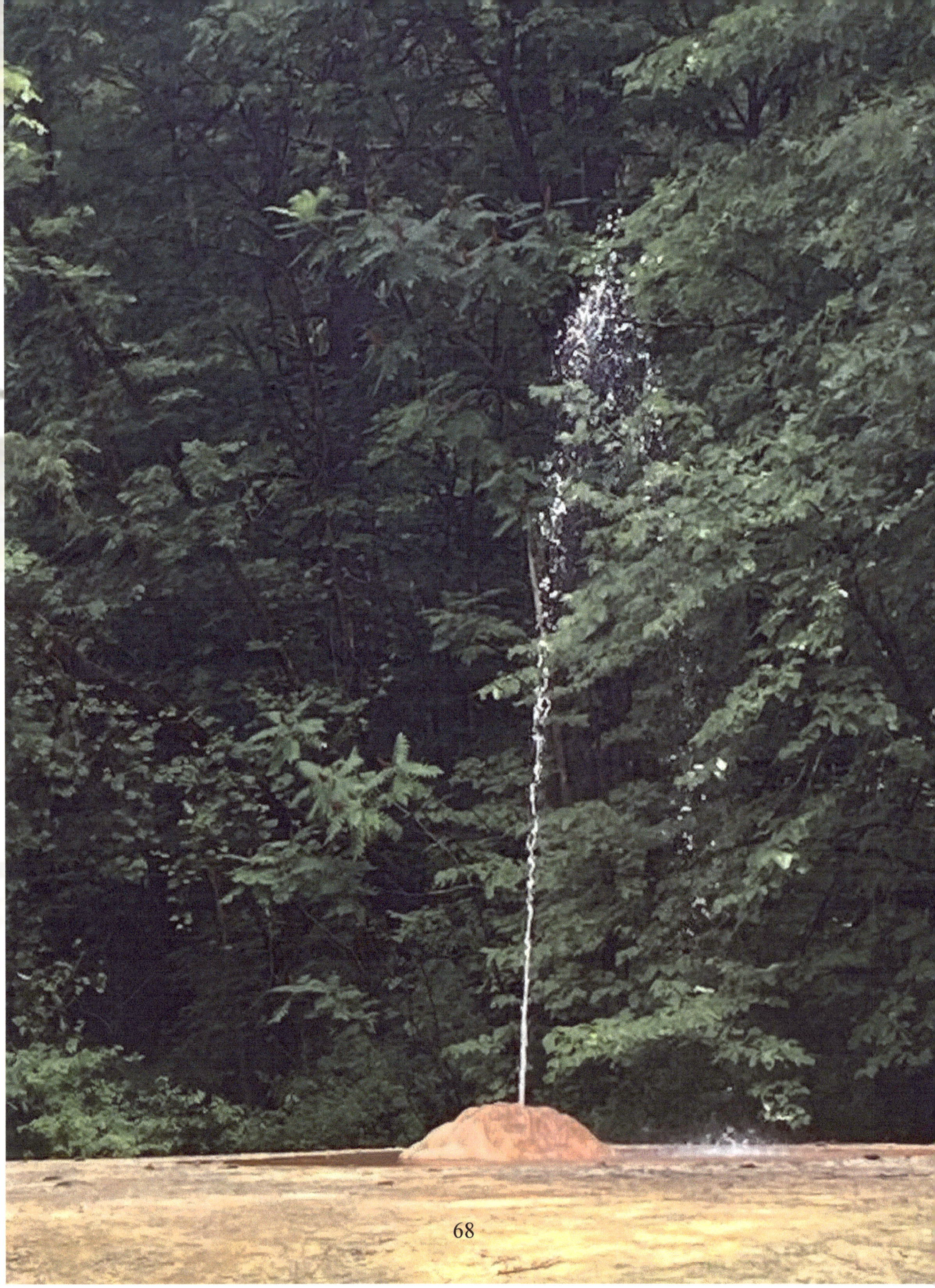

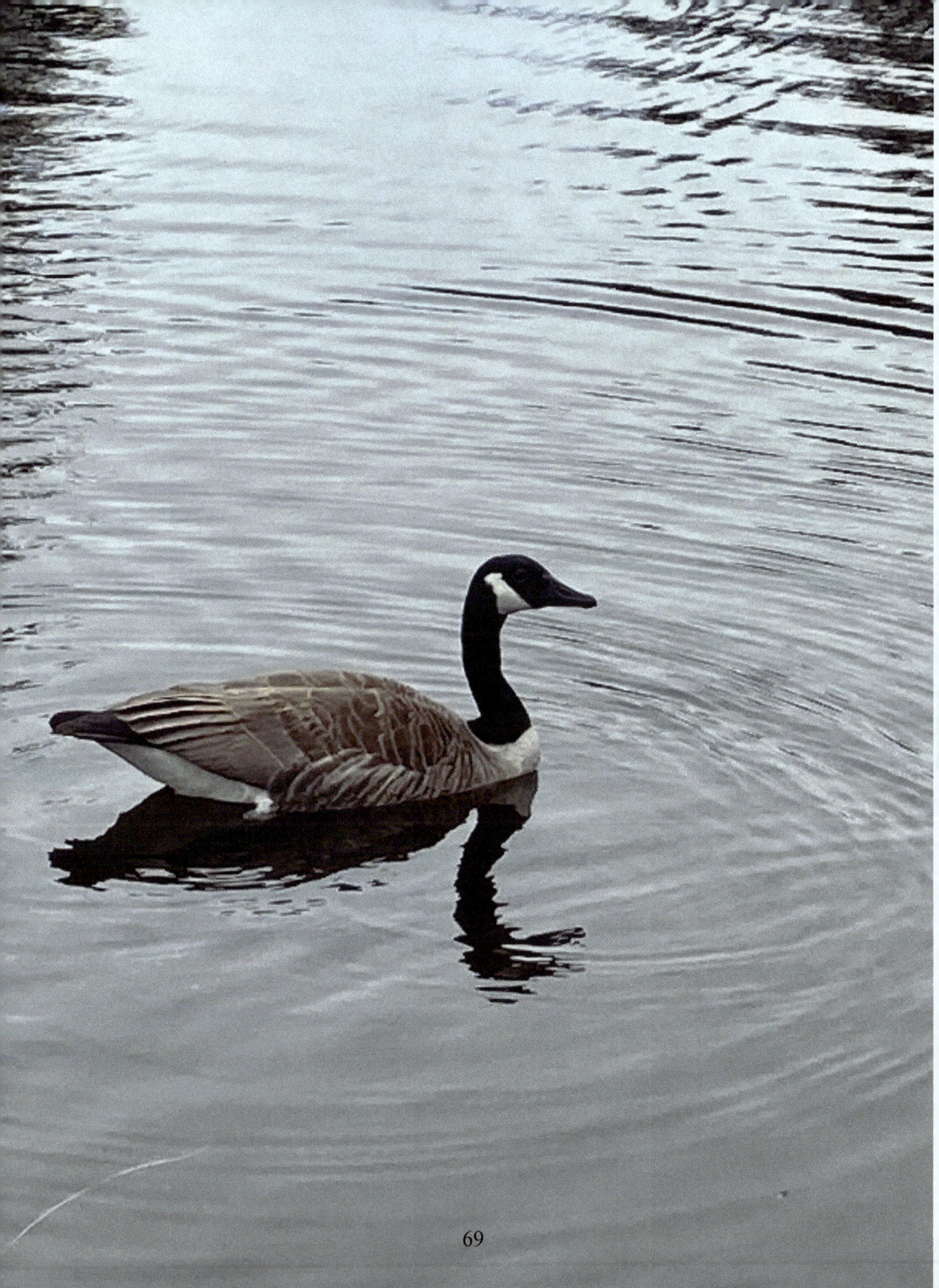

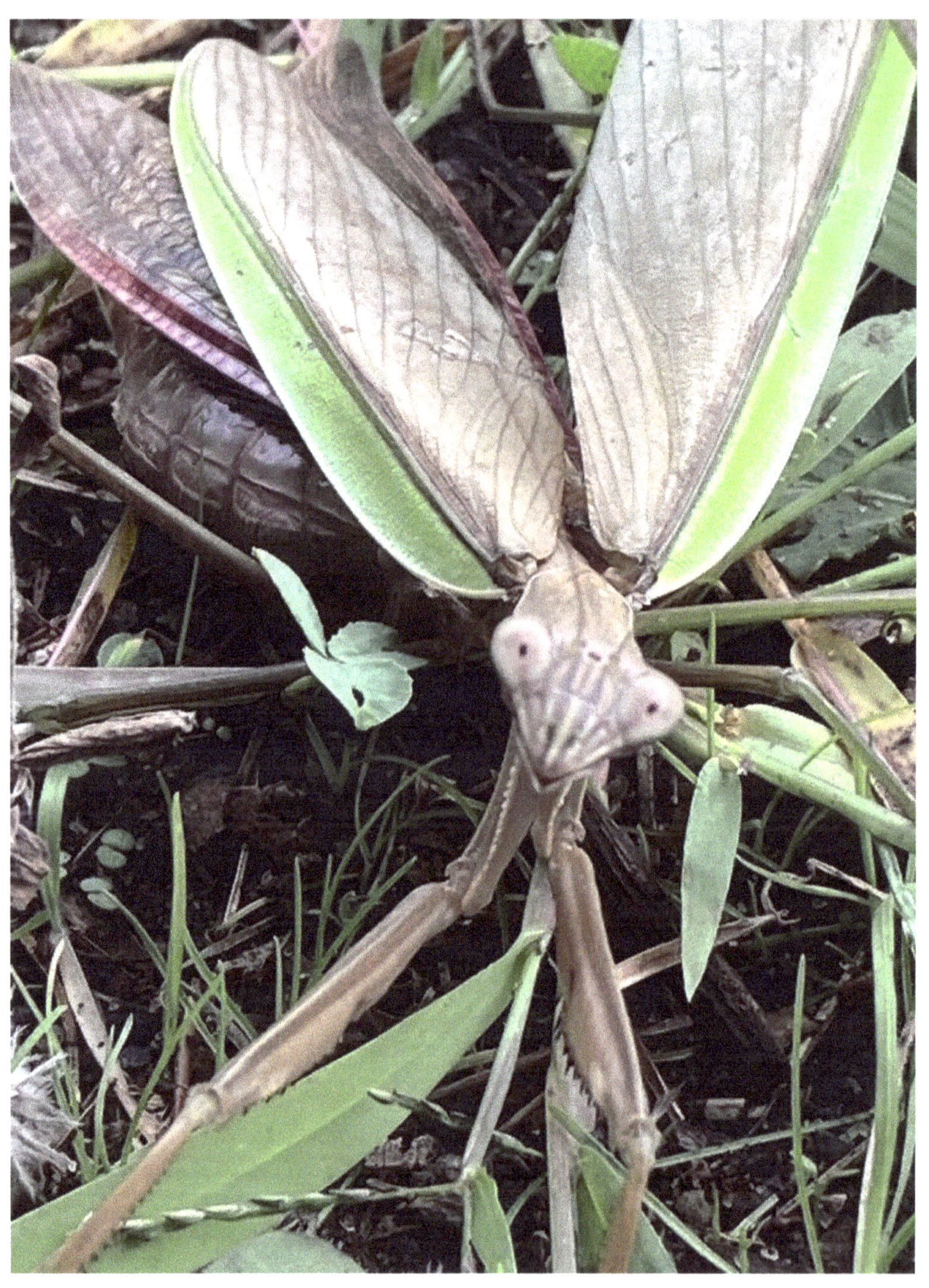

"The earth has music for those who will listen."

William Shakespeare

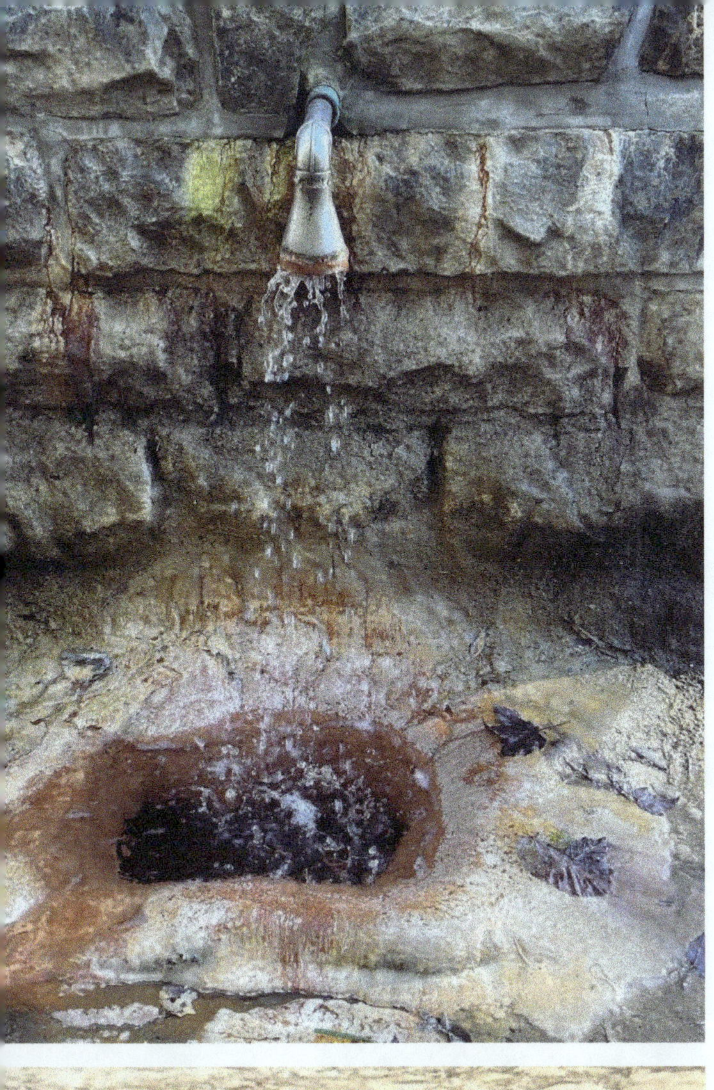
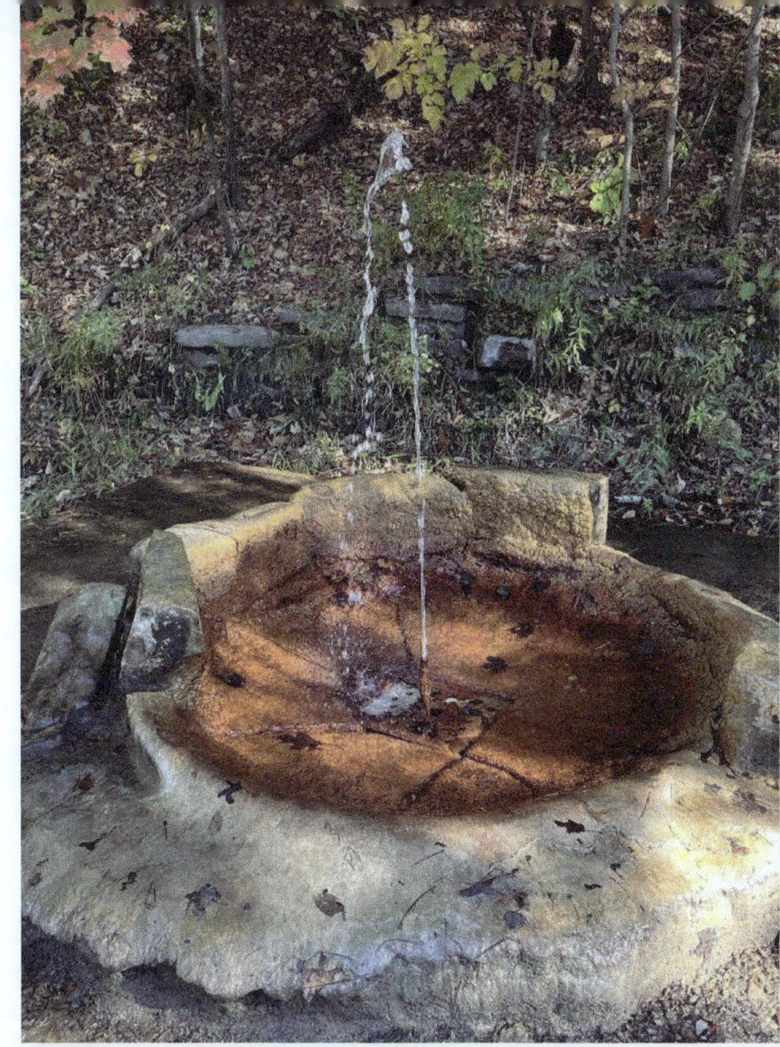
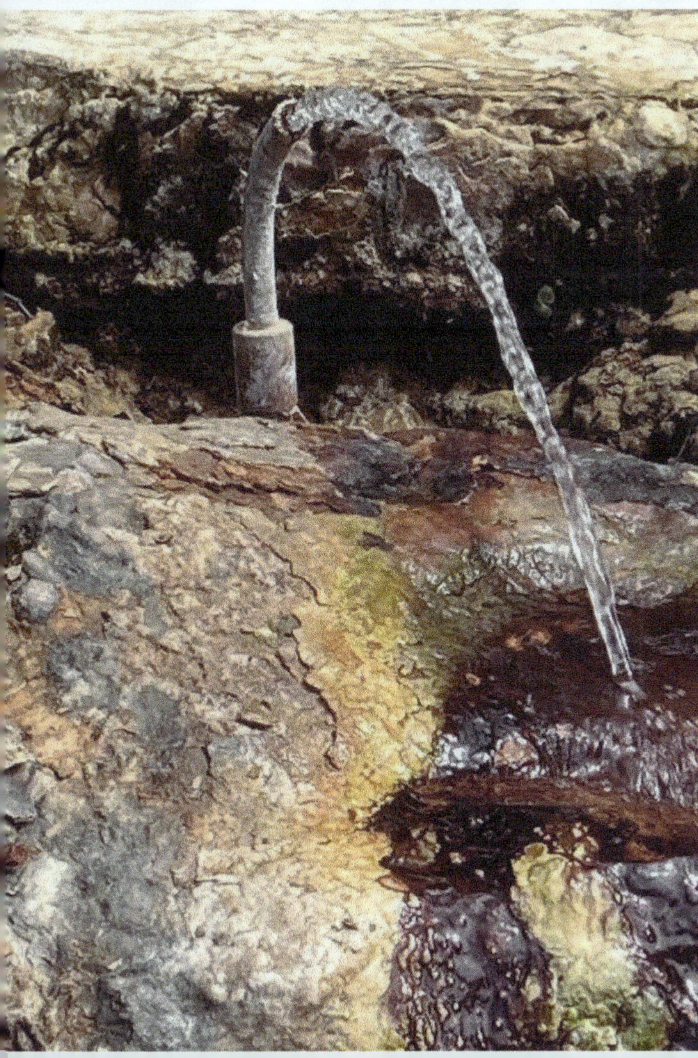
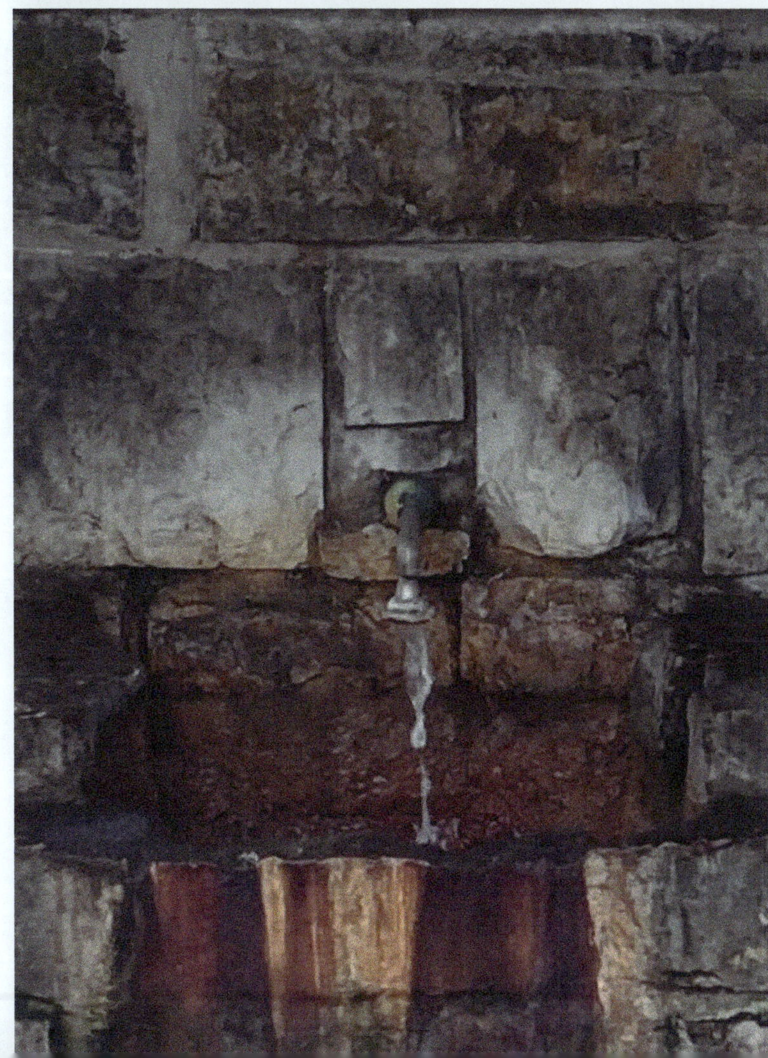

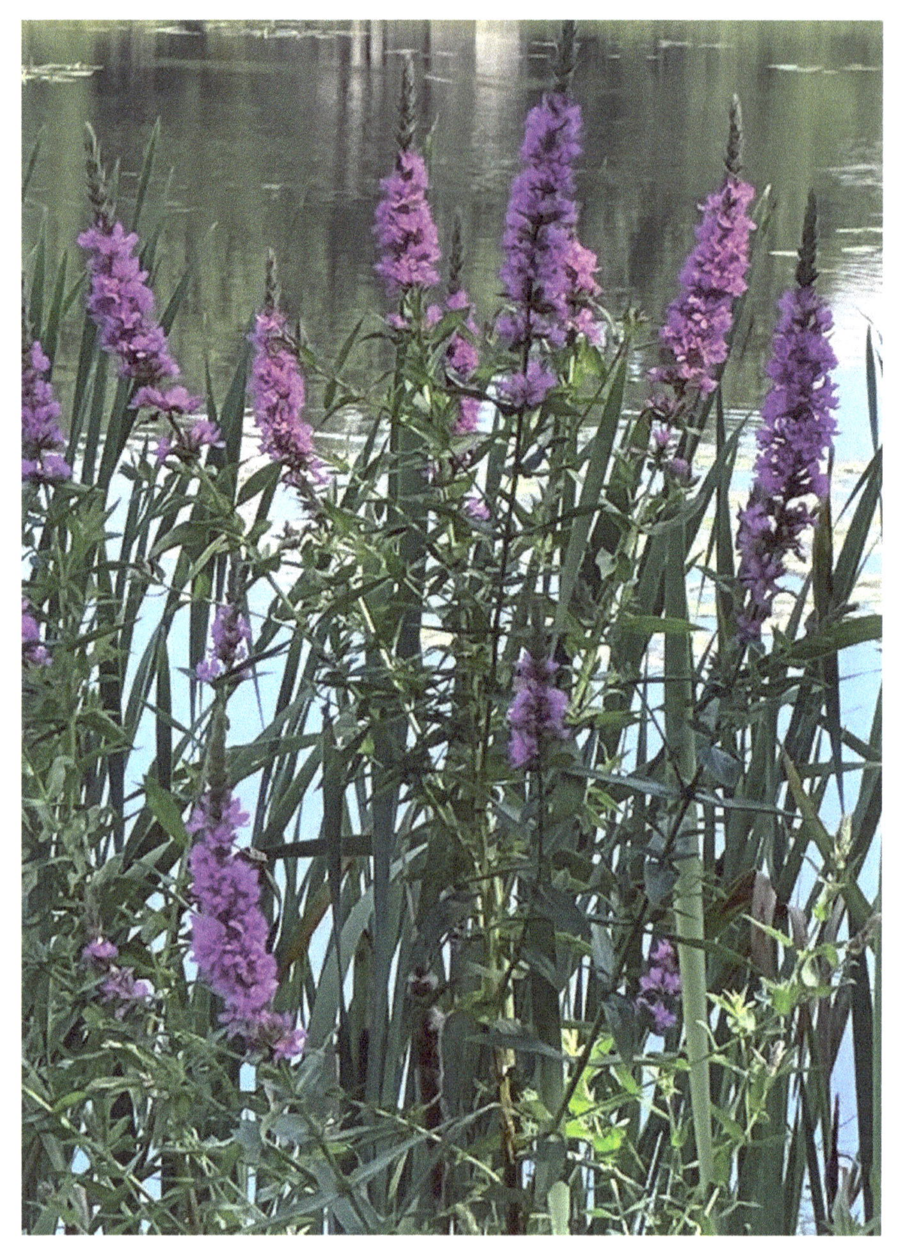

Bog Meadow Brook Nature Trail

Of all the artists
Who have graced our world,
However great they were,
No one can compete with Mother Nature,
Her beauty is beyond compare . . .

John P. Read

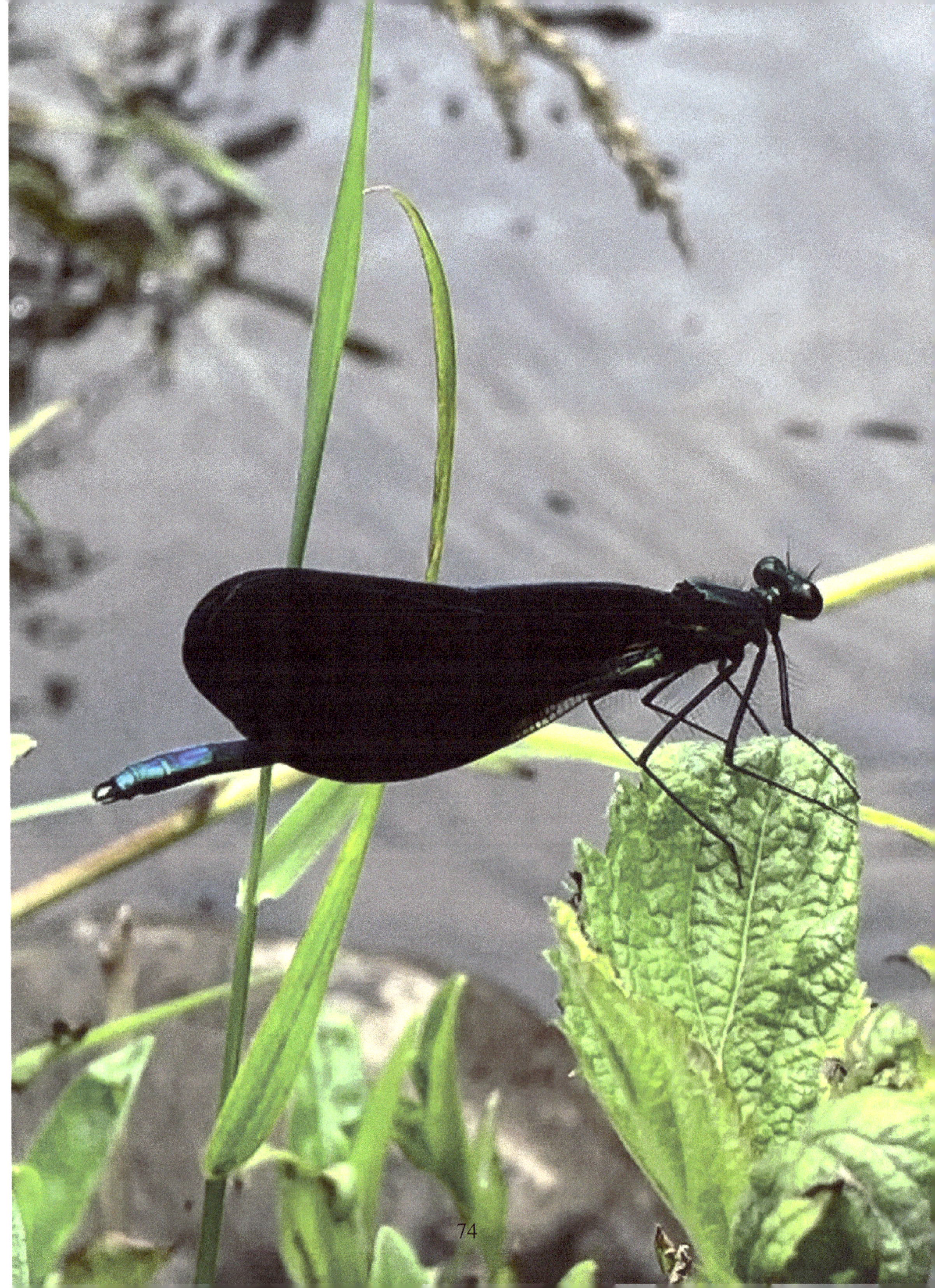

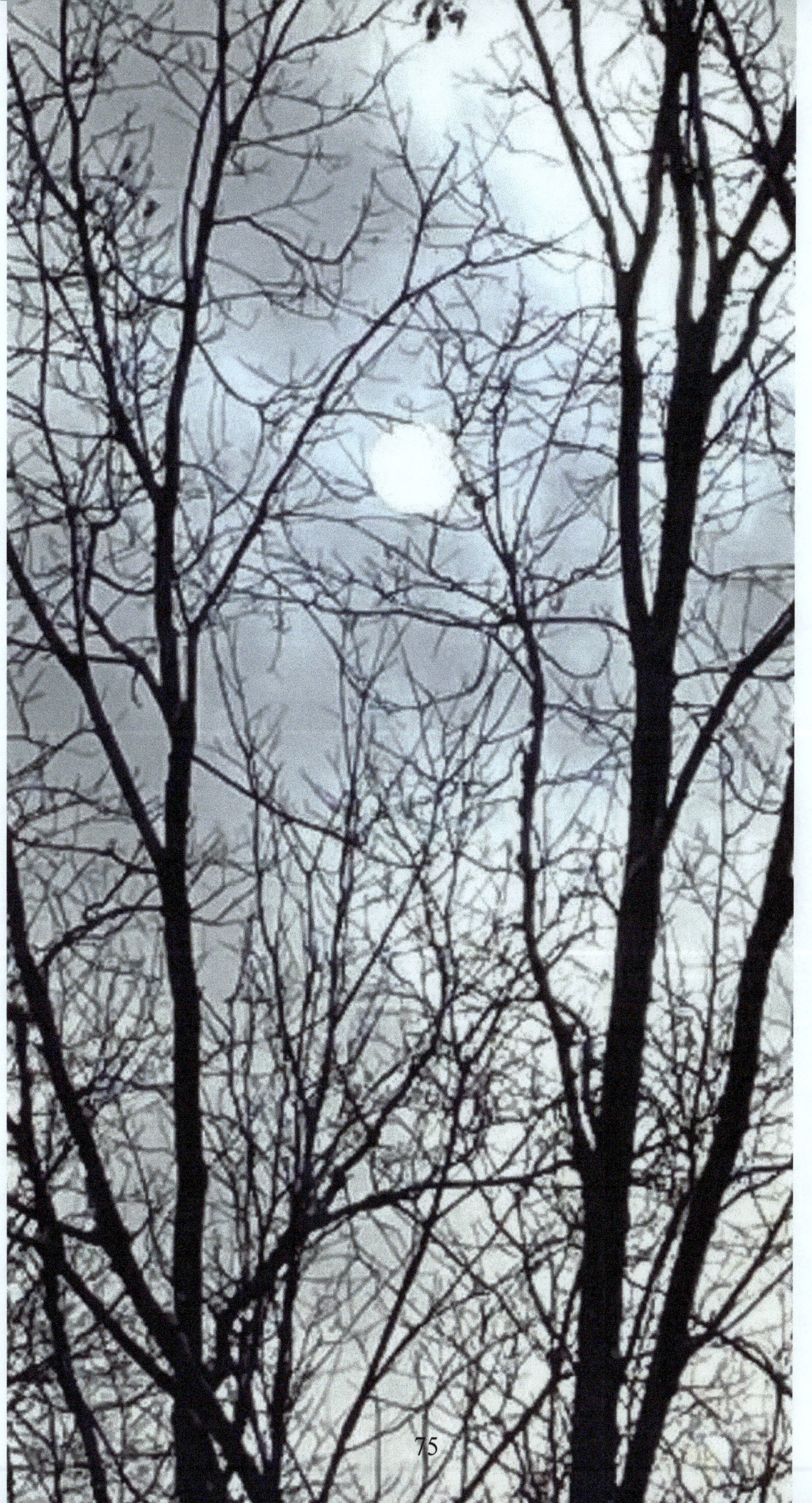

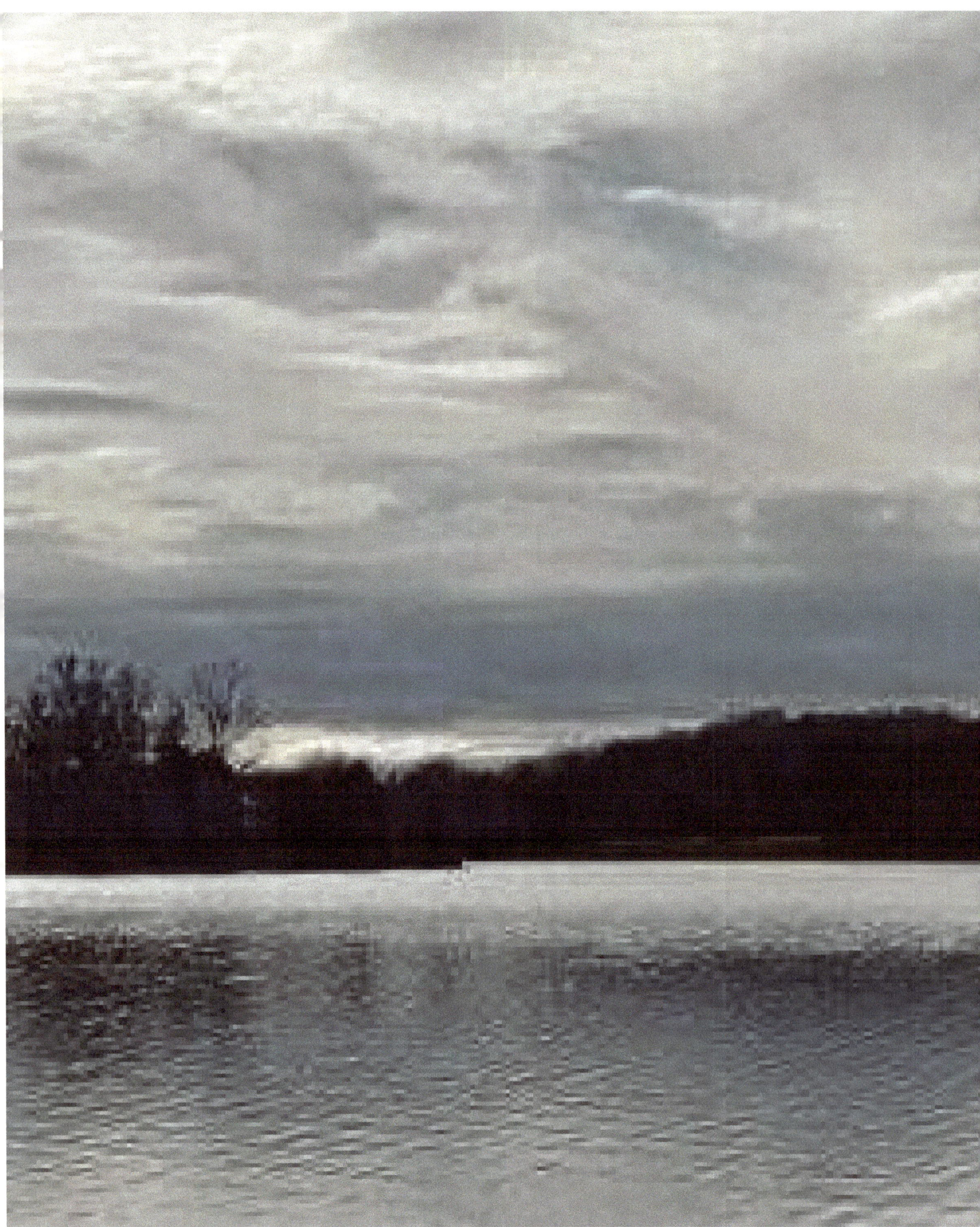

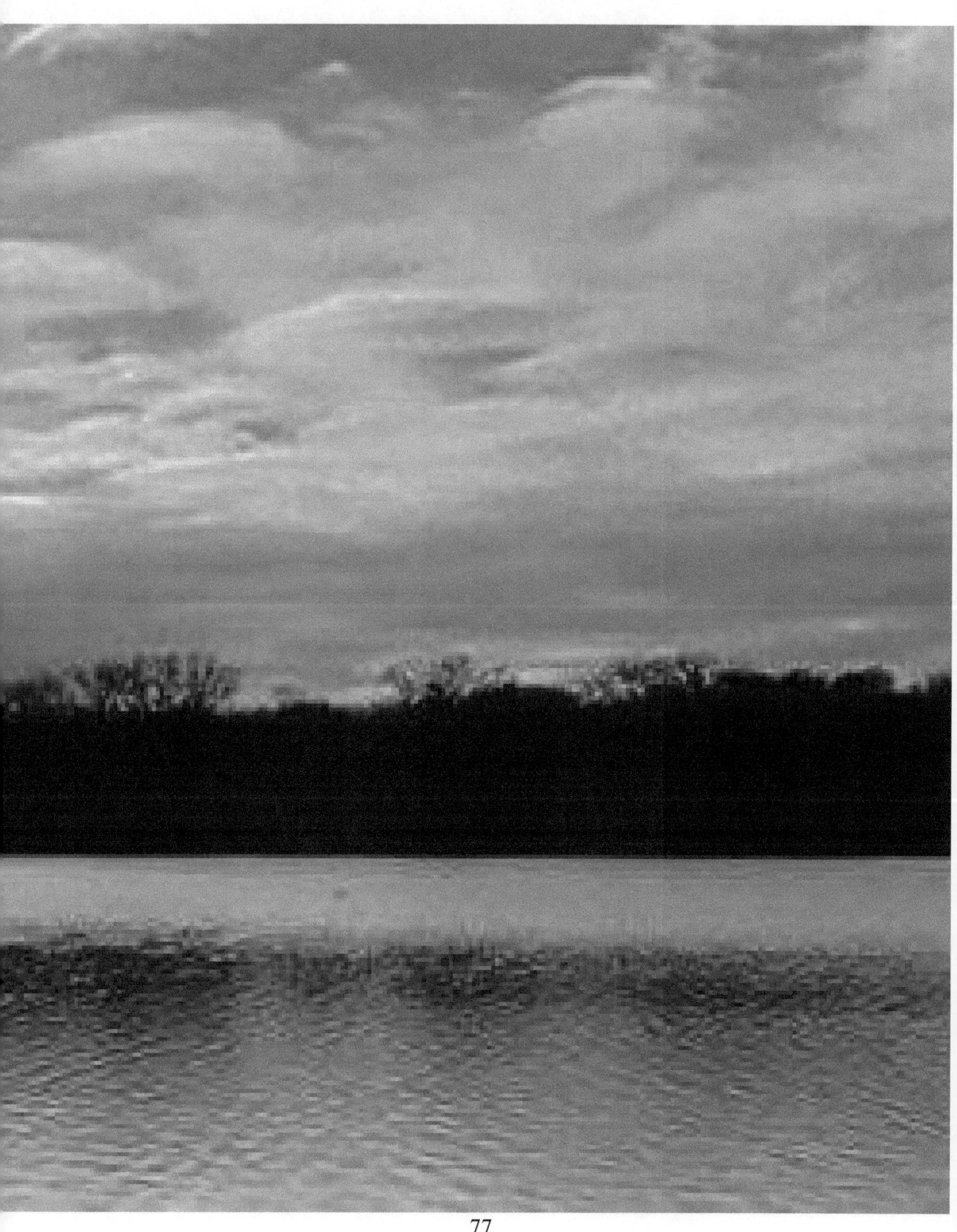

Two roads diverged in a yellow wood,
And sorry that I could not travel both
And be one traveler, long I stood
And looked down one as far as I could . . .

Then took the other, as just as fair,
And having perhaps the better claim,
Because it was grassy and wanted wear . . .

Two roads diverged in a wood, and I —
Took the one less traveled by,
And it made all the difference.

Robert Frost

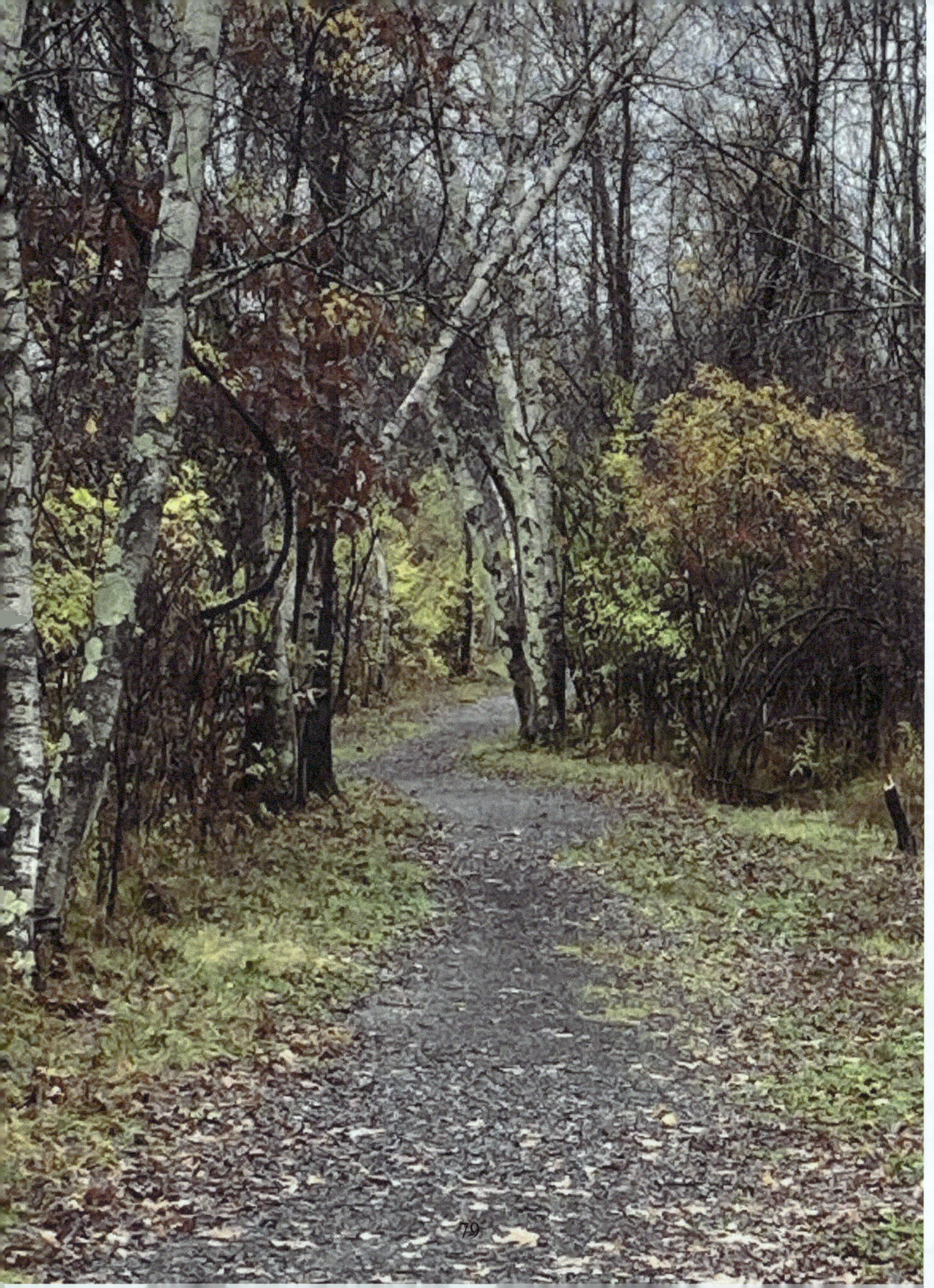

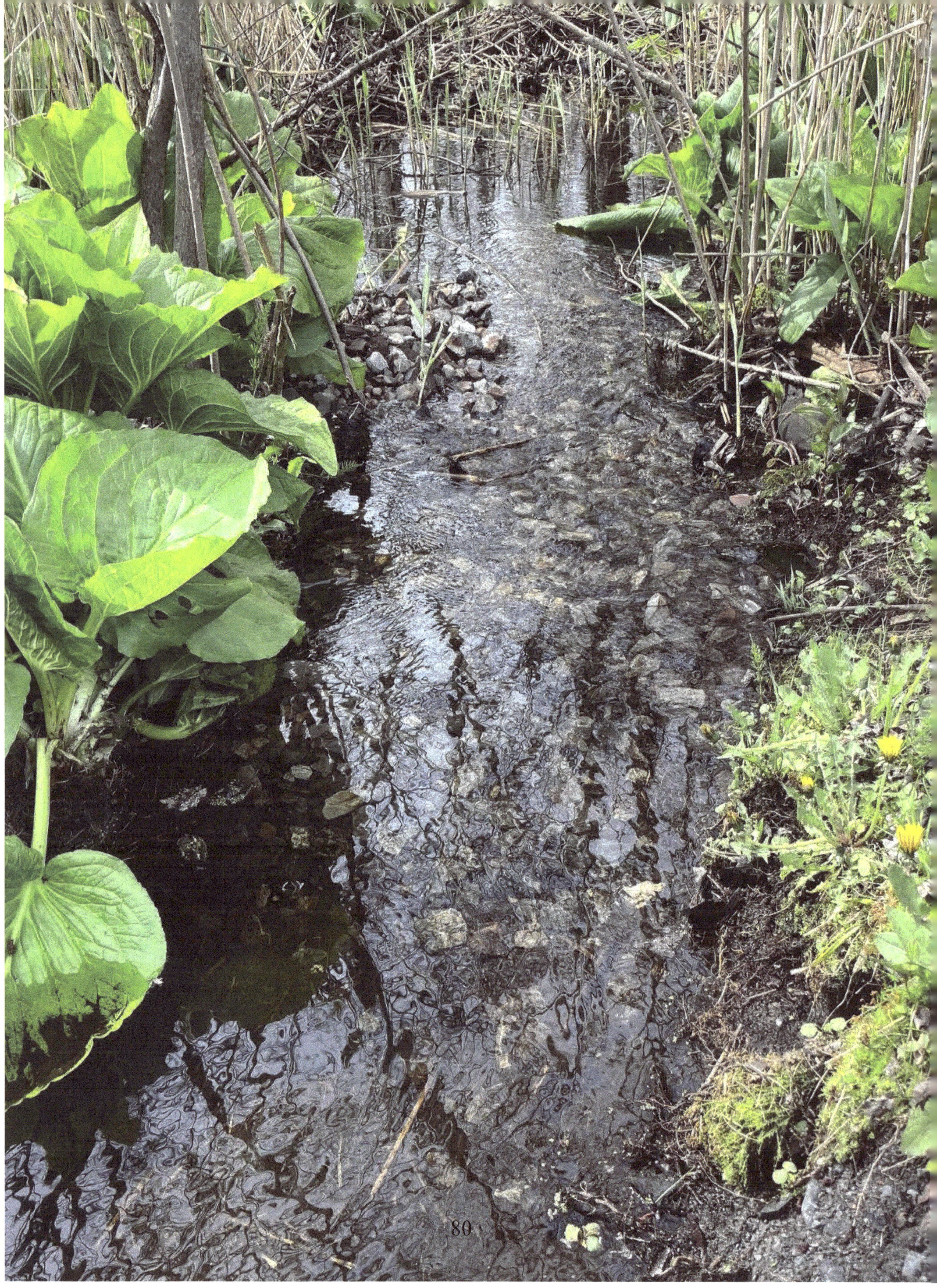

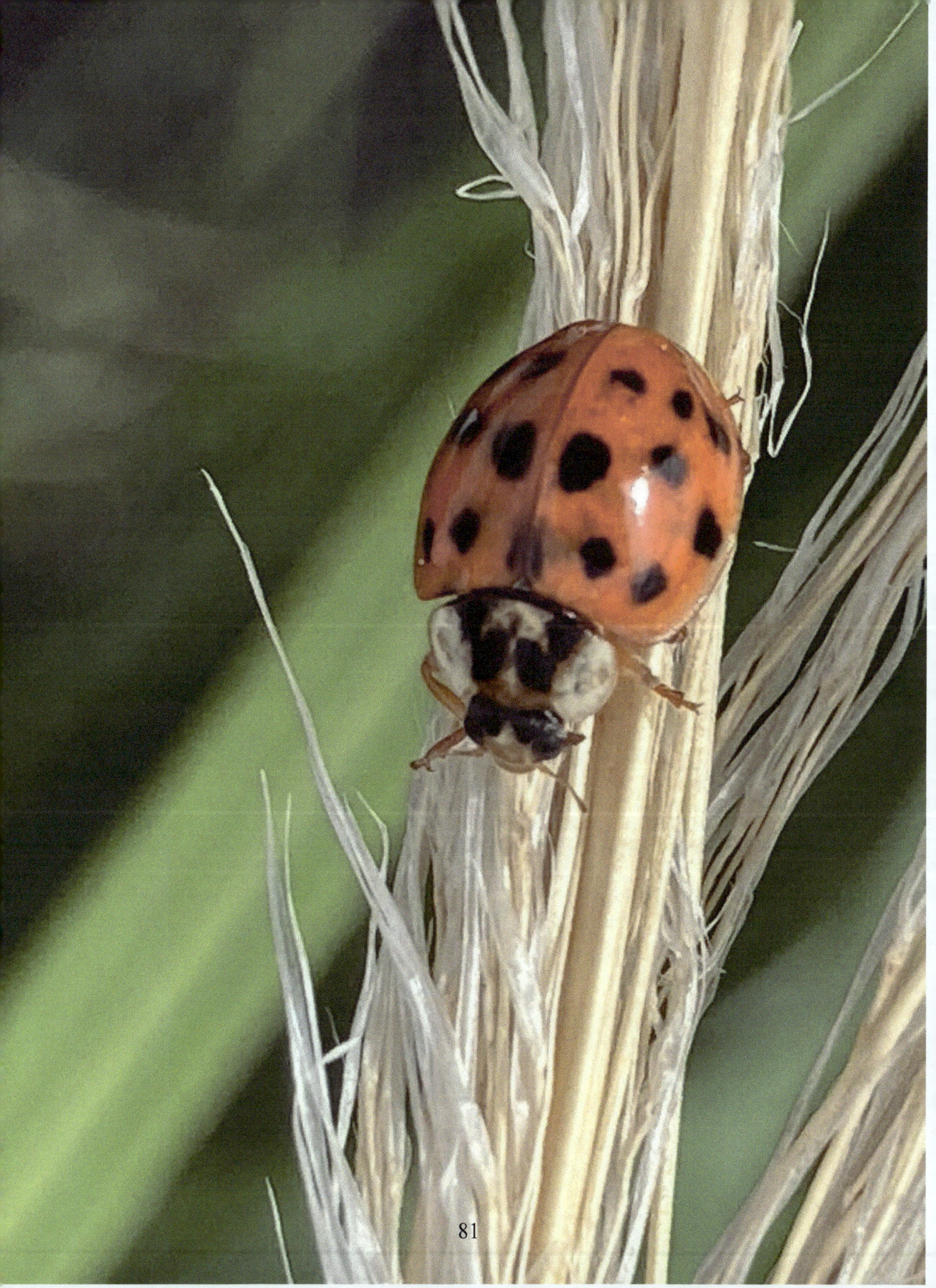

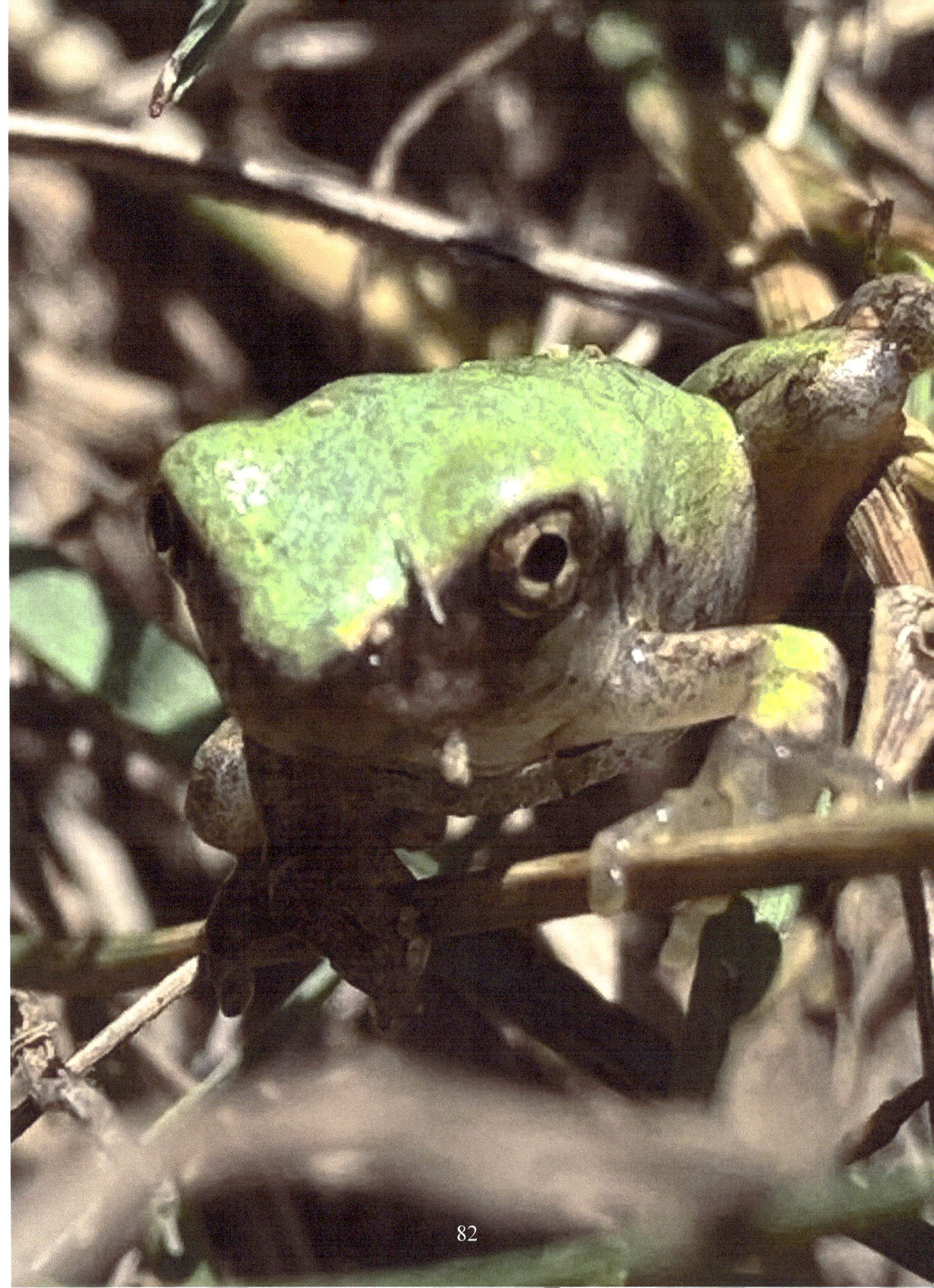

"Being in Nature is the antidote for everything."

Anonymous

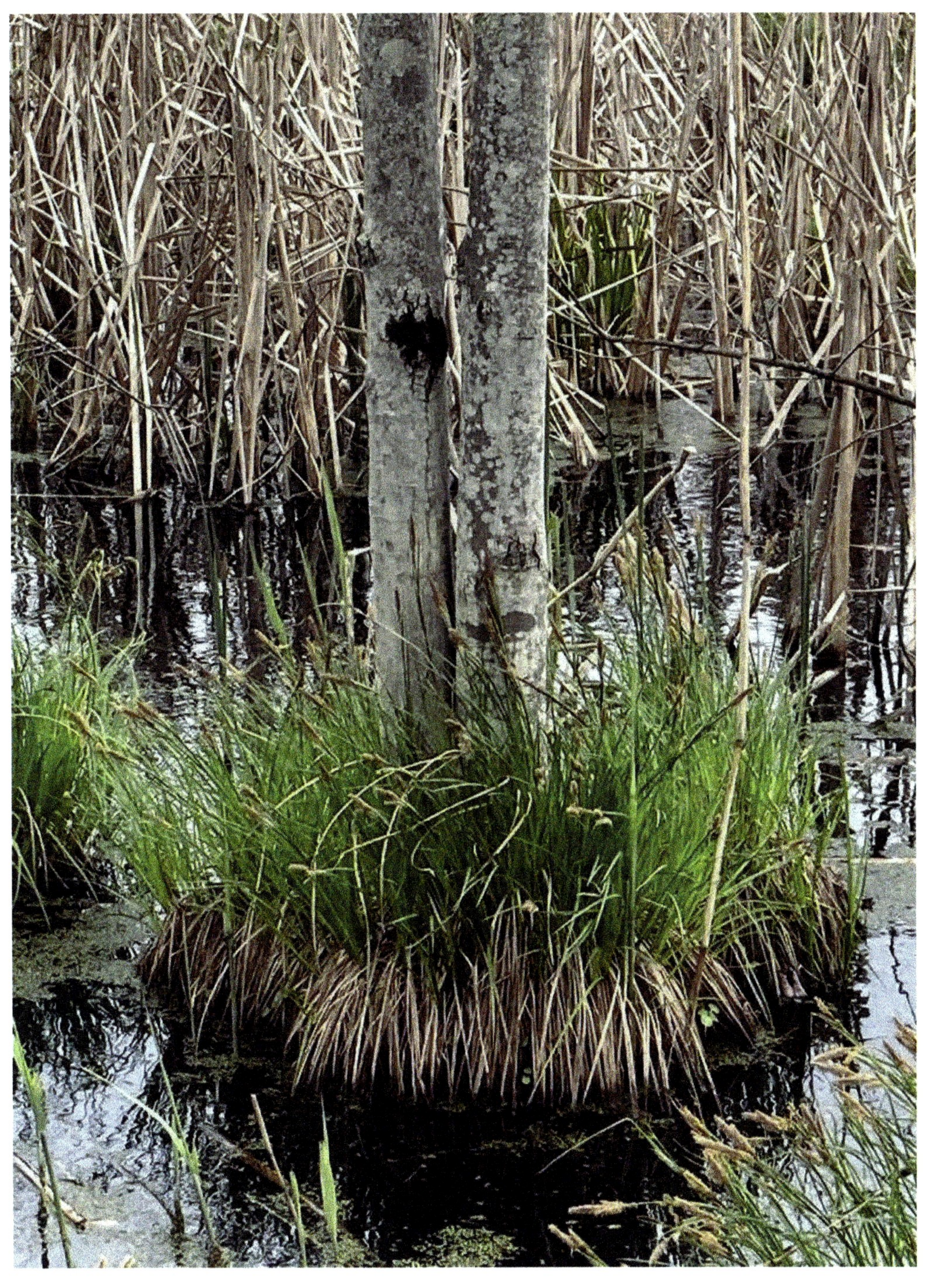

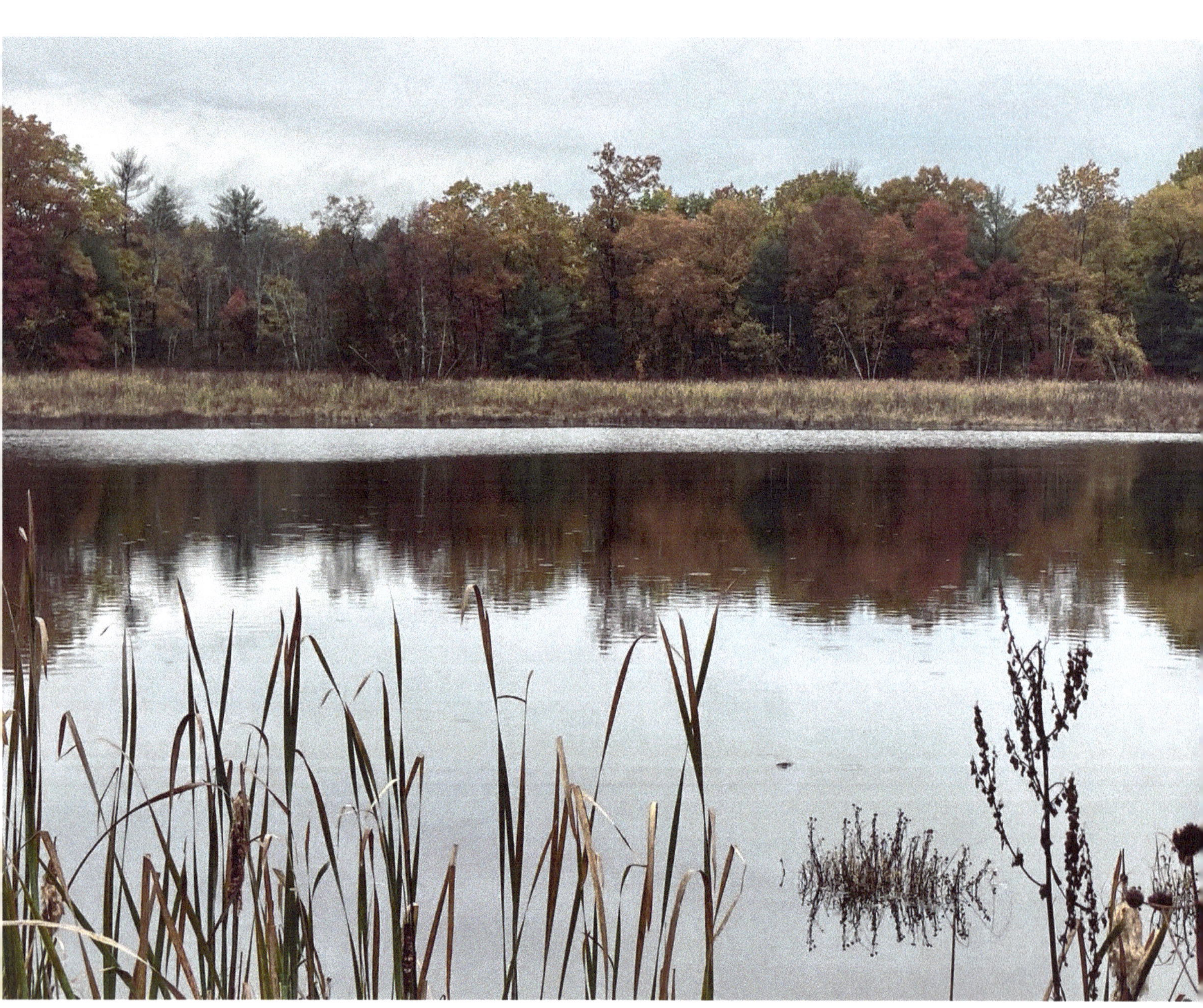

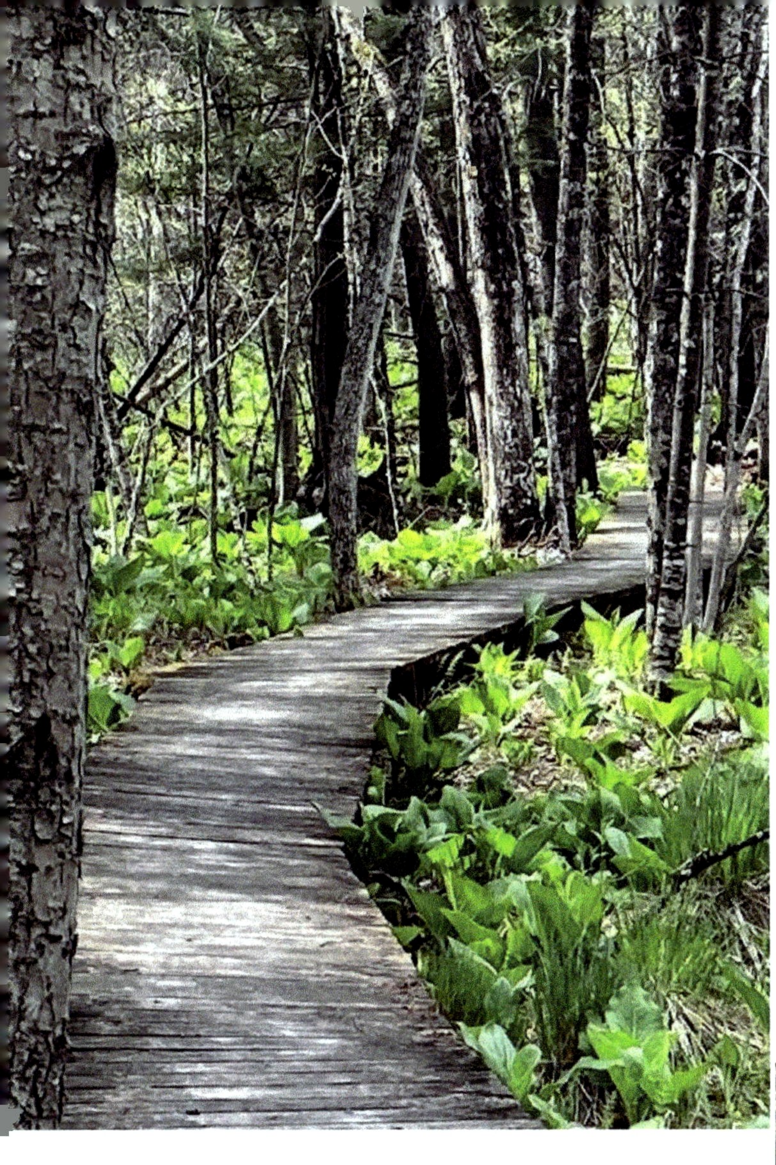

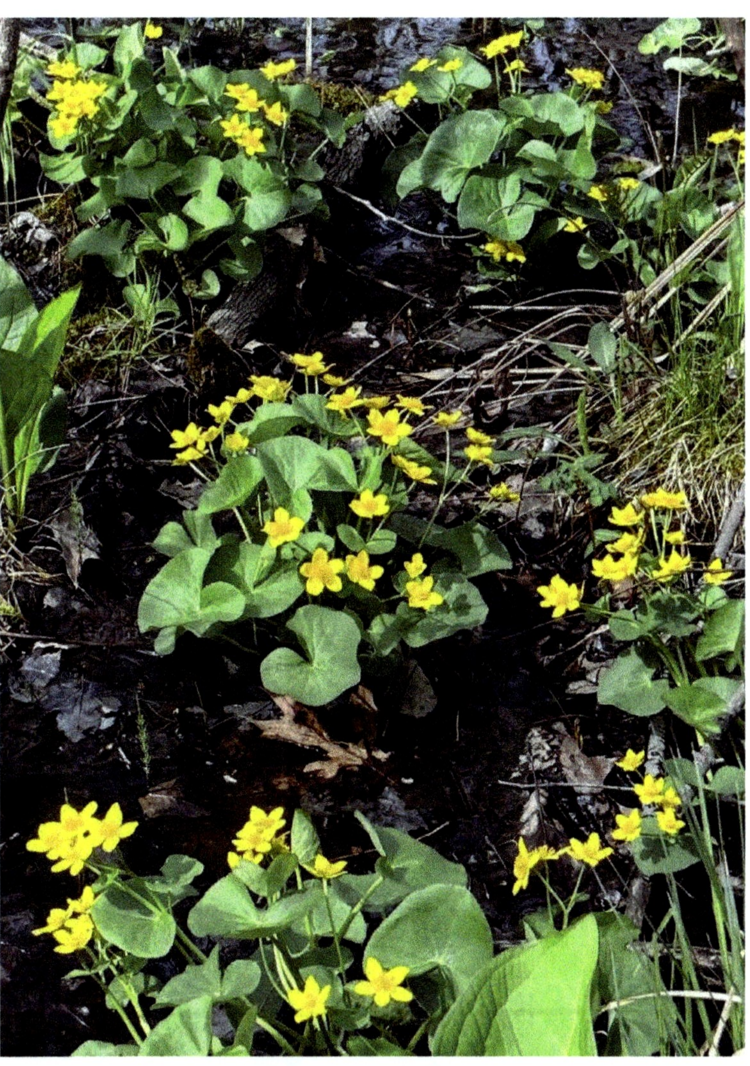

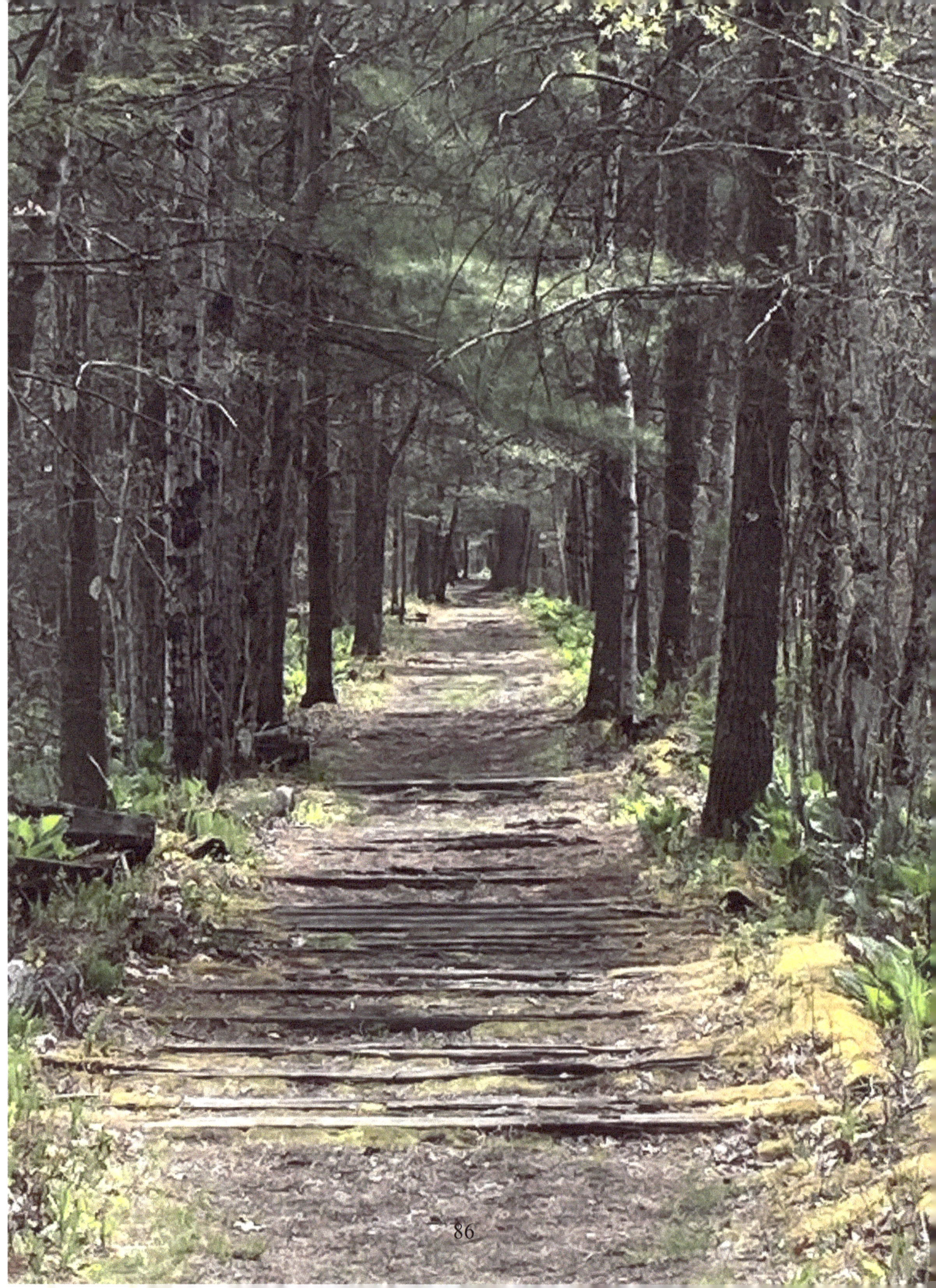

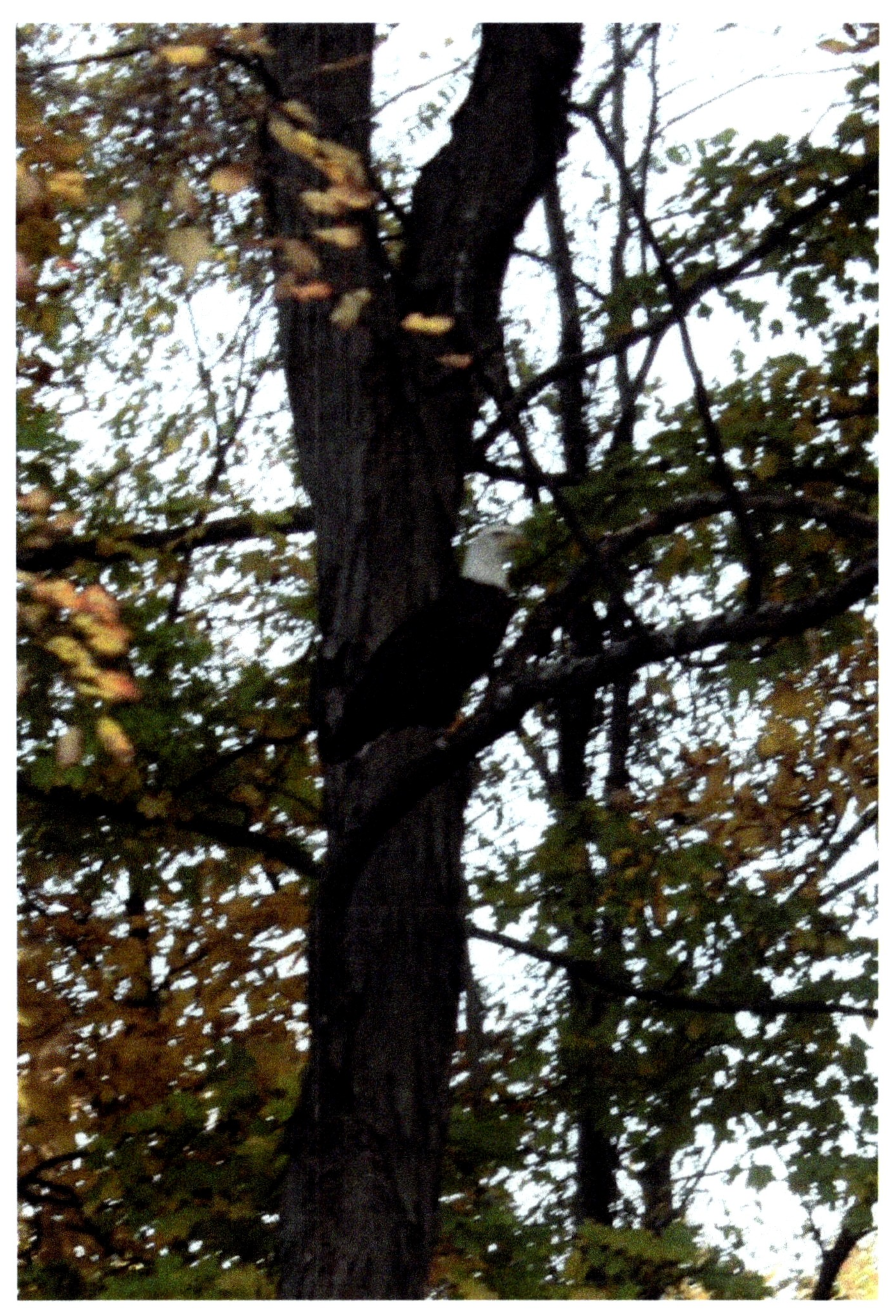

The miracle is not to fly in the air.
The miracle is to walk
on the green earth
and connect with Nature.

Chinese Proverb

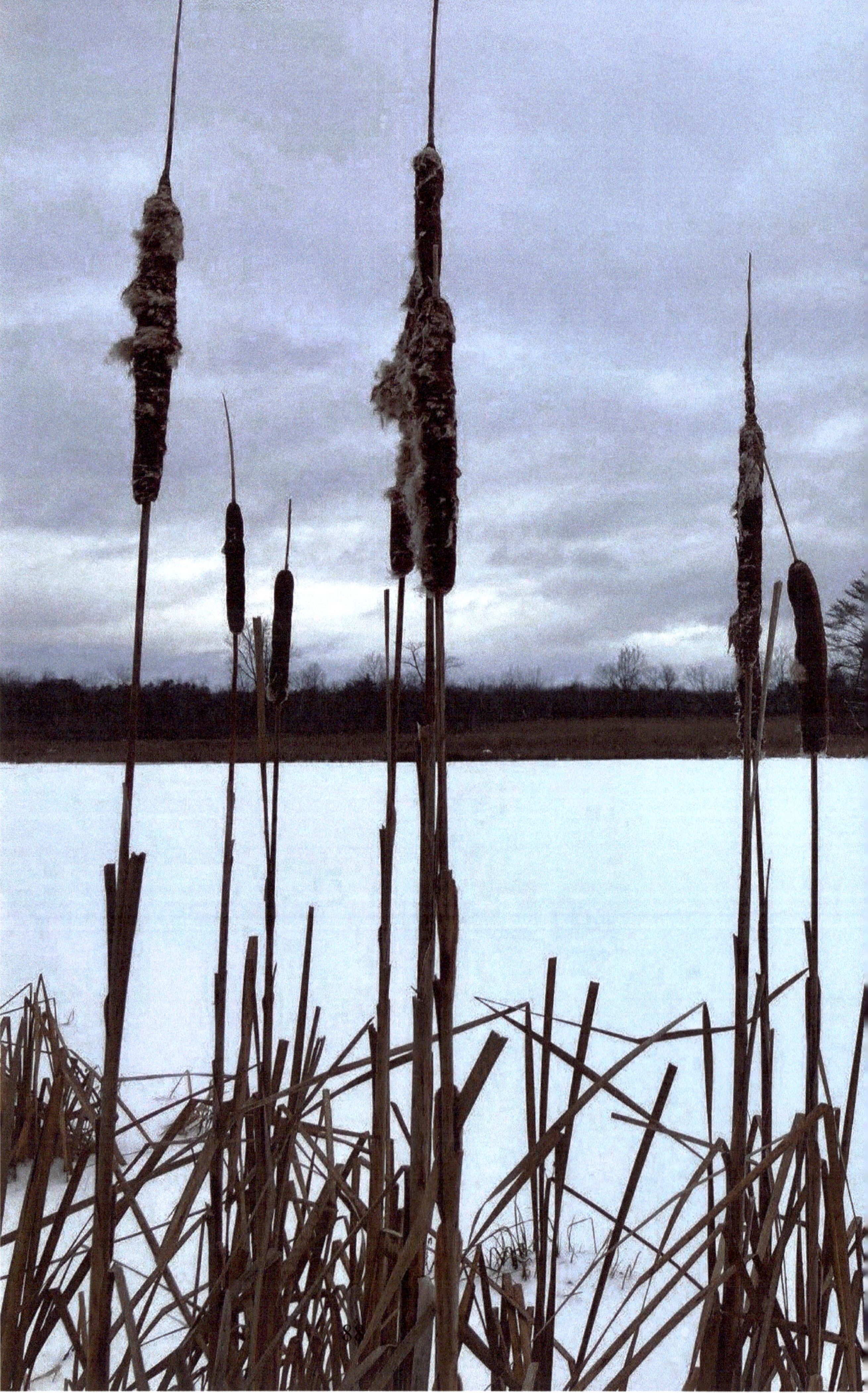

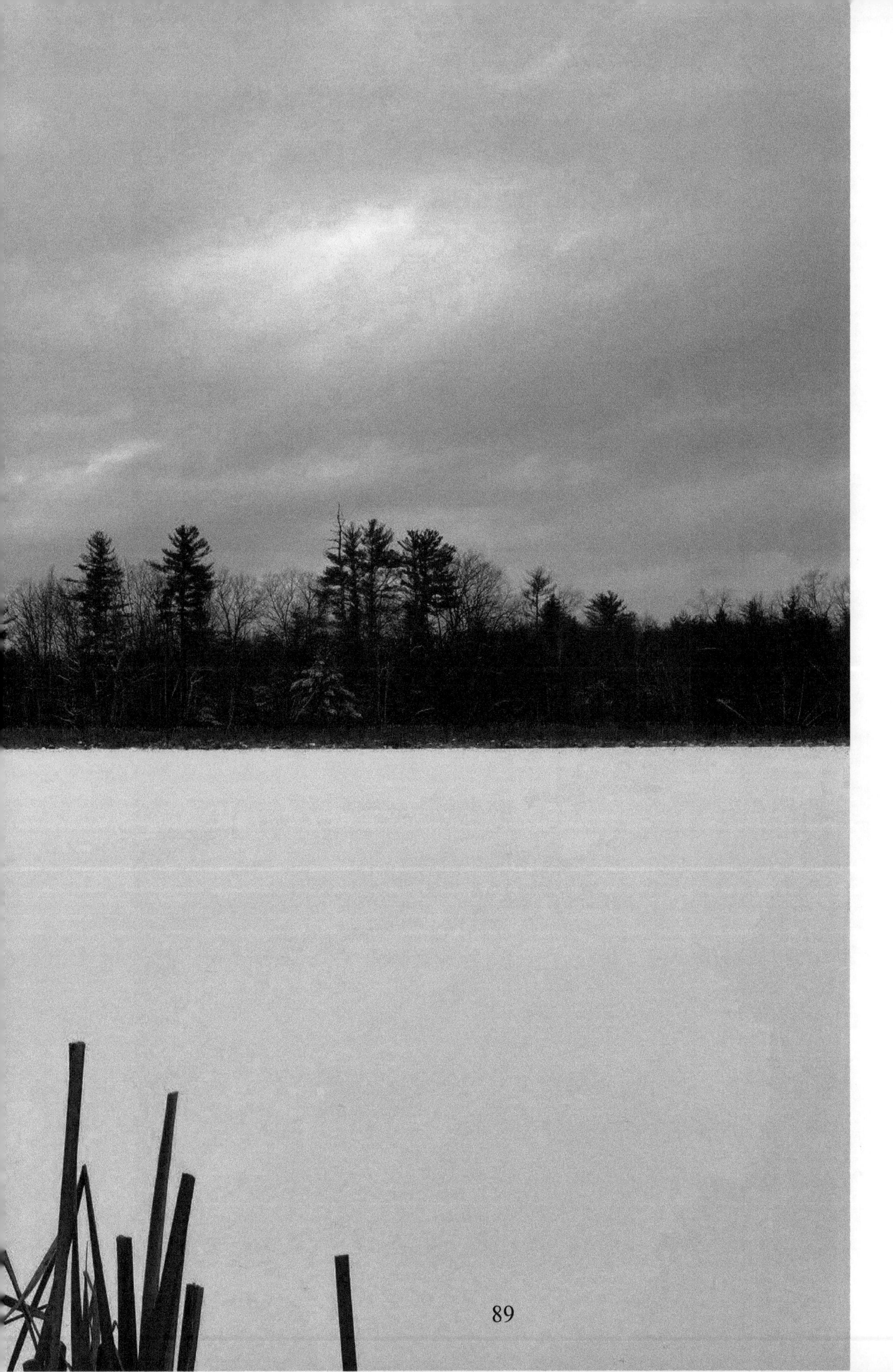

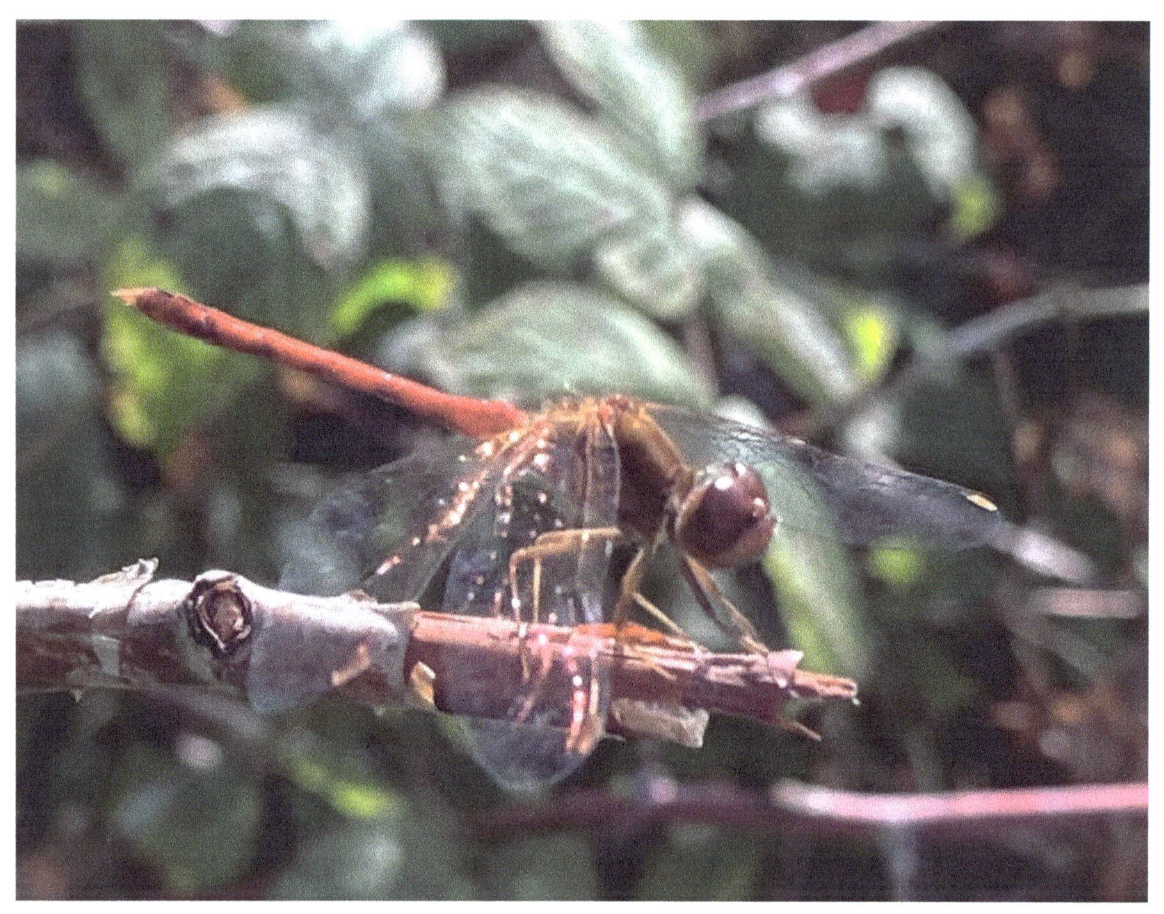

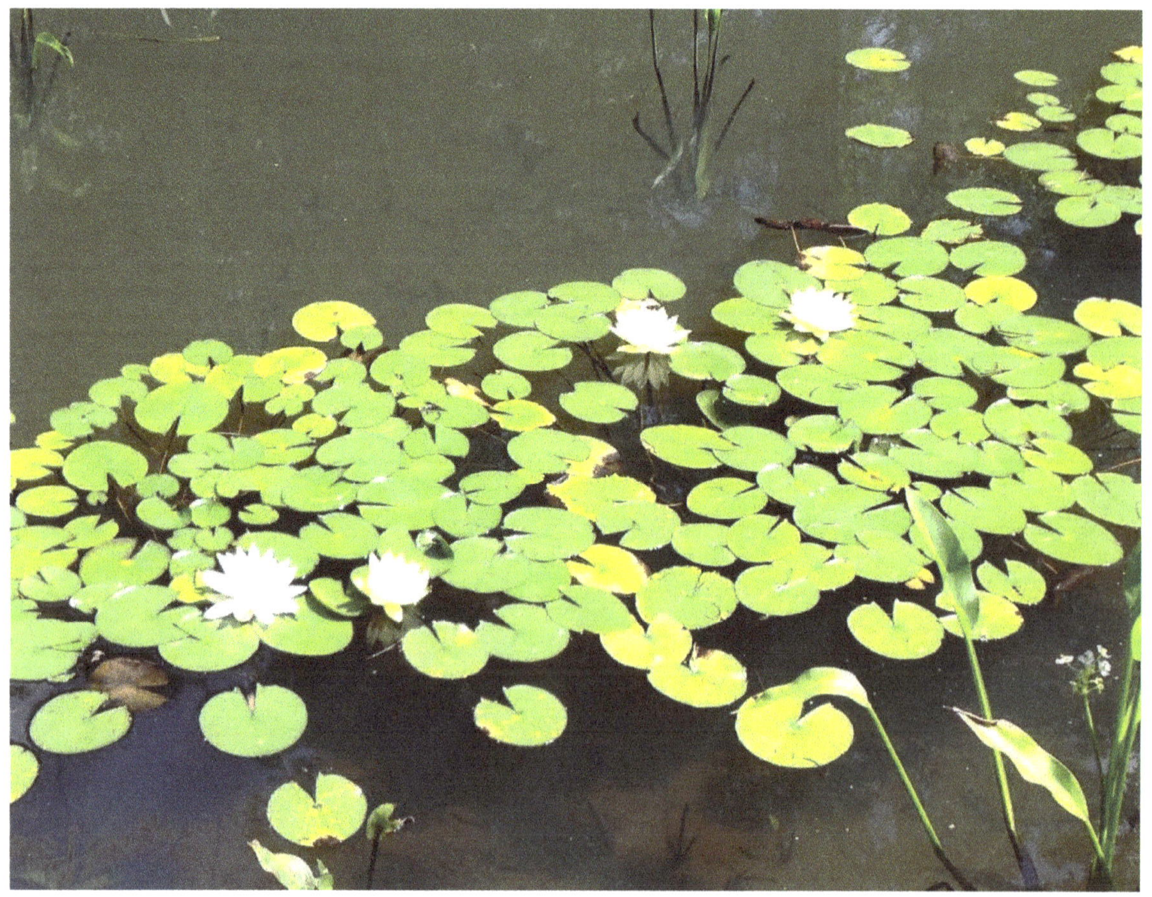

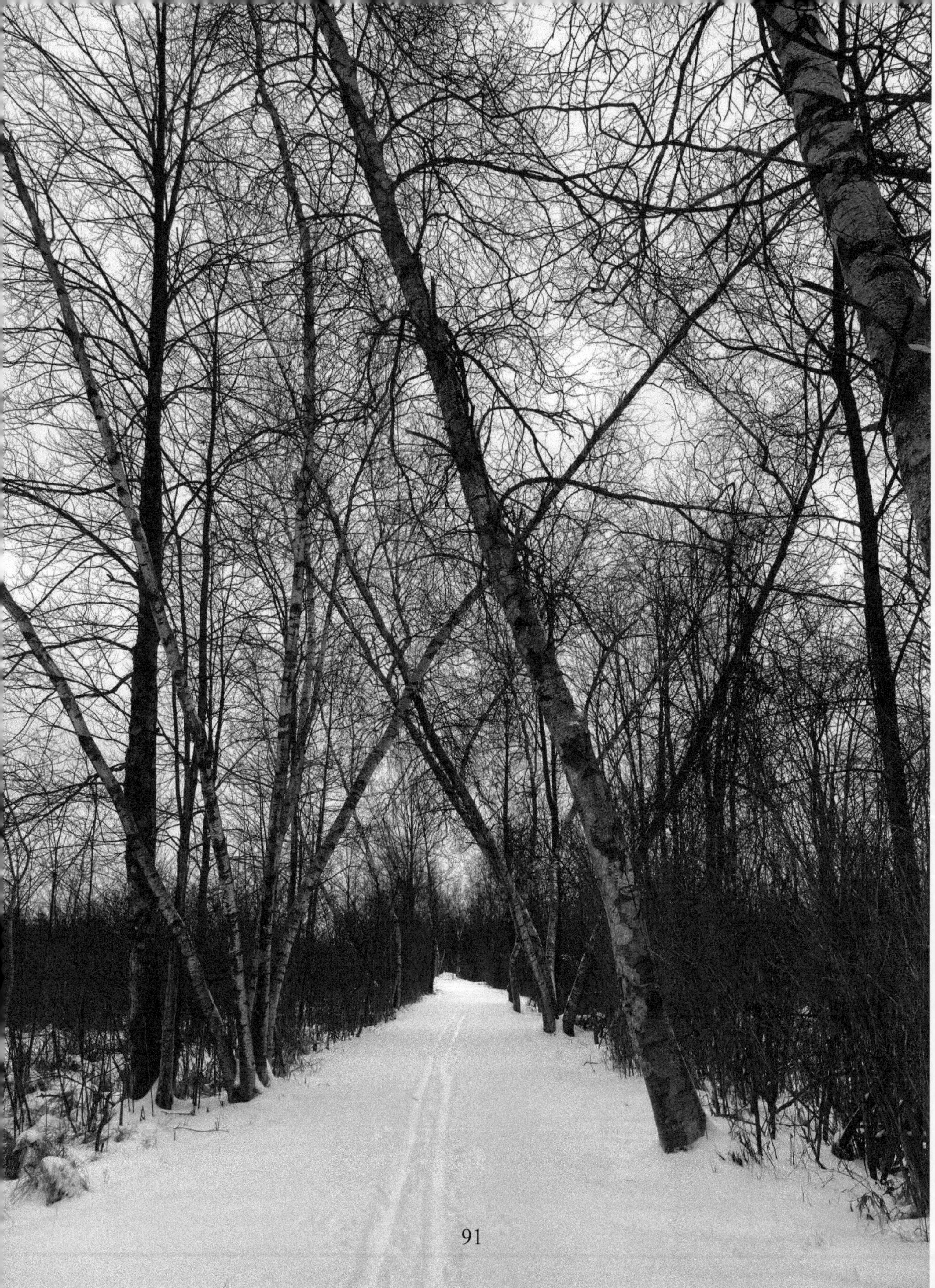

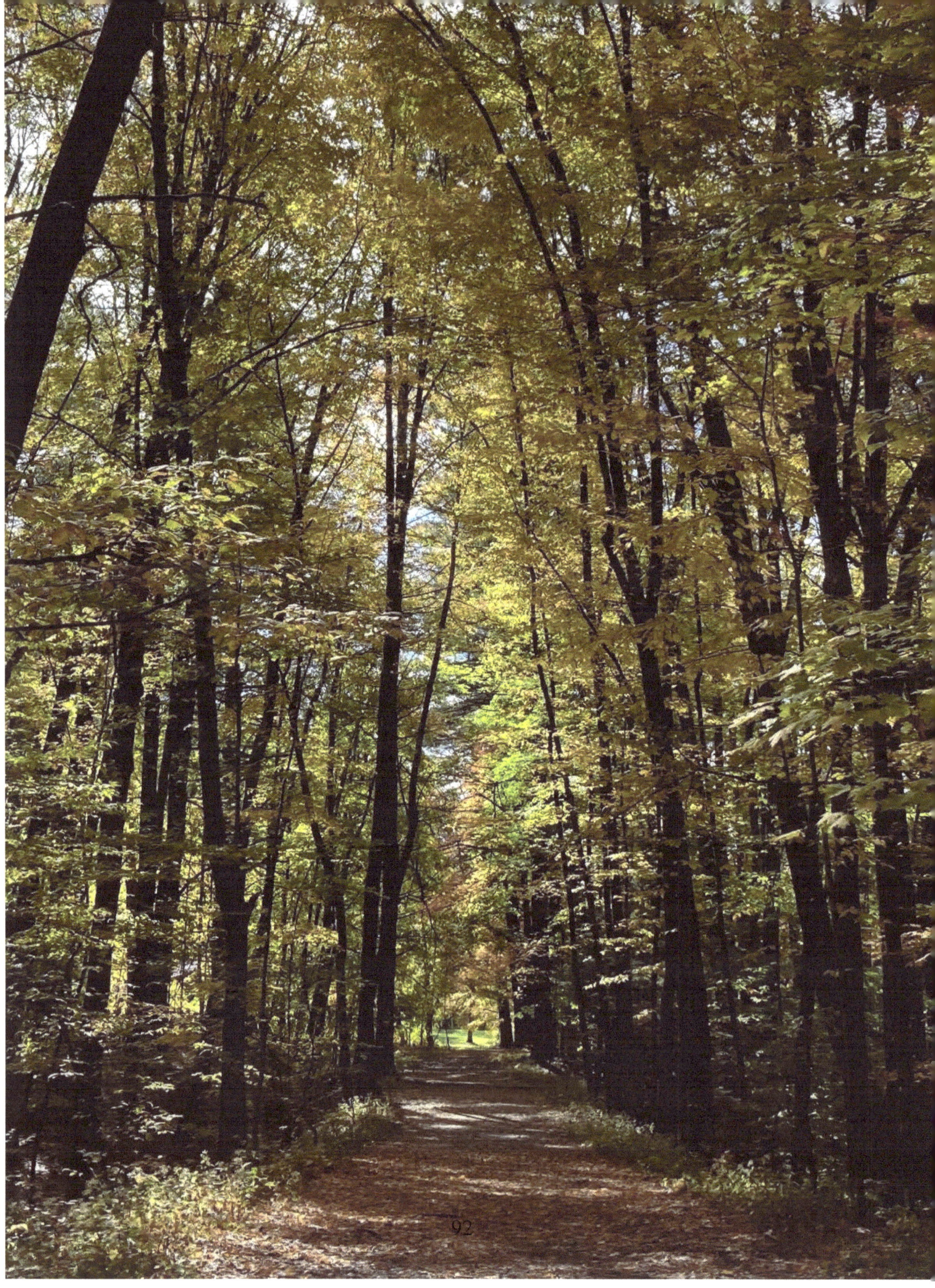

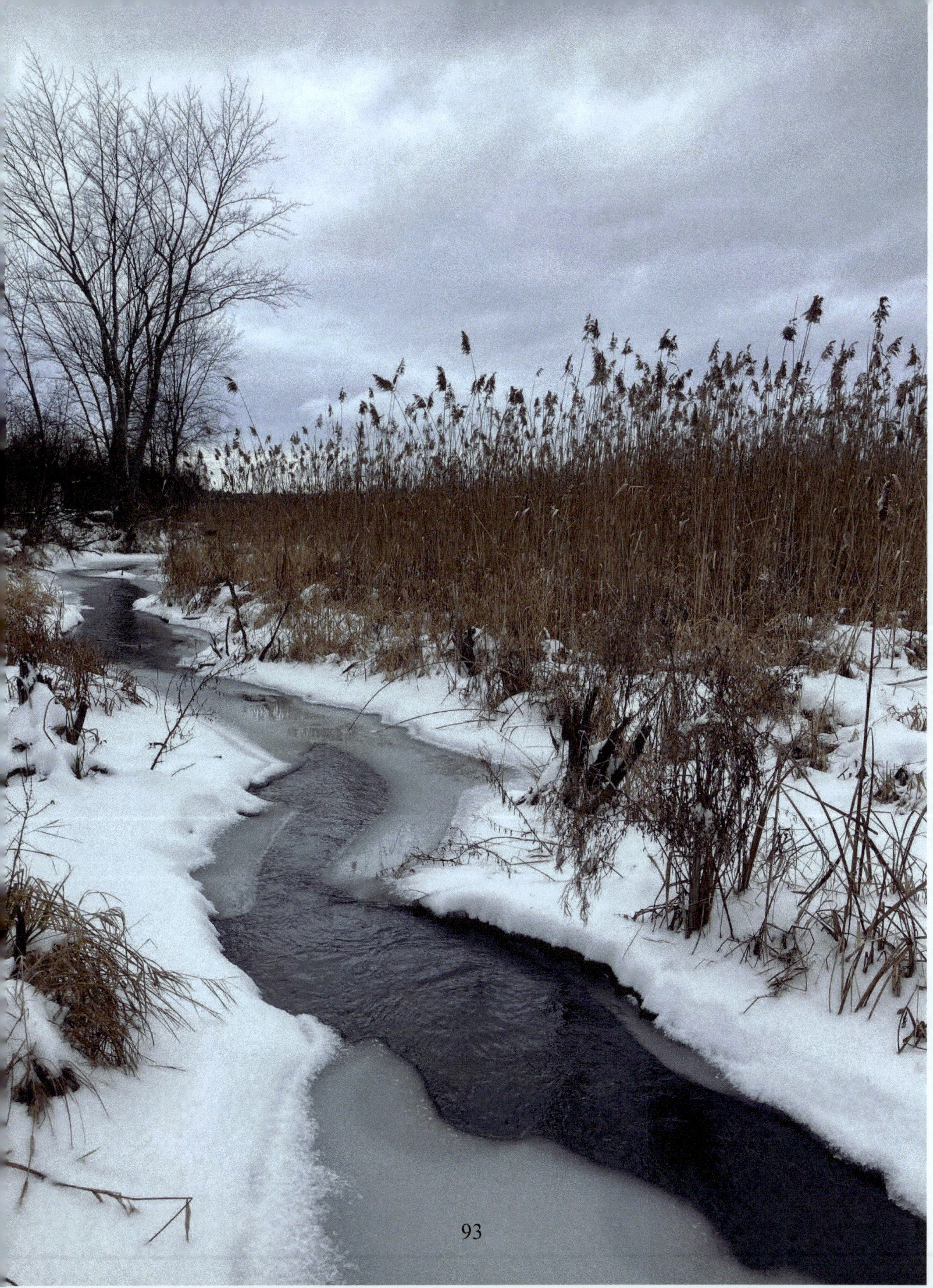

"We are not surrounded by the ordinary – we are surrounded by the extraordinary."

Thich Nhat Hanh

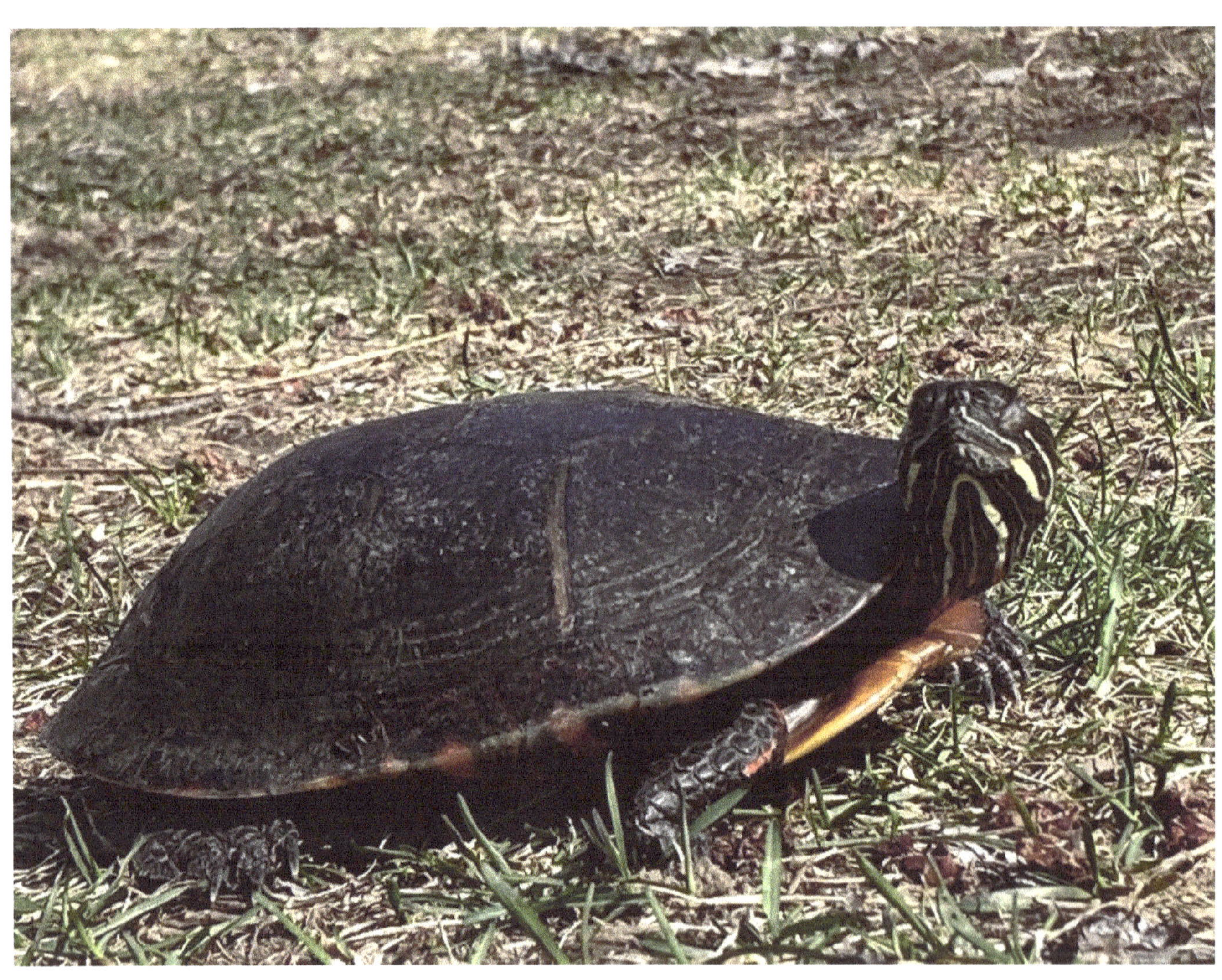

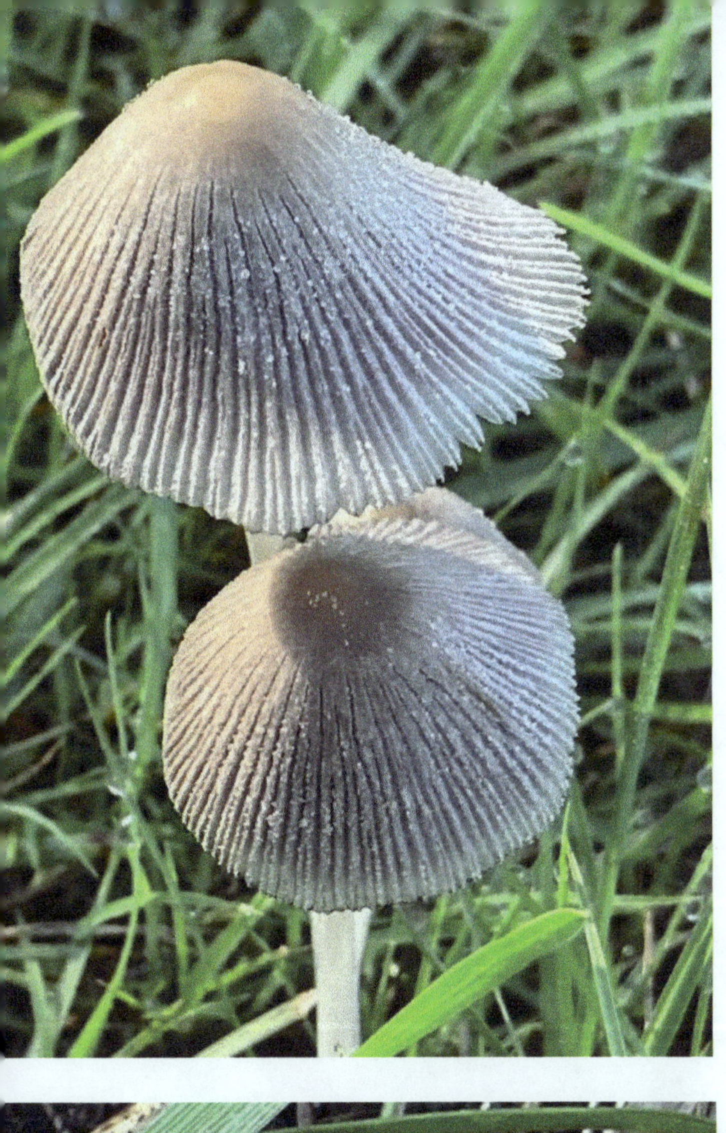
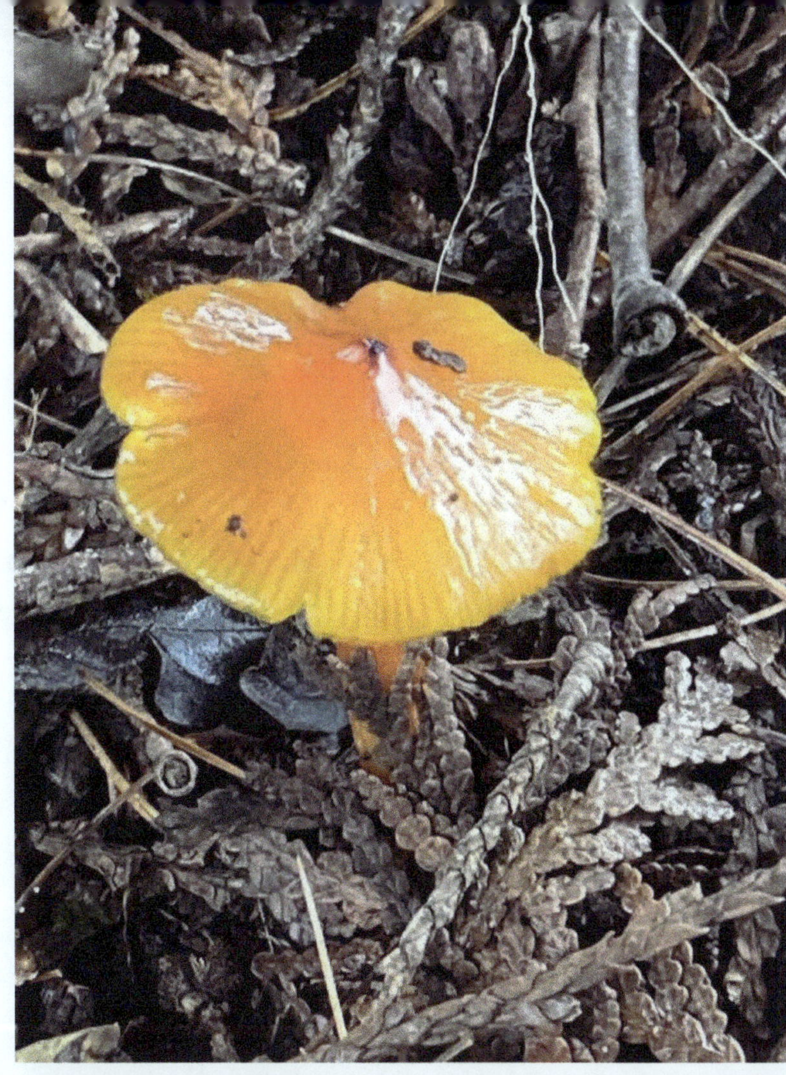
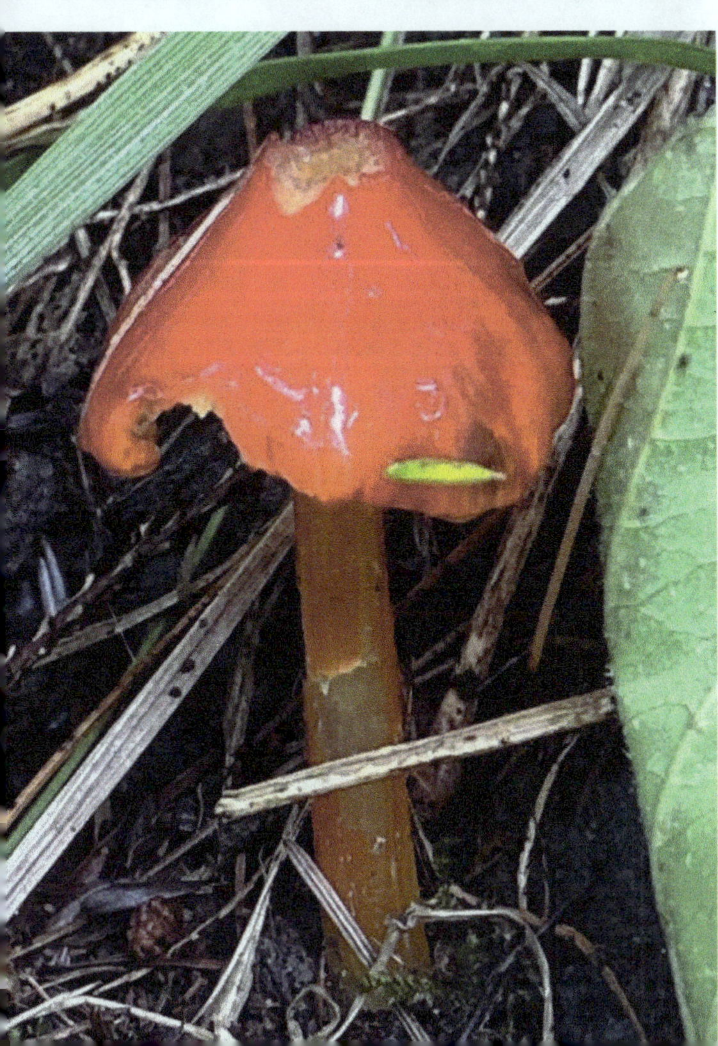
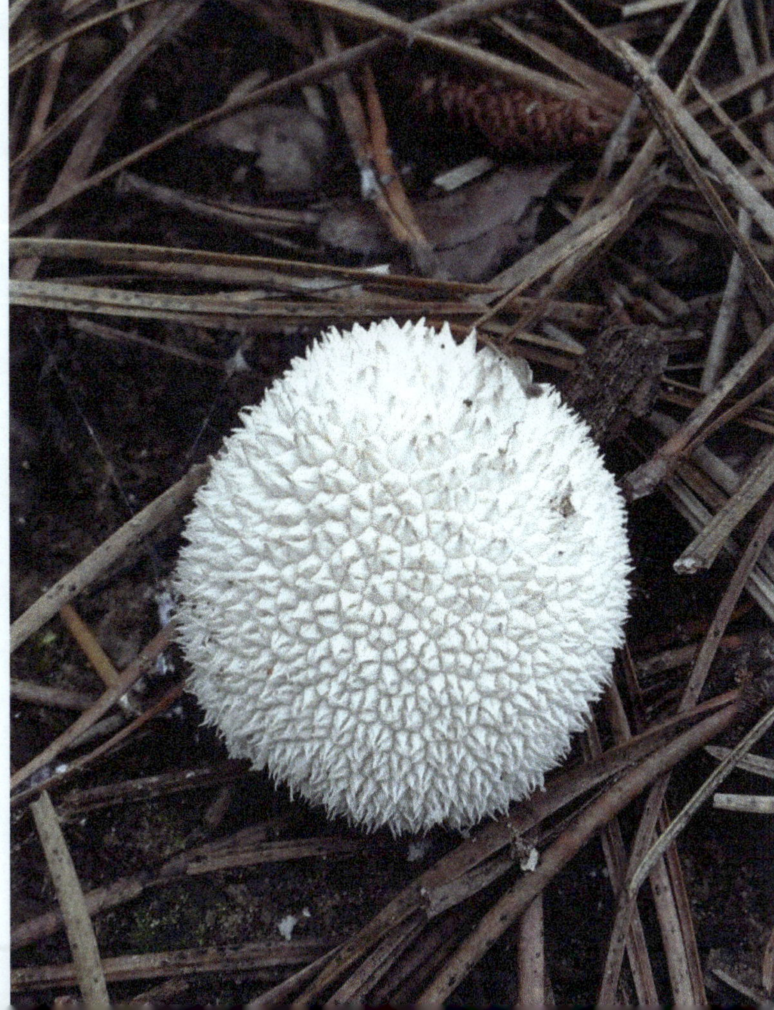

Saratoga National Historical Park and Battlefield

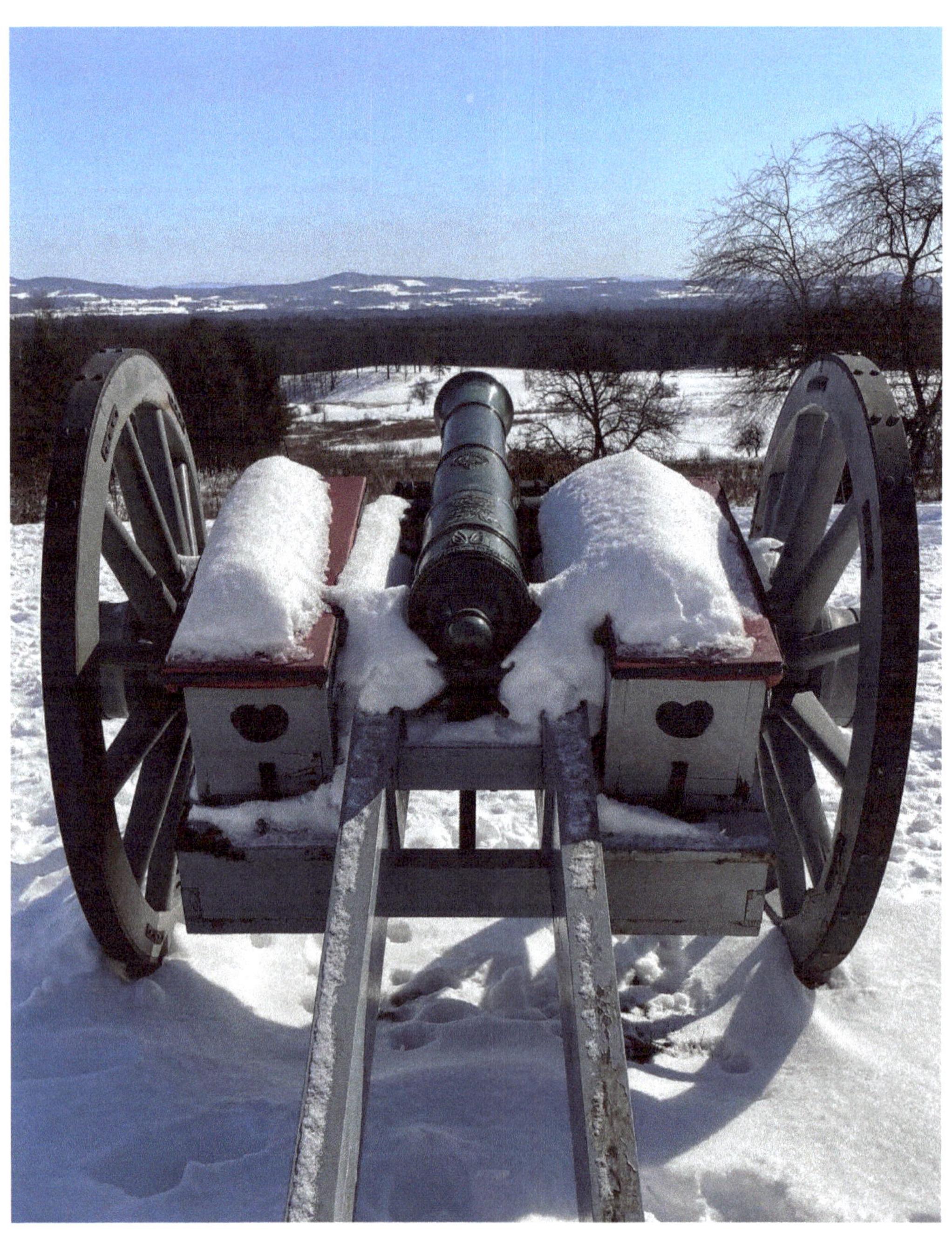

All this he saw, for one
Moment breathless and intense,
Vivid on the morning sky;
And still, as he looked, he lived,
And still, as he lived, he wondered.

Kenneth Grahame

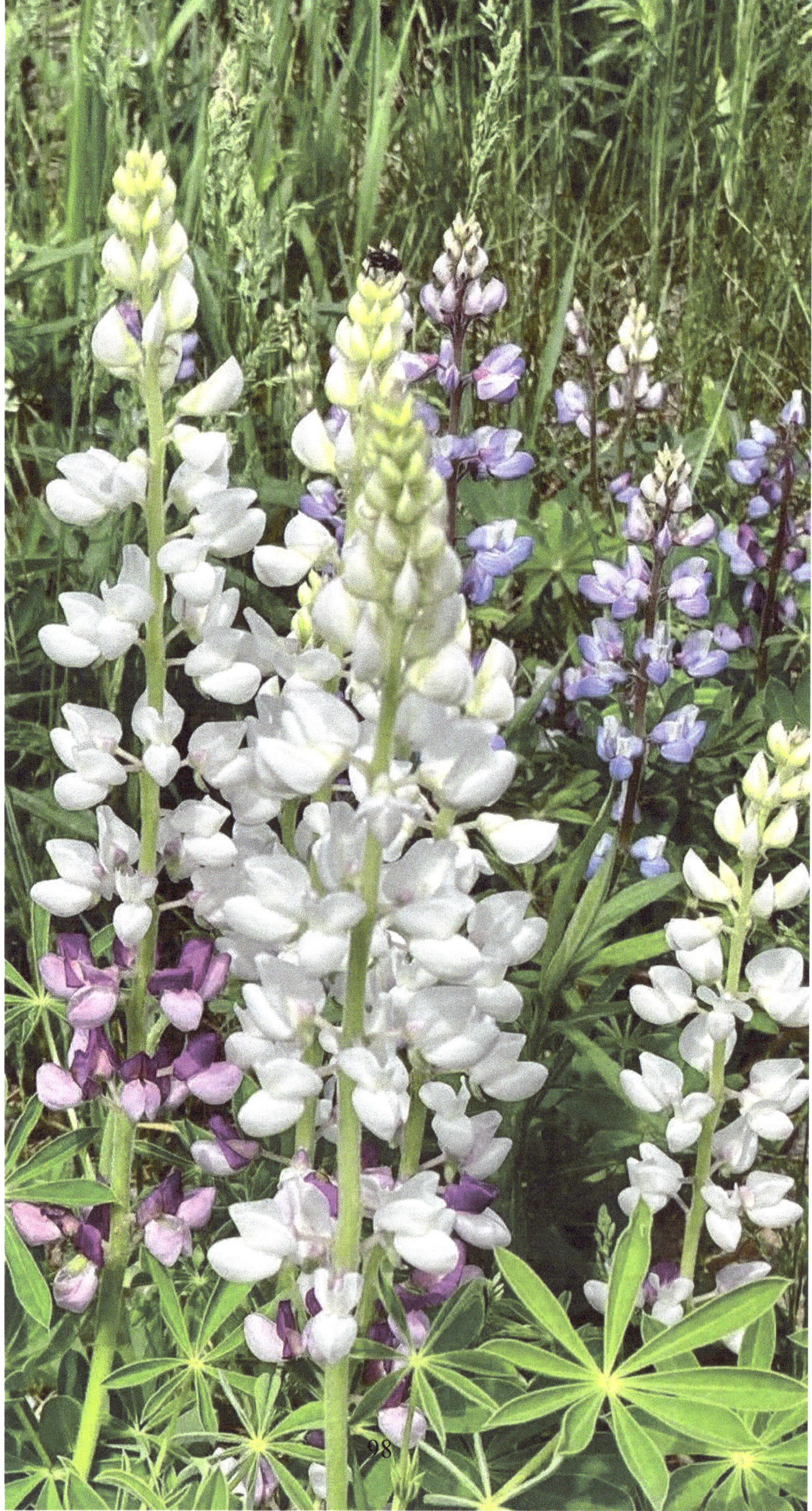

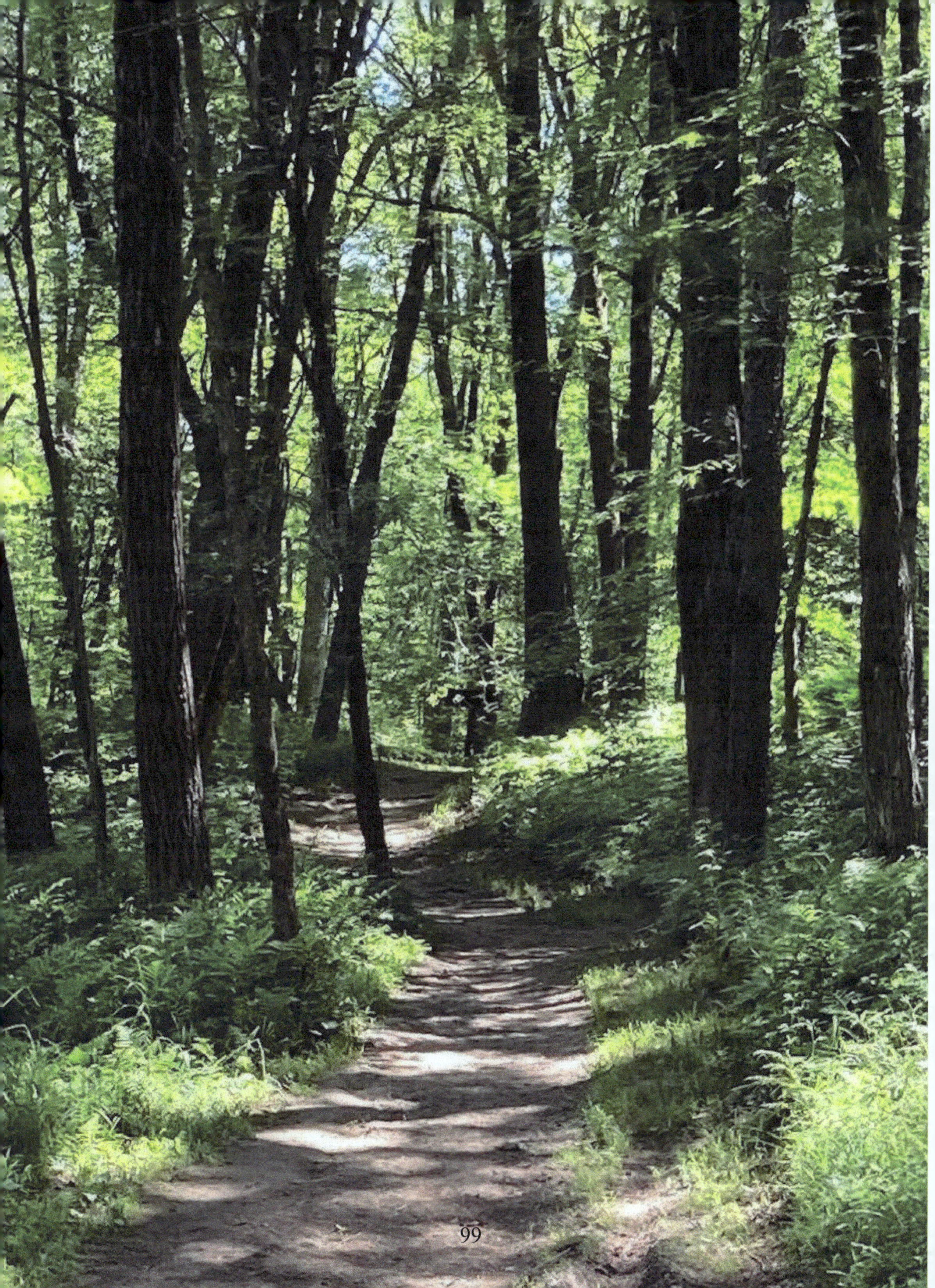

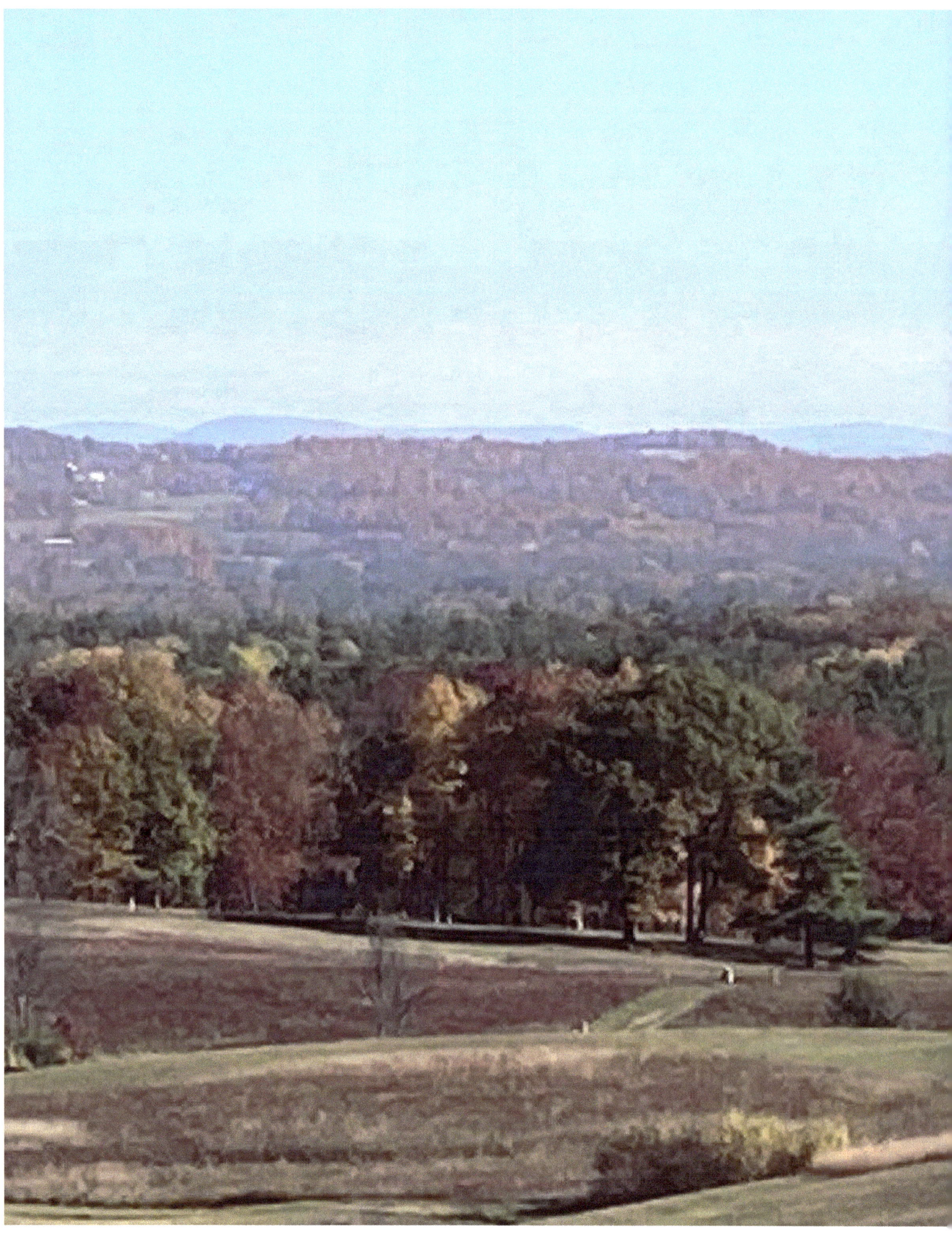

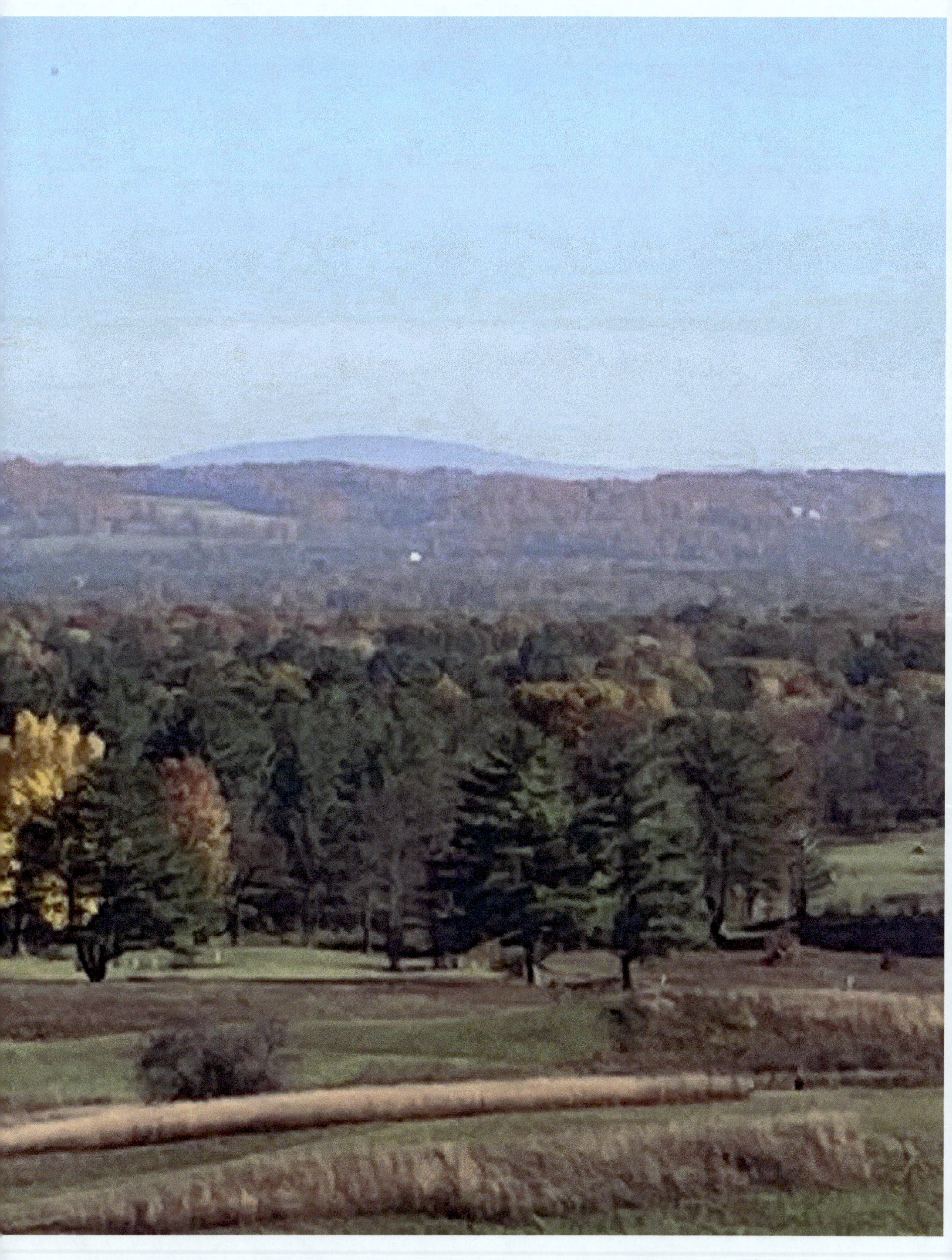

"The beauty of the natural world lies in the details."

Natalie Angier

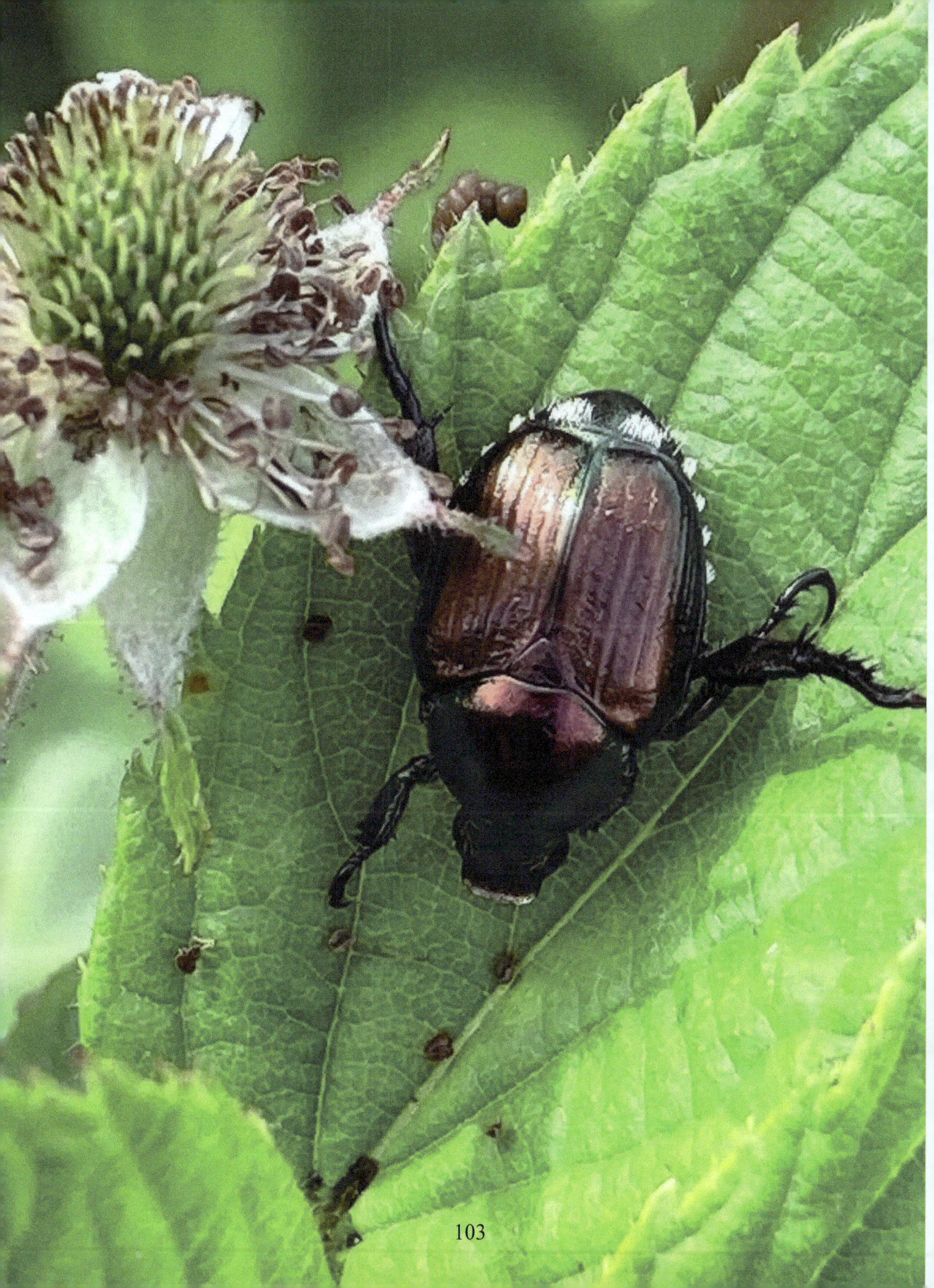

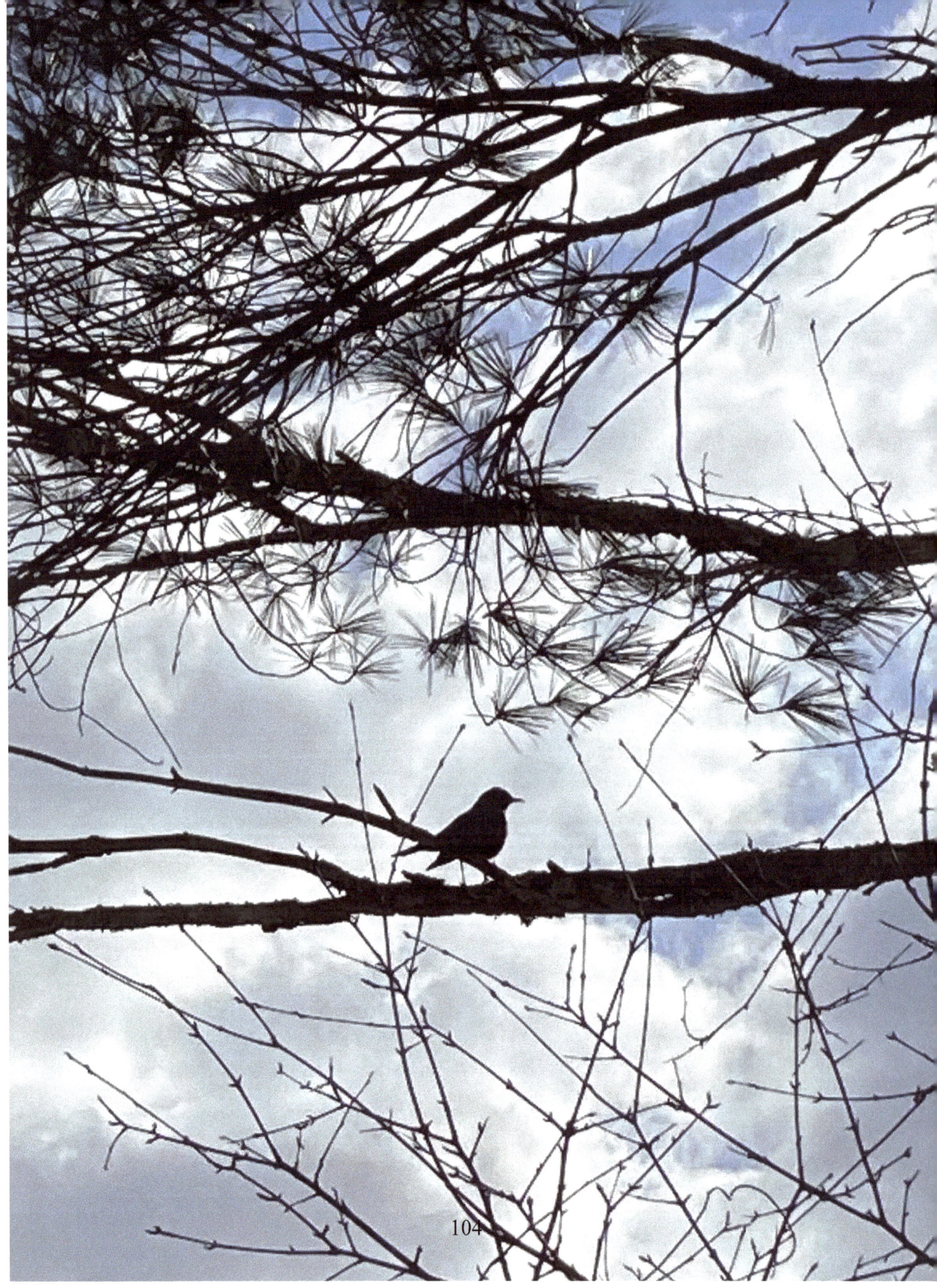

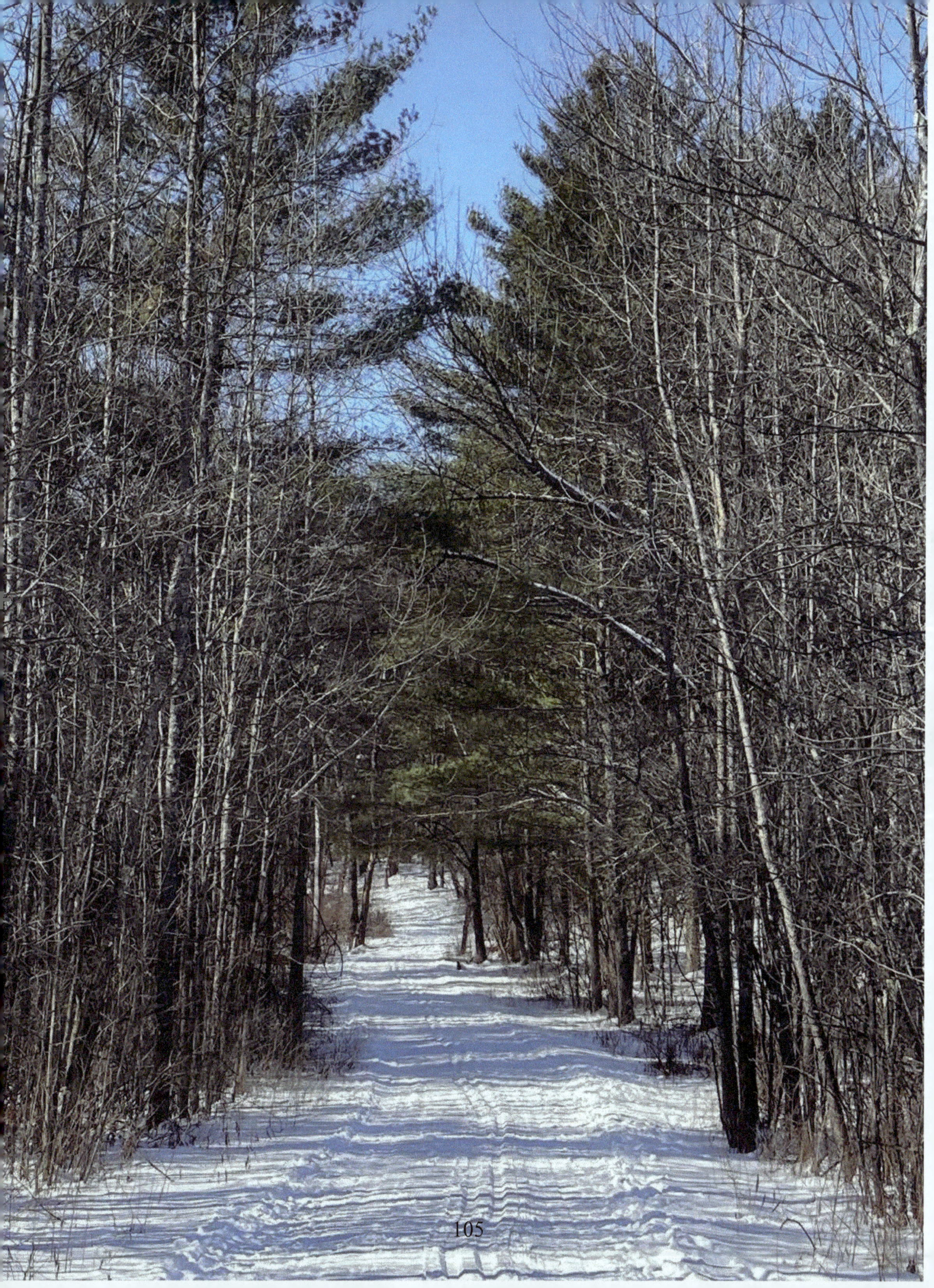

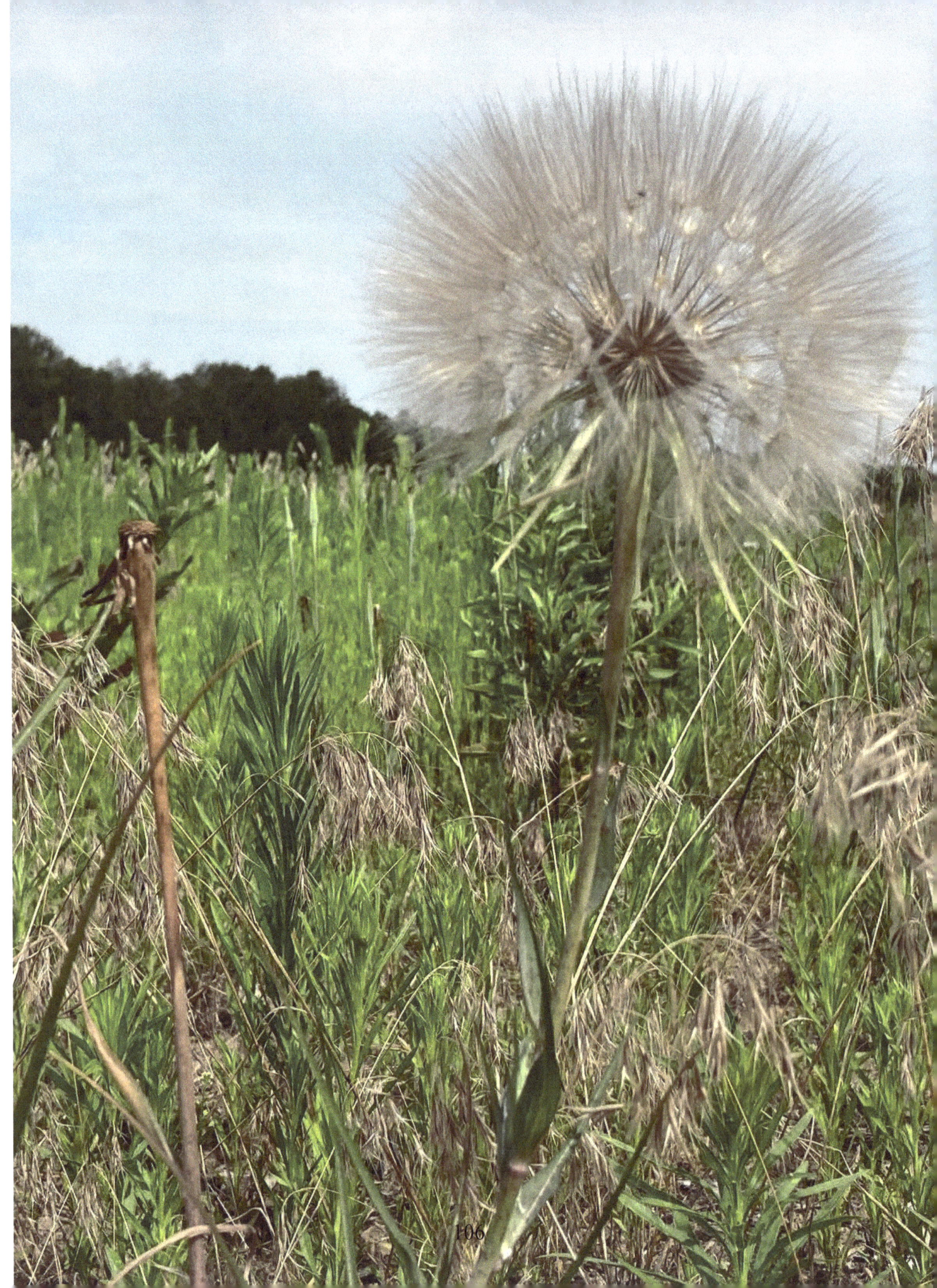

"All good things are wild and free."

Henry David Thoreau

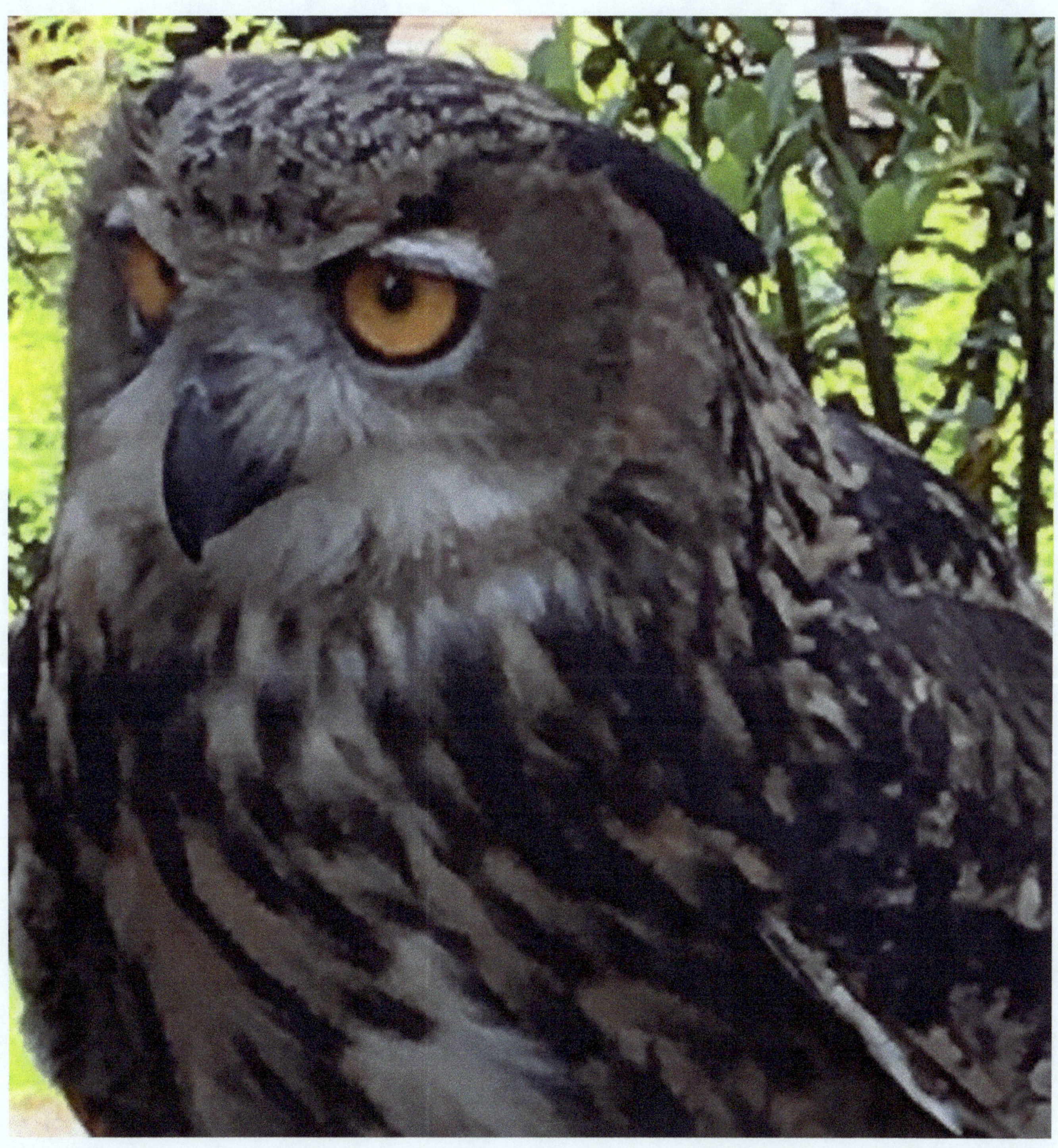

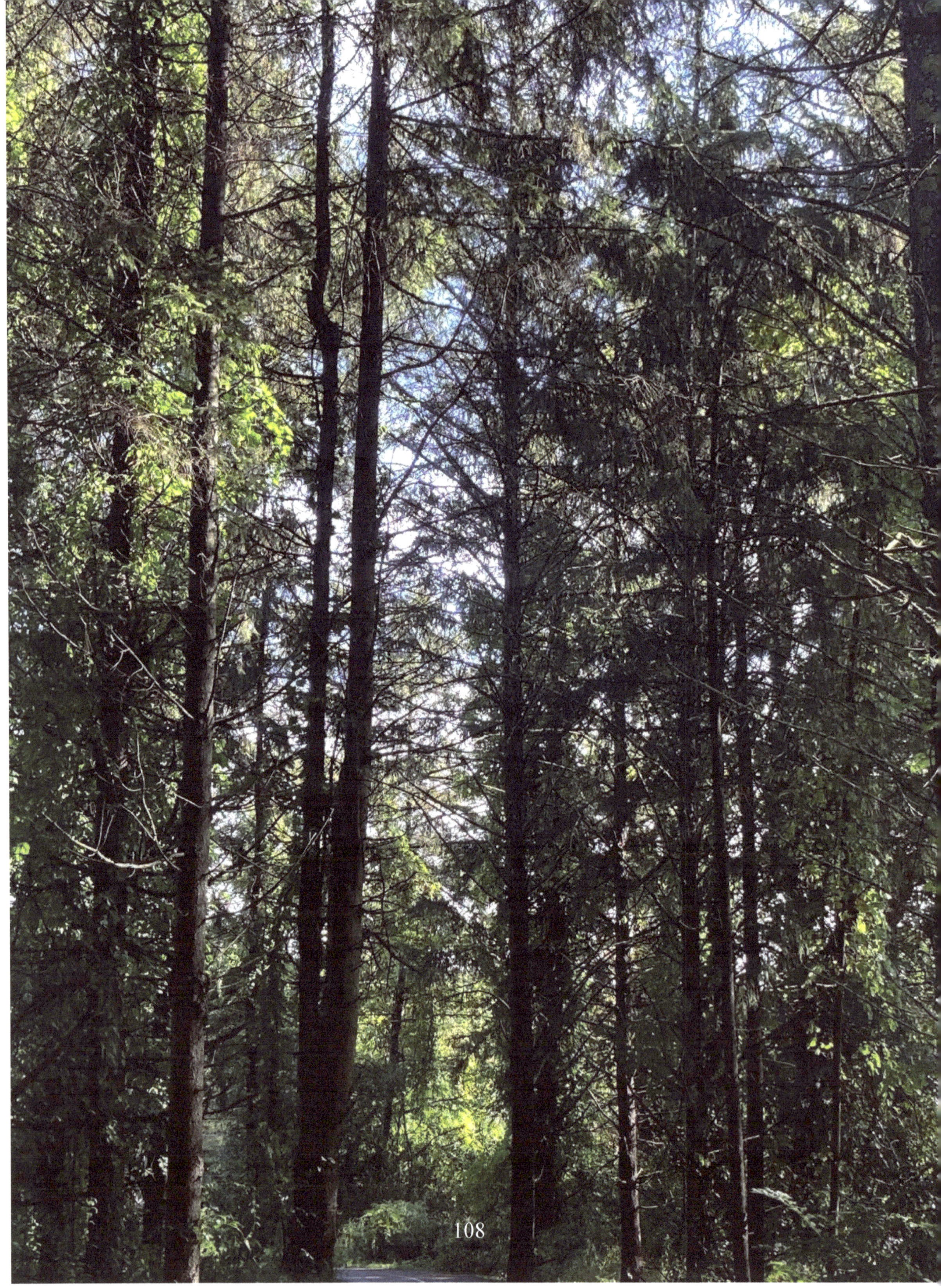

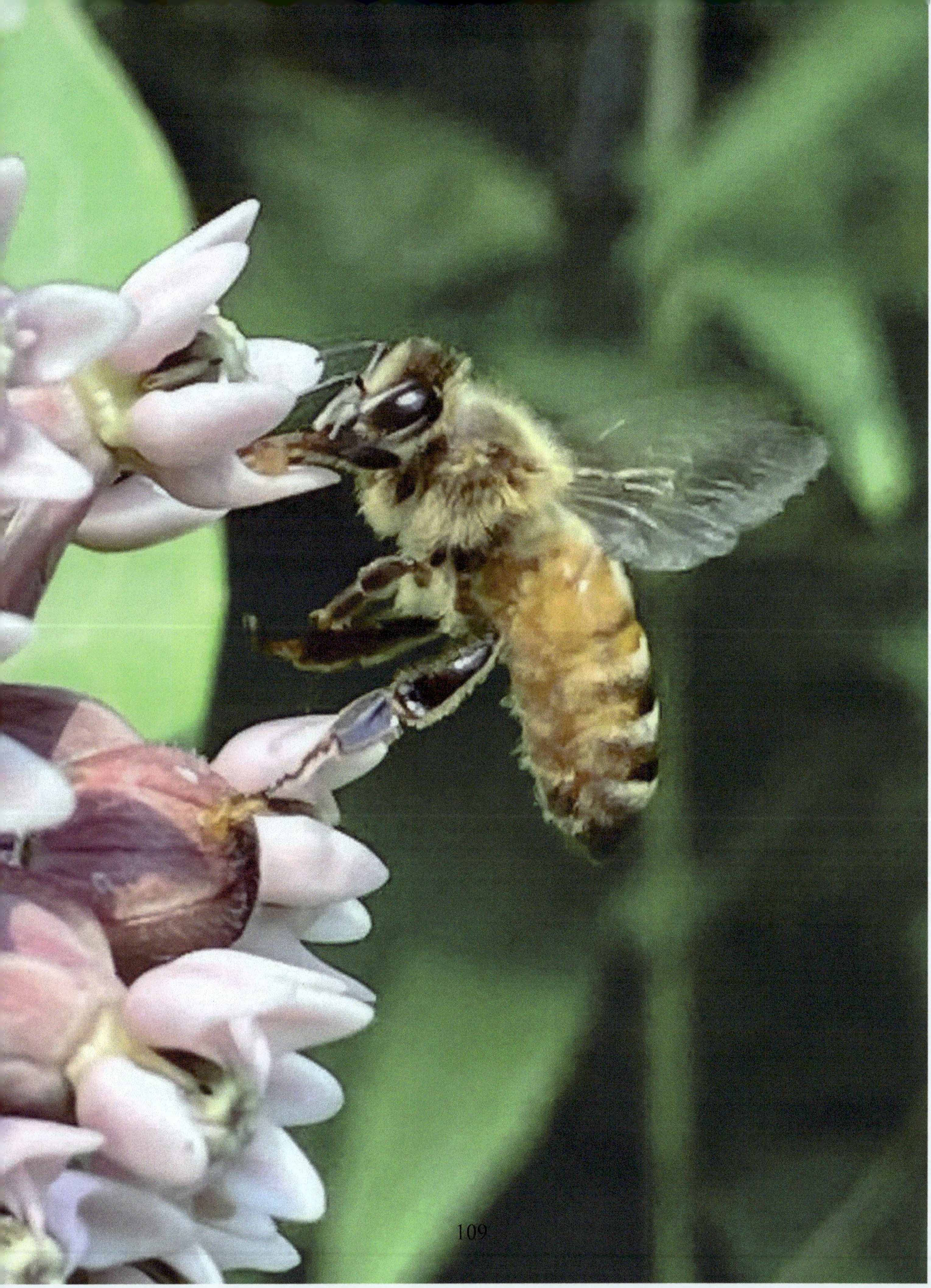

I think that I should never see
A poem as lovely as a tree.

A tree whose hungry mouth is prest
Against the earth's sweet flowing breast:

A tree that looks at the Heaven's all day,
And lifts her leafy arms to pray;

A tree that may in Summer wear.
A nest of robins in her hair . . .

Joyce Kilmer

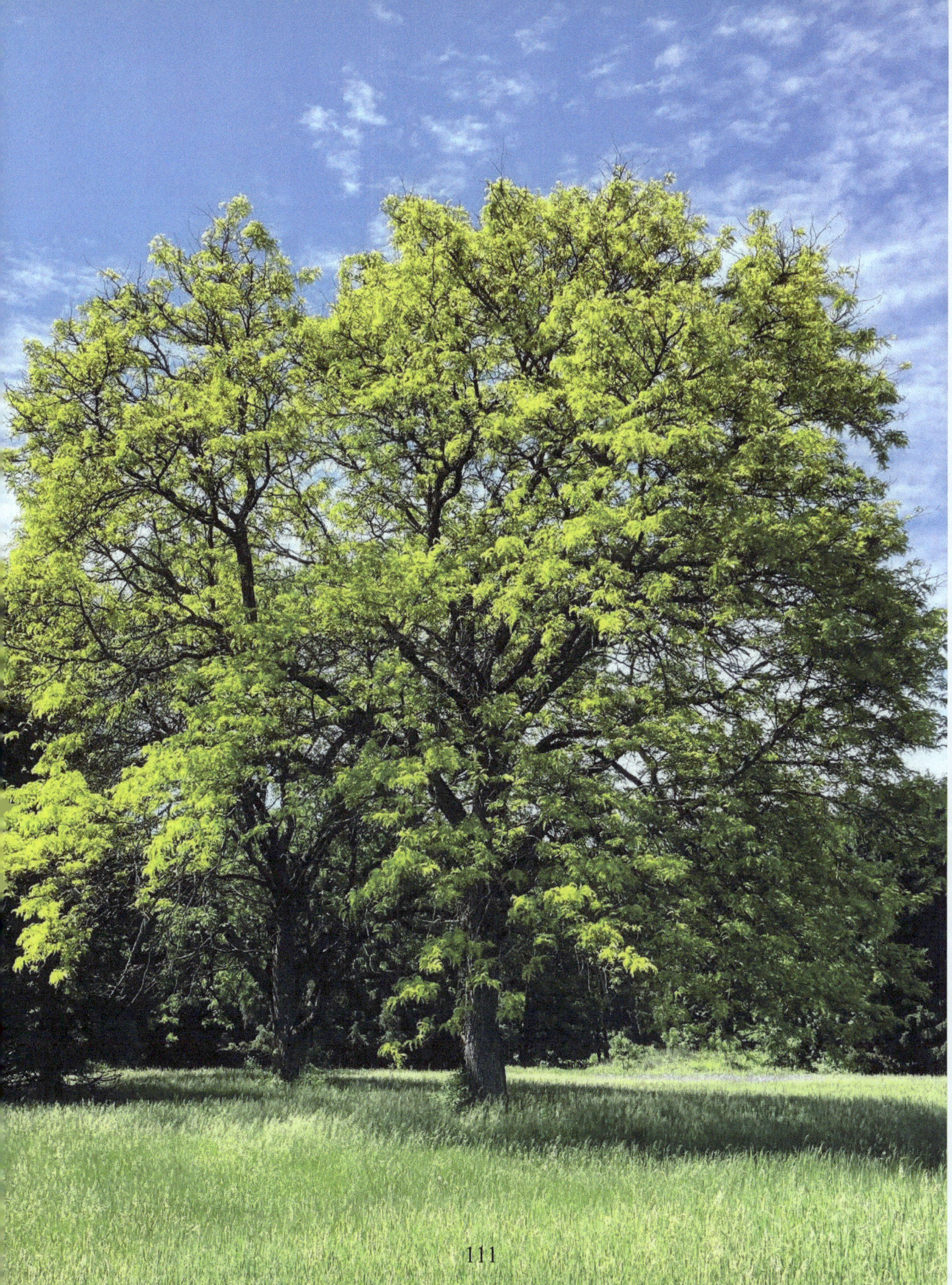

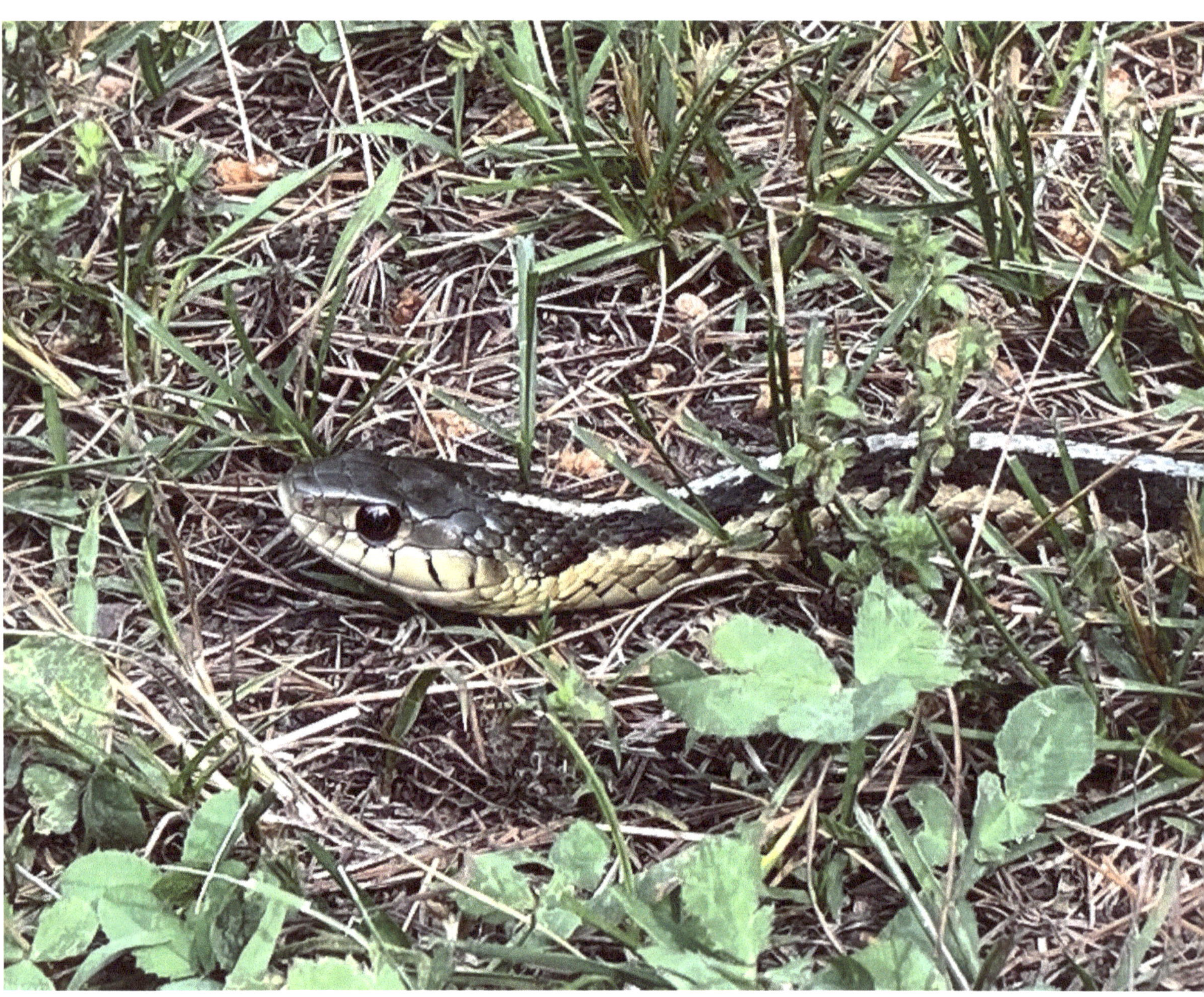

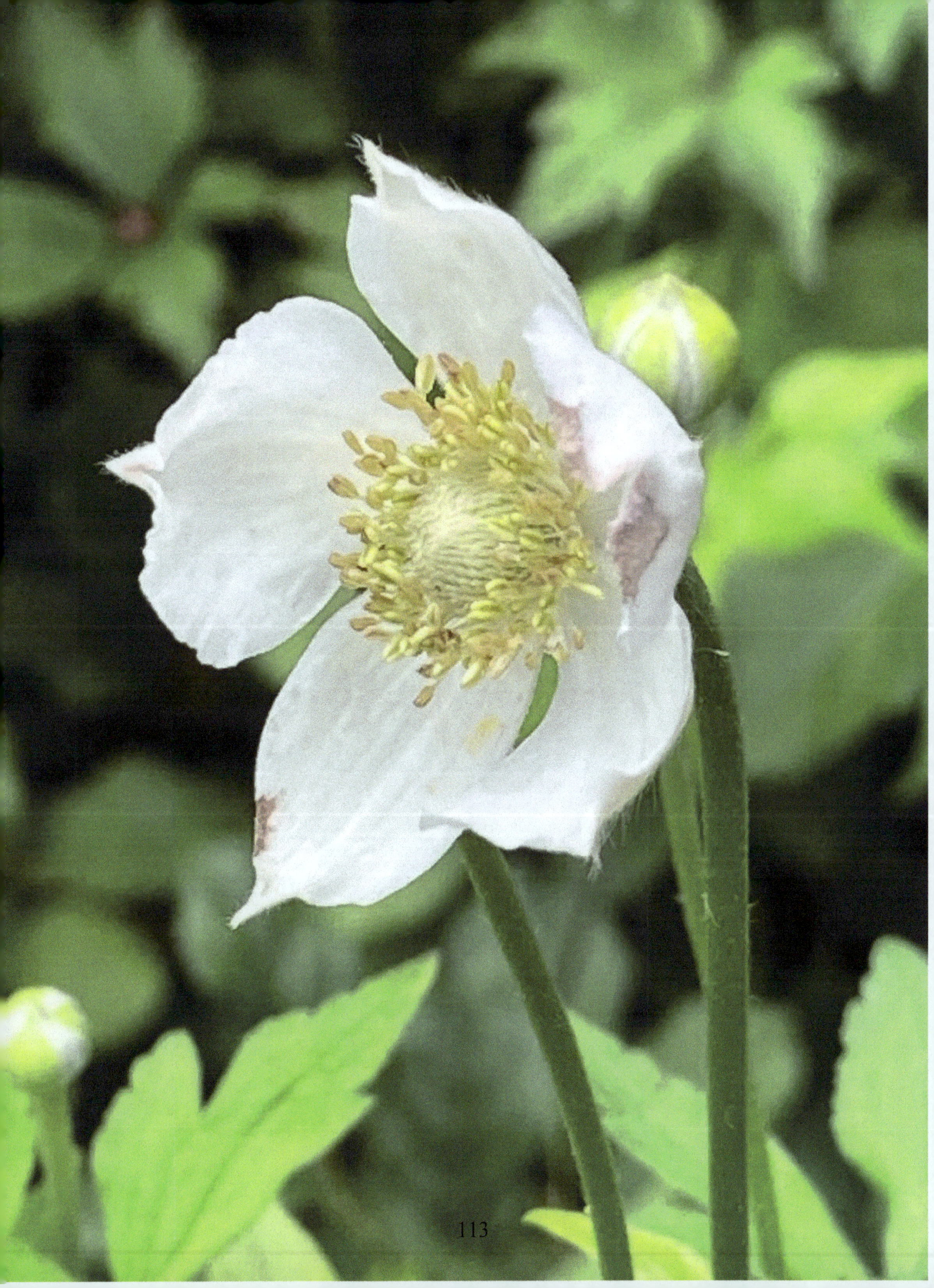

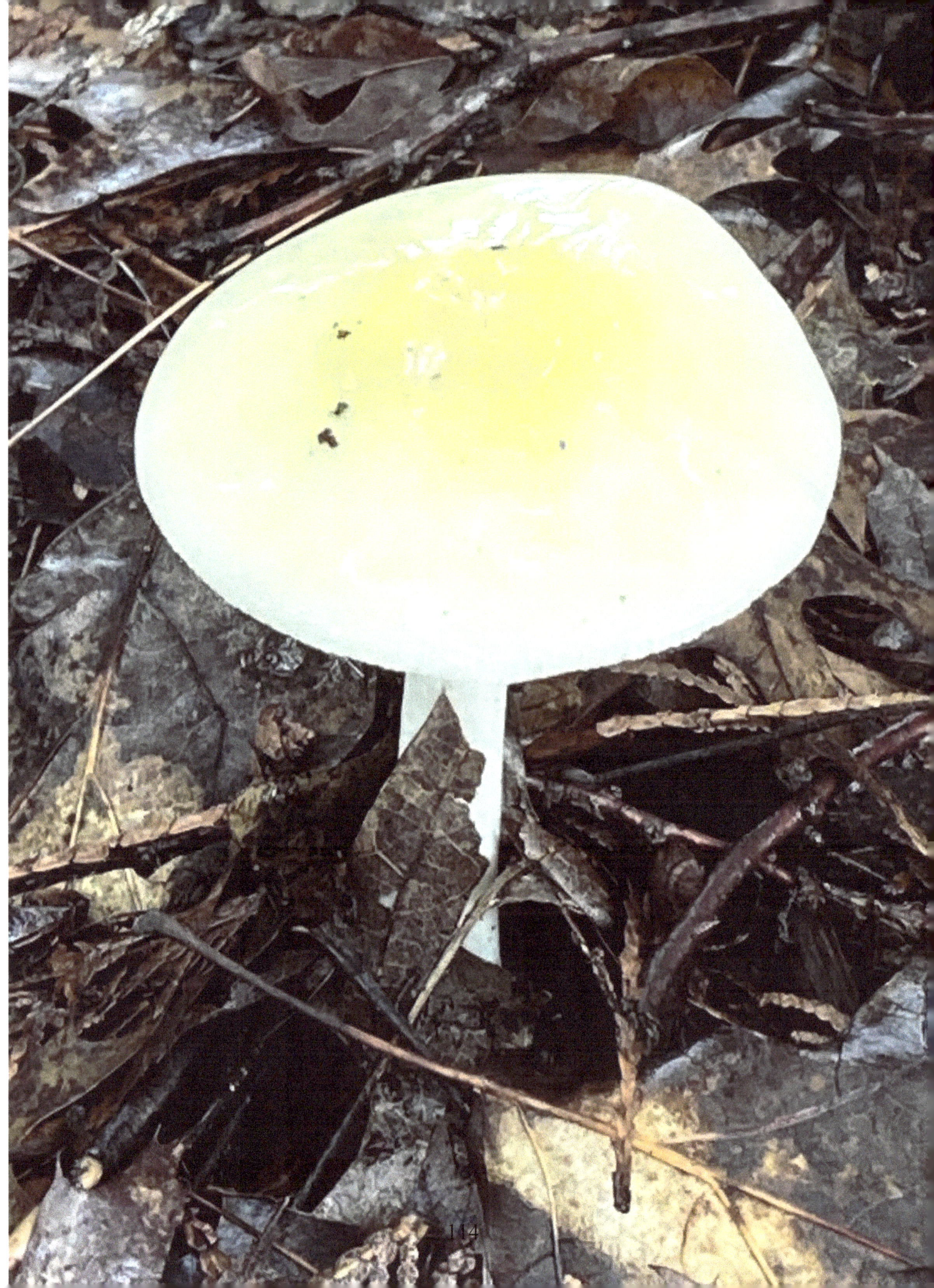

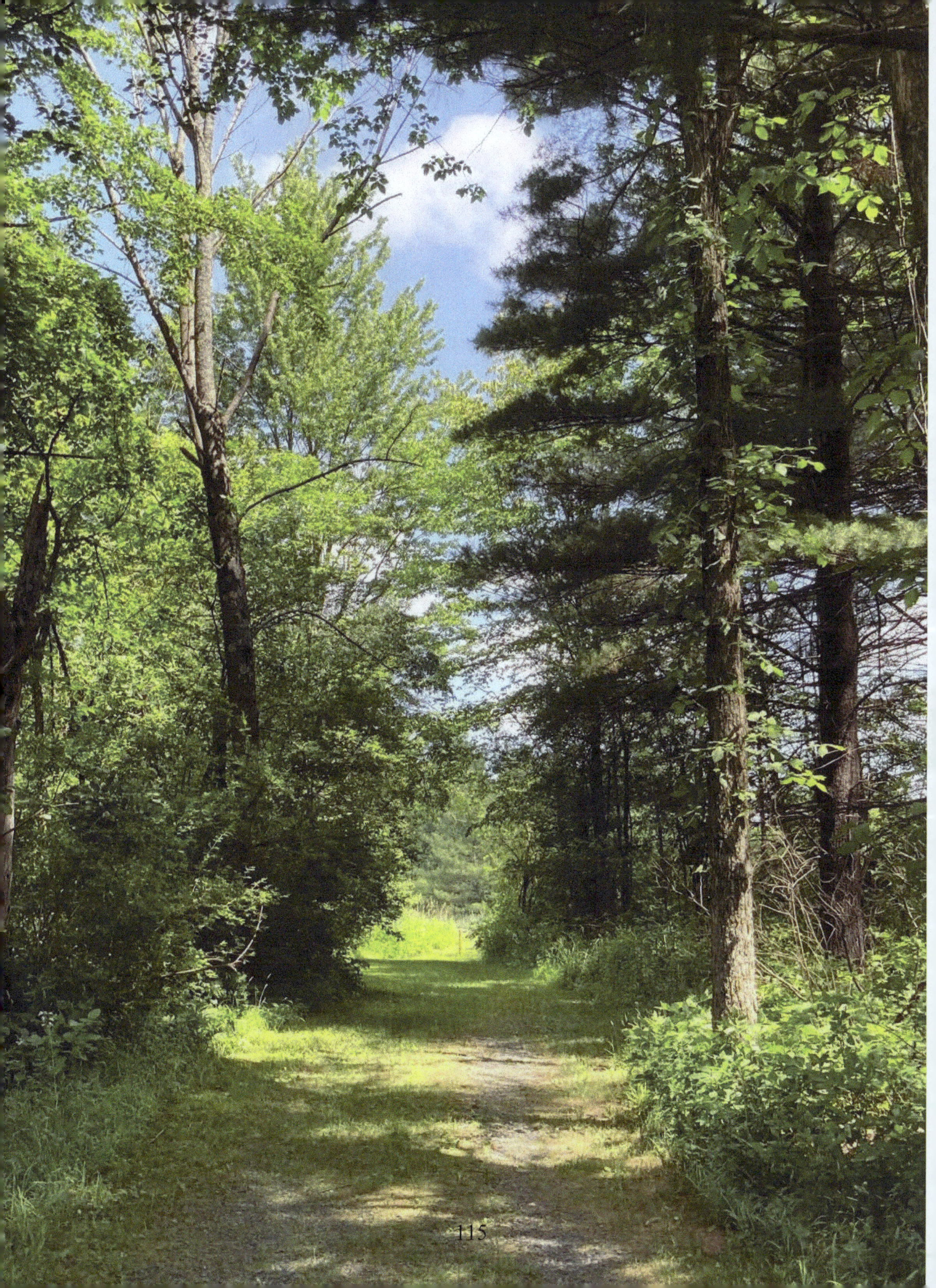

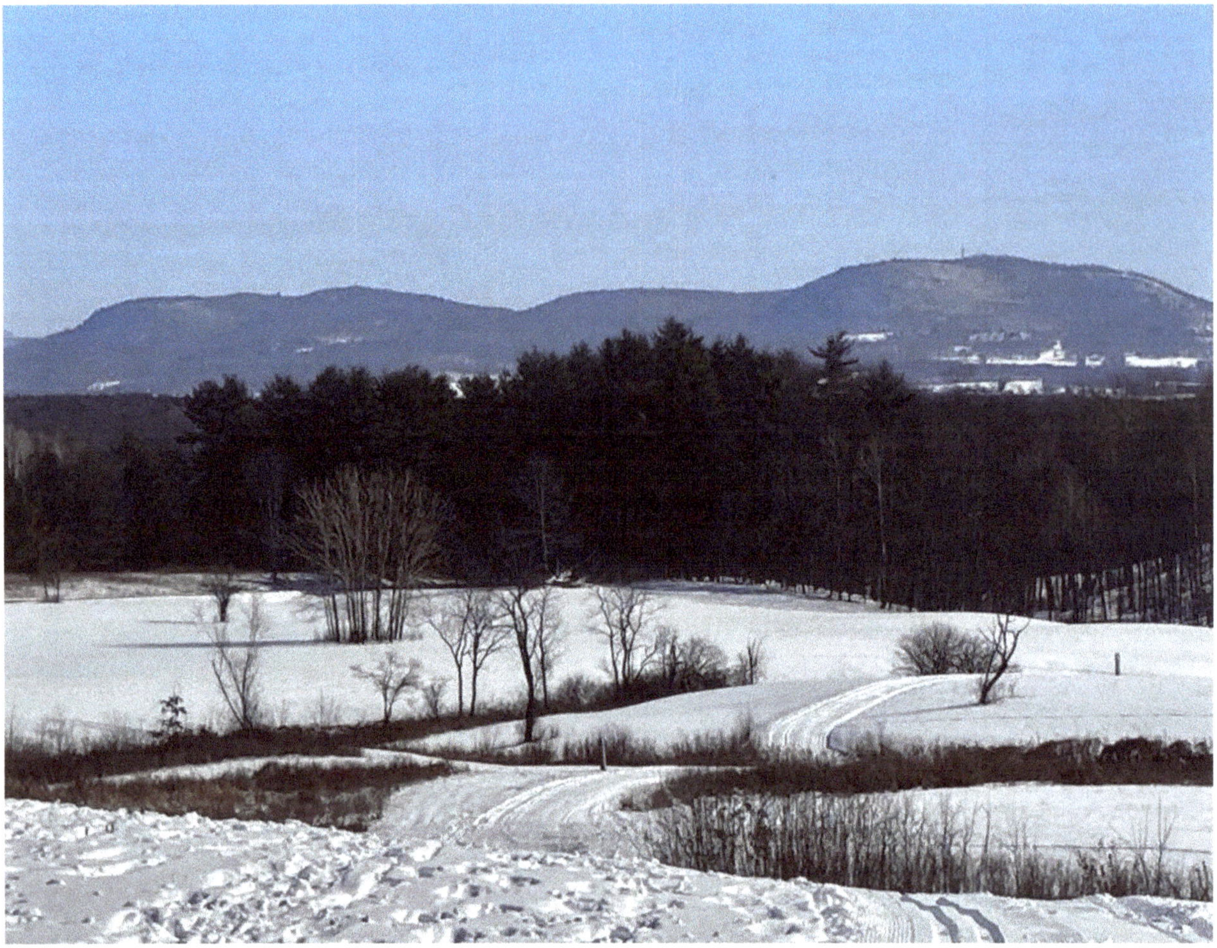

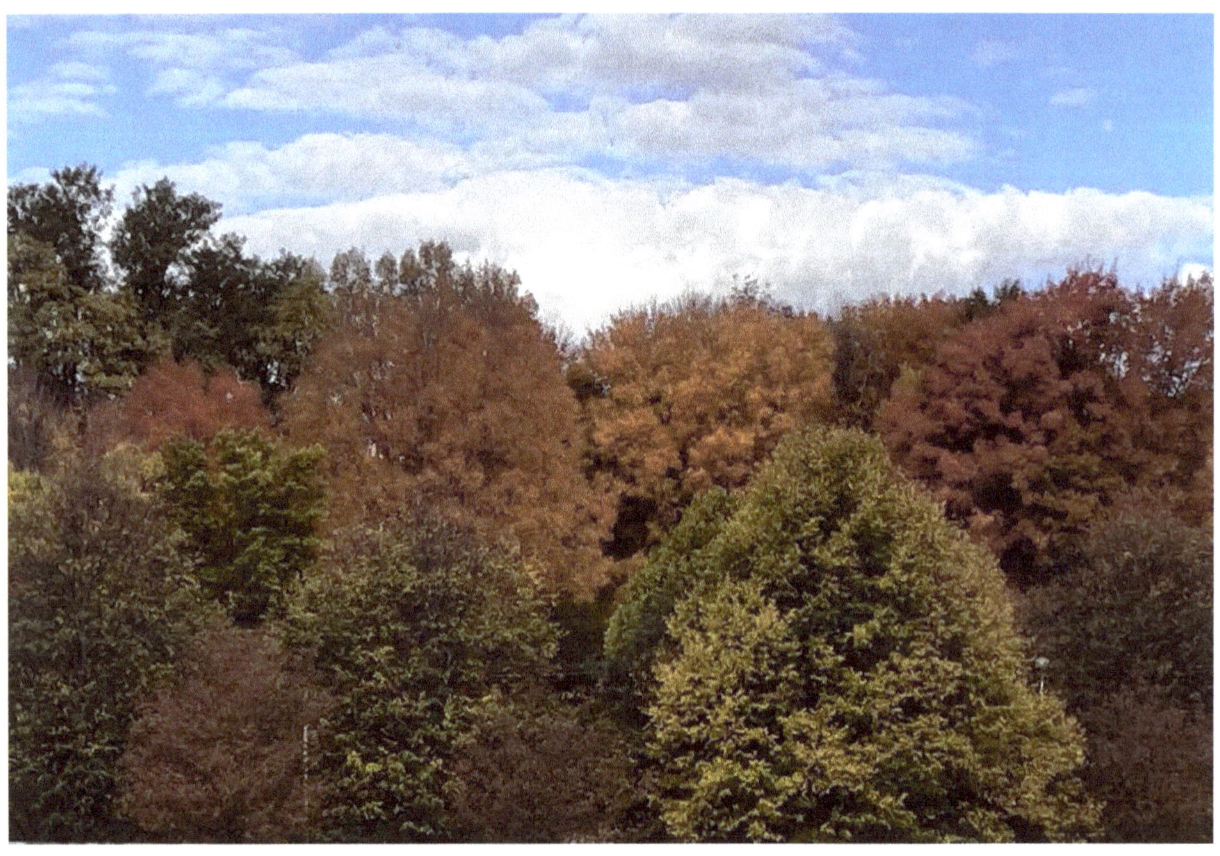

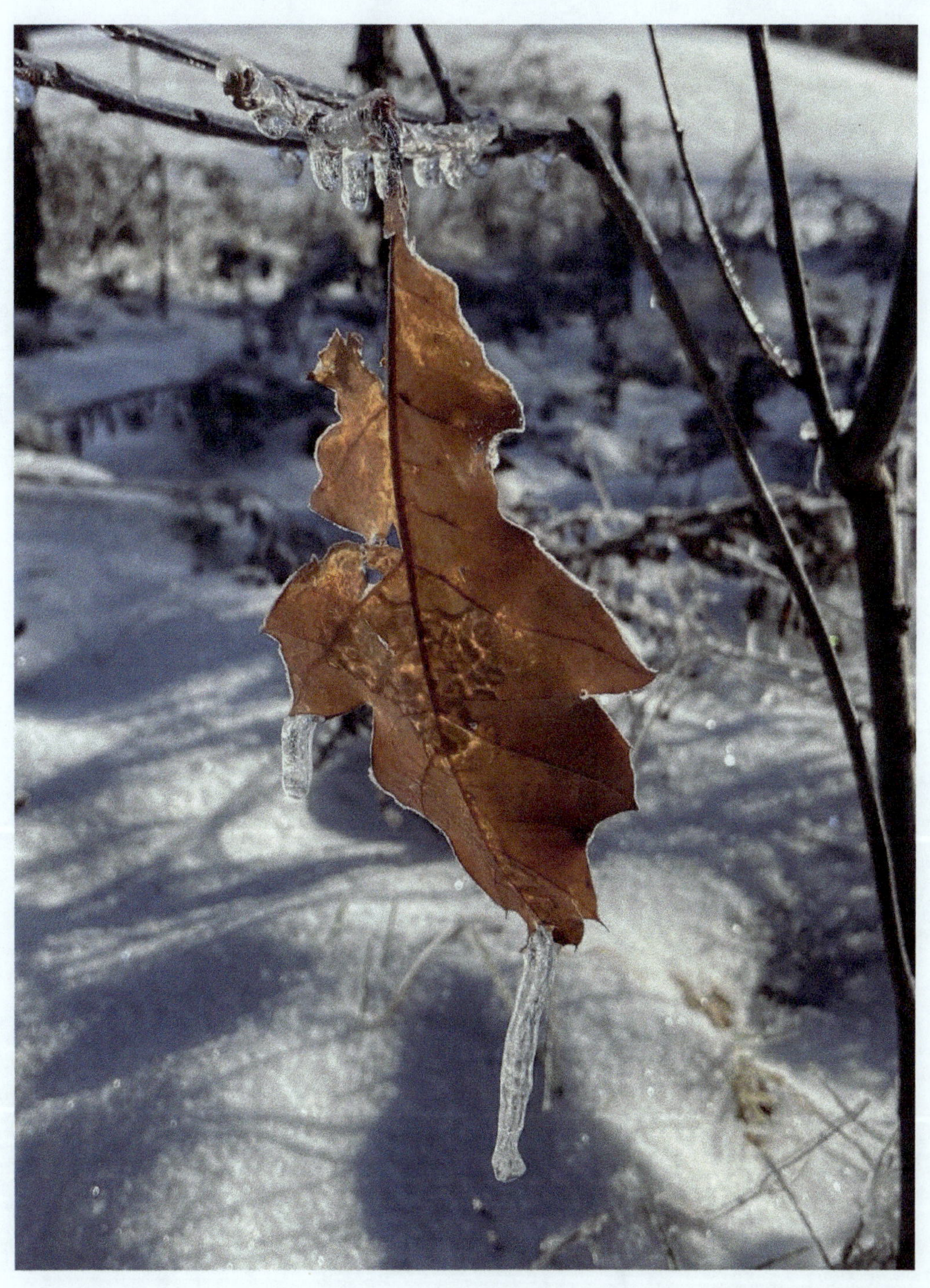

"Live each season as it passes, breathe the air, drink the drink,
Taste the fruit, and resign yourself to the influence of the earth."

Henry David Thoreau

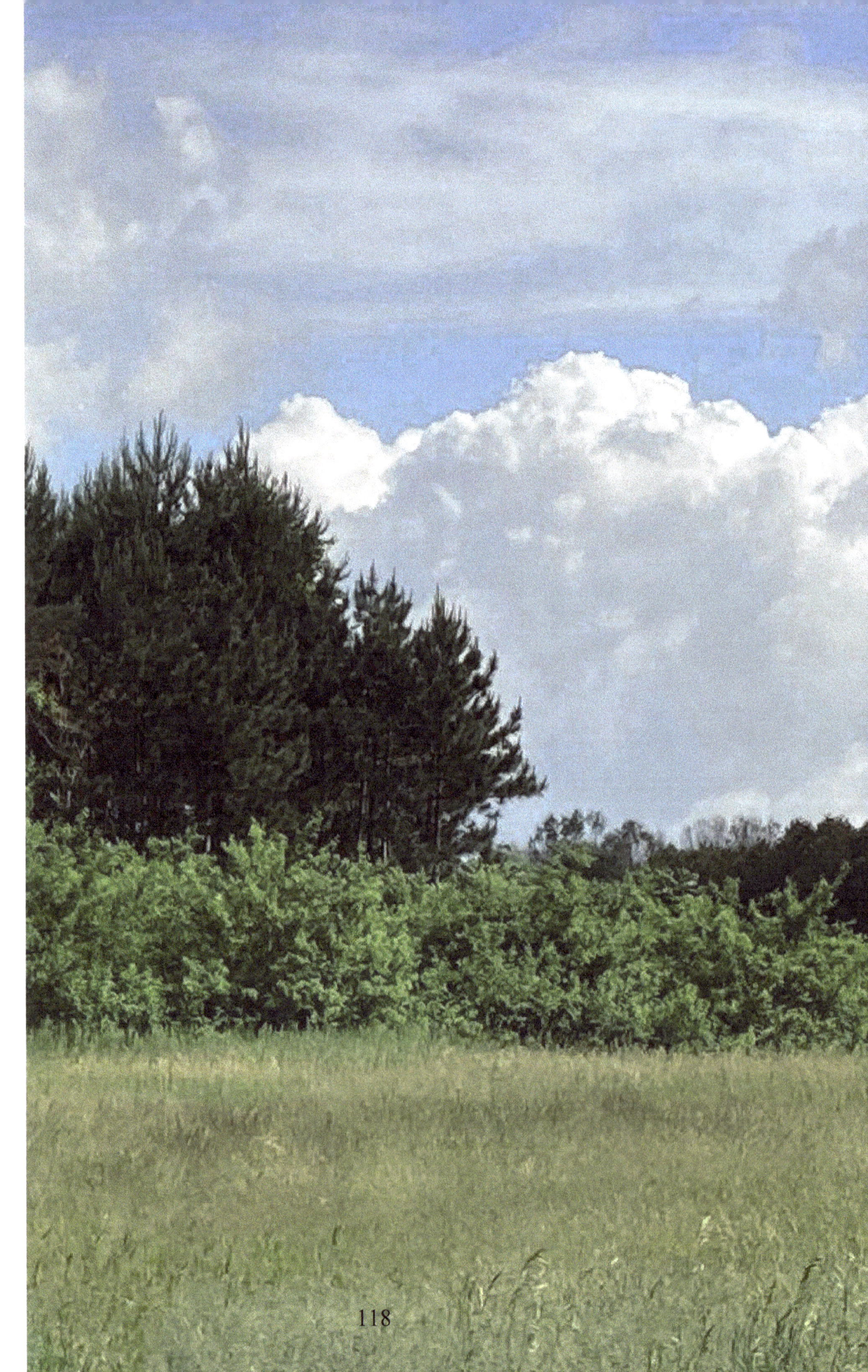

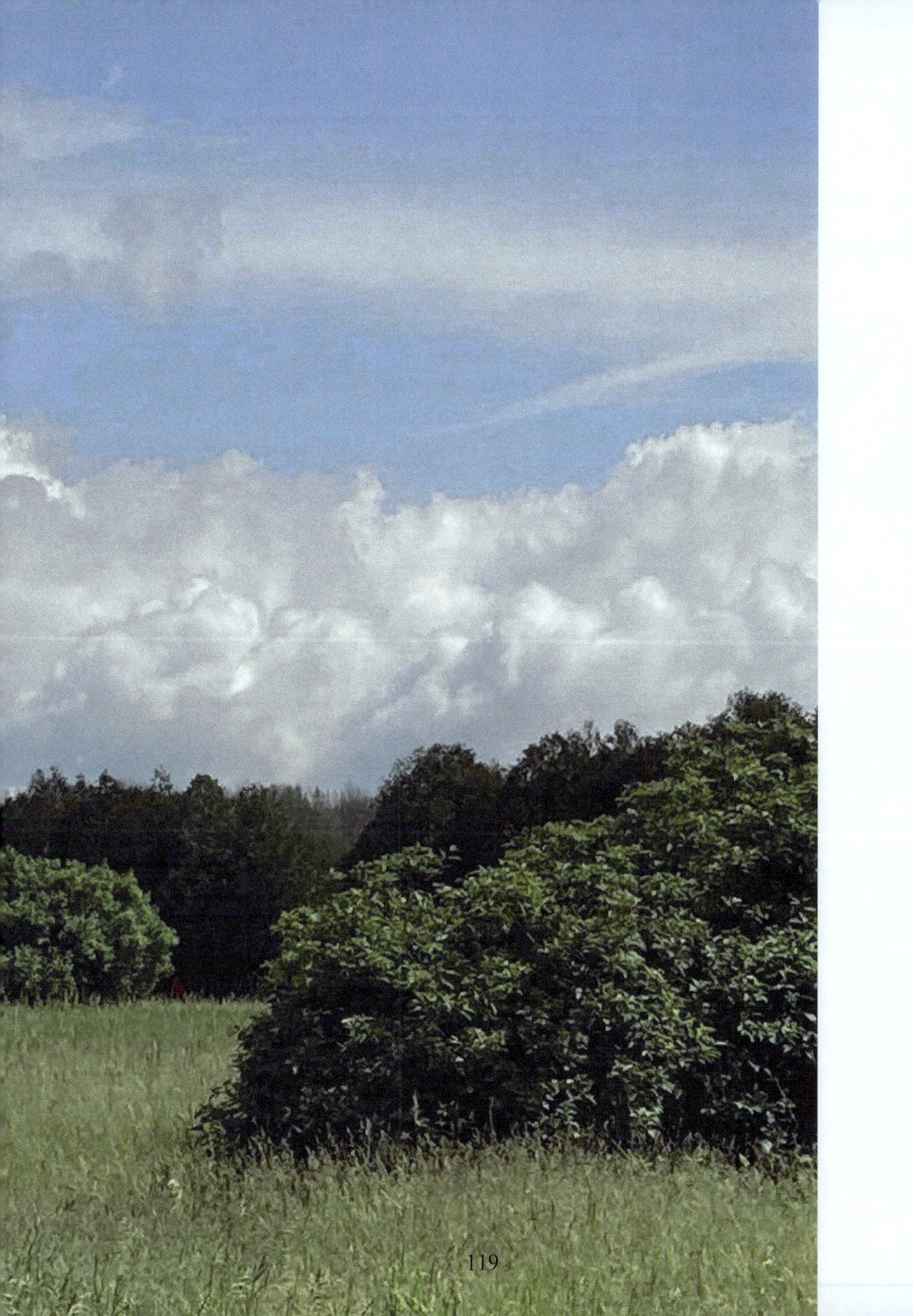

As I walk with beauty
As I walk, Nature is walking with me
In beauty walking before me, behind me,
Below me and above me,
Beauty on every side of me.

Navajo Prayer

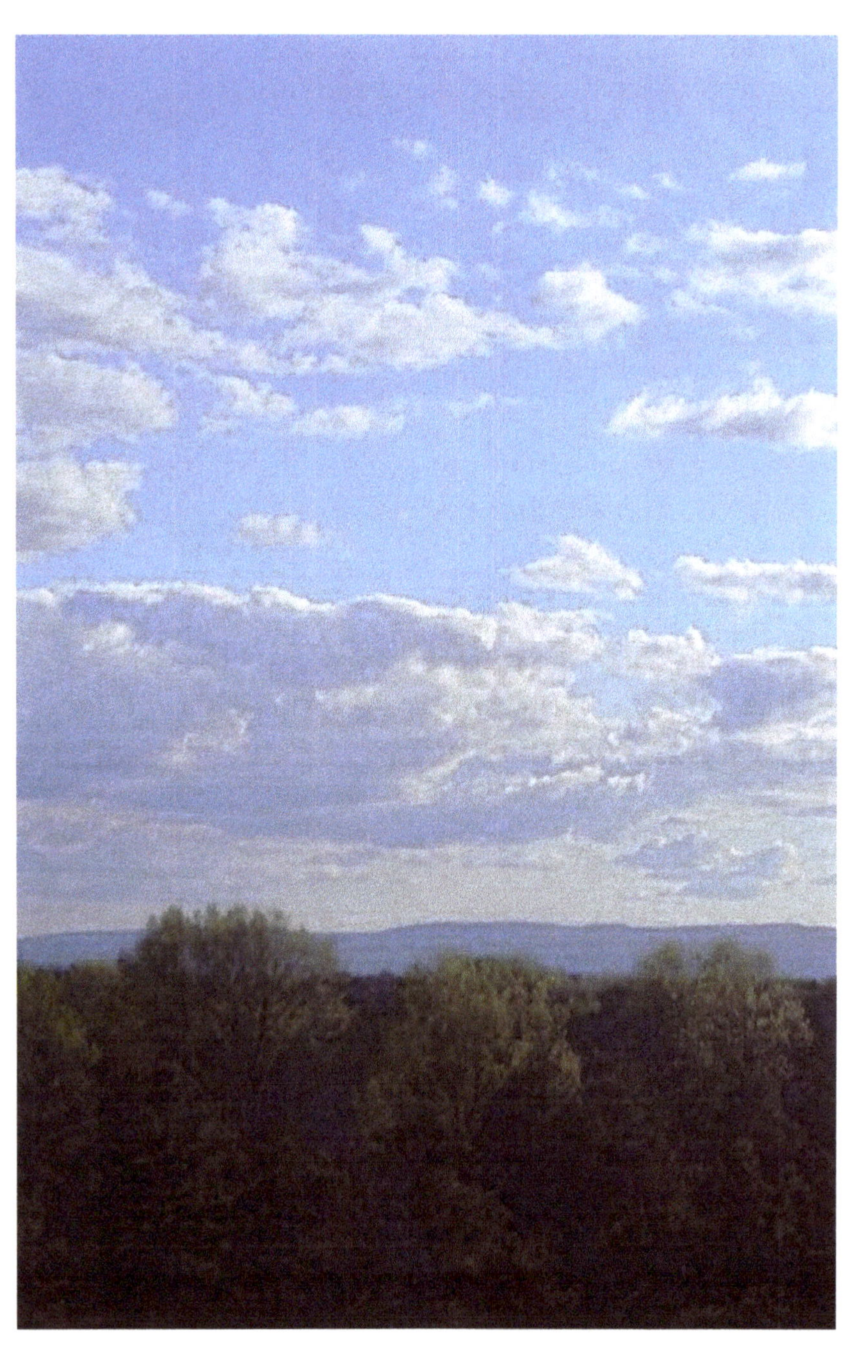

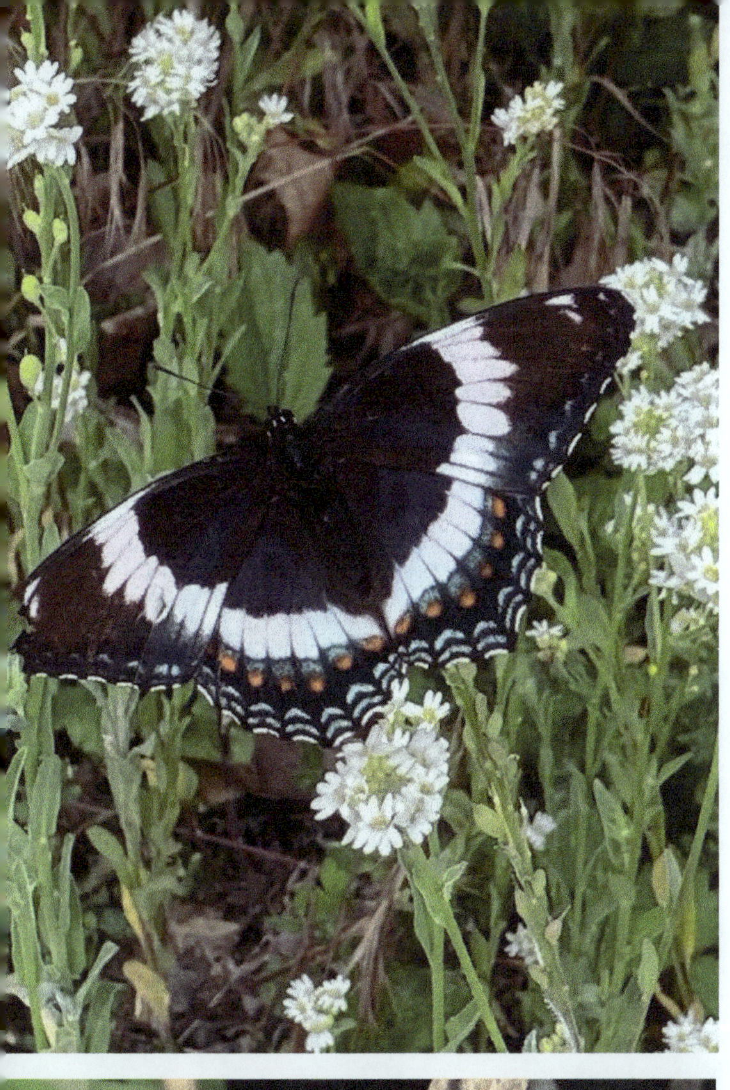
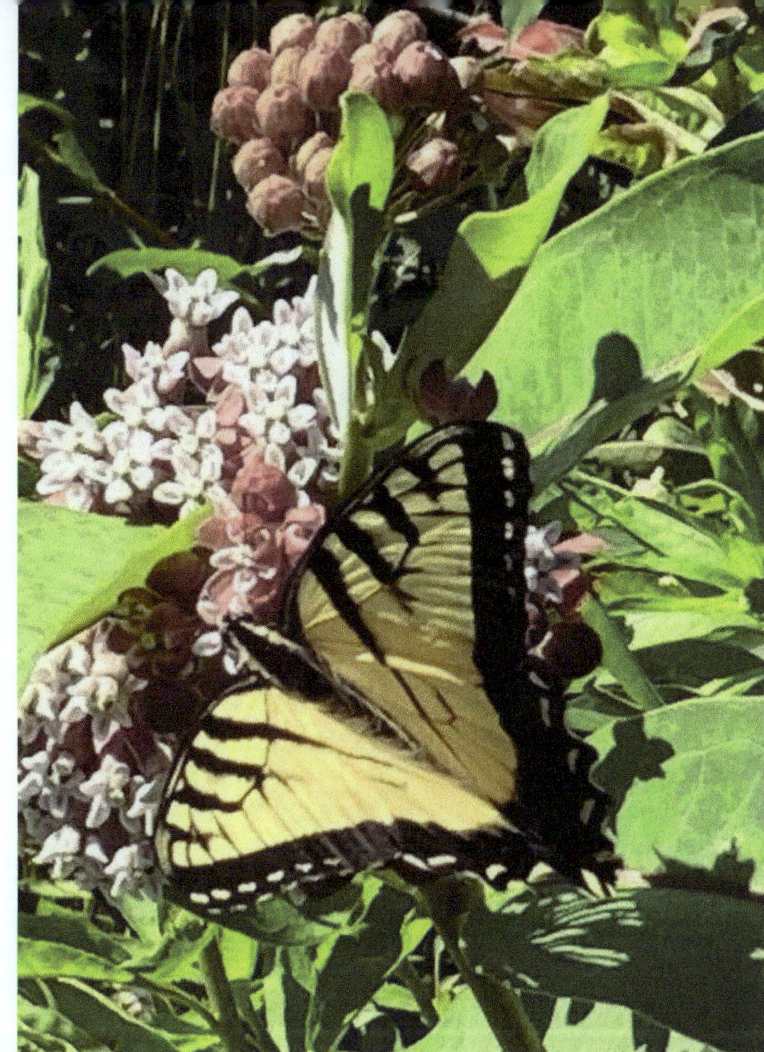
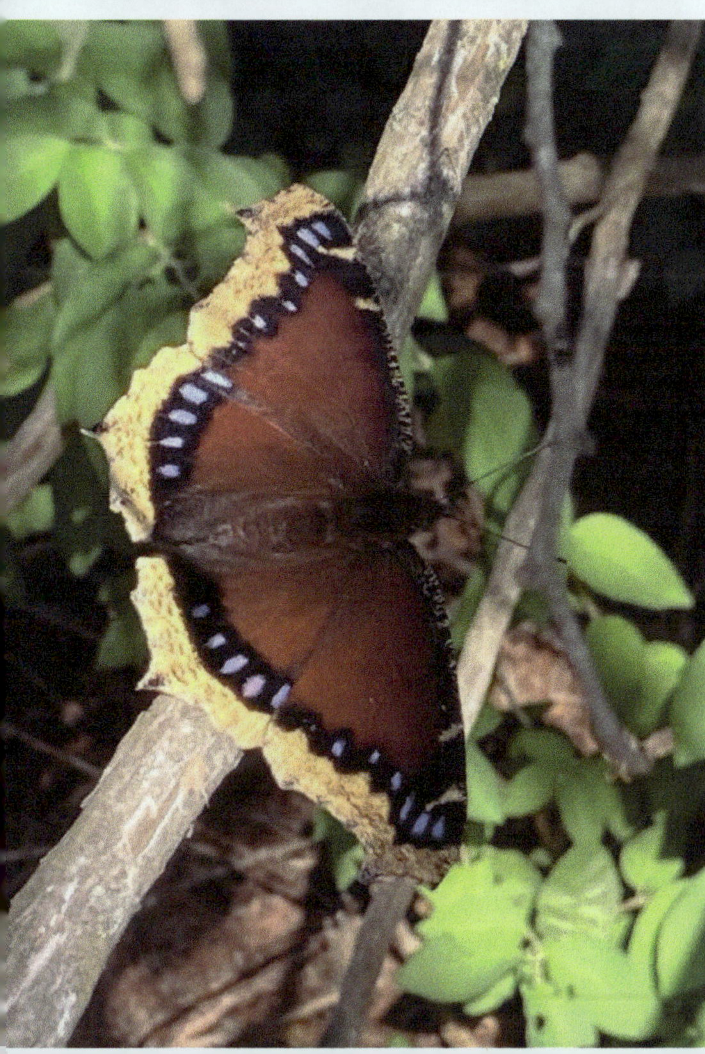
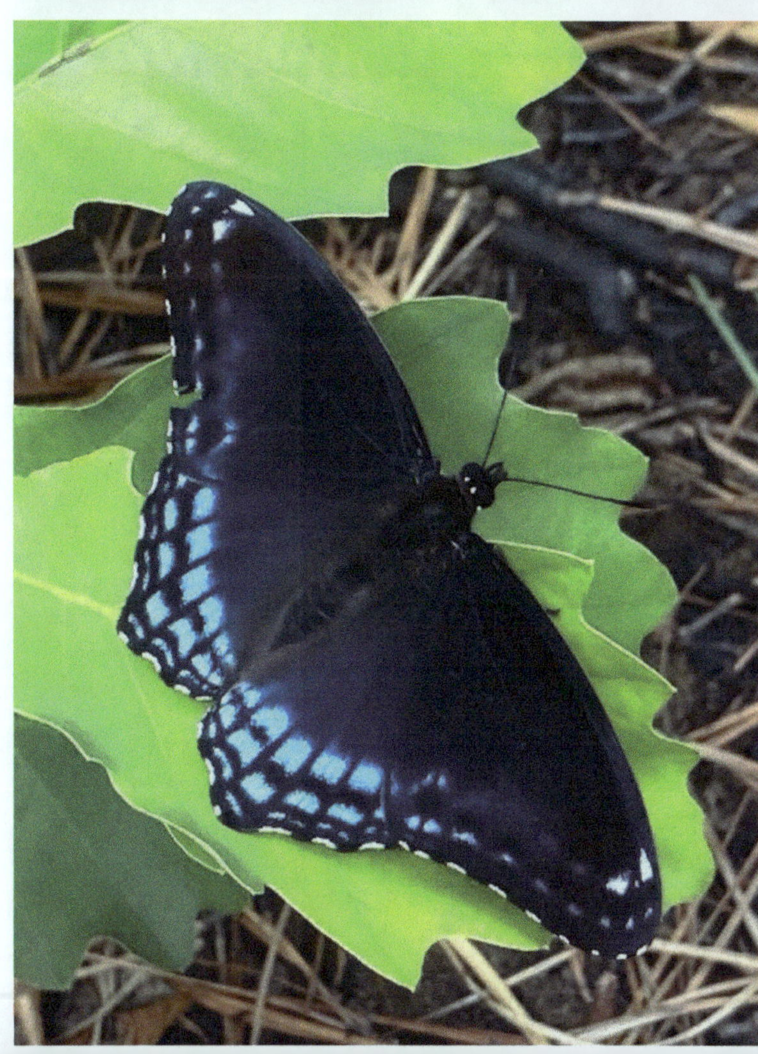

Bibliography

Dunbar, Paul Laurence. *In Summer:* The Complete Poems of Paul Laurence Dunbar: Dodd, Meadow & Co., 1913.

Pollack, LeRoy. *The Secret.* Lapham's Quarterly, 1928.

Anonymous. *Walk My World.* Inspirational Moon Quotes, 2021.

Ruskin, John. *Nature is a Painter.* Reader's Digest, 2022.

Muir, John. *Walk In With Nature: Steep Trails.* Boston: Houghton, 1918.

Longfellow, Henry Wadsworth. *Flowers in the Sunlight*: Voices of the Night, 1839.

Kwong, Jakusho. *No Beginning, No End:* The intimate Zen, 2007.

Einstein, Albert. *Look Deep Into Nature*: Poem Hunters.com, 2019.

Tzu, Lau. *Nature Does Not Hurry:* Lau Tzu Quotes, Up Journey, 2020 .

Tolle, Eckhart. *A New Earth:* The Power of Now, 2005.

Frank, Anne. *Nature Brings Solace in Trouble*: Diary of a Young Girl, originally published, 1947.

Bronte, Emily. *Spellbound:* The Medici Society Ltd., London, 1837.

Rilke, Rainer Maria (c.1875-1926). *Close to Nature*: Selected Poems.

Yanagihara, Hanya. *Kindness: A Little Life.* New York: Anchor Books, 2015.

Tolstoy, Leo (c.1828–1910). *One of the First Conditions of Happiness.*

Plath, Sylvia. *Appreciating Nature:* The Collected Poems, 1956.

Shakespeare, William. *The Earths Music:* The Complete Works, first published 1623.

Read, John P. *Mother Nature Is An Artist.* PoemHunt.com, 2020.

Frost, Robert. *The Road Not Taken.* First published in the Atlantic Monthly, August 1915.

Anonymous. *Beauty:* ShortNatureQuotes.com, 2020.

Chinese Proverb. *Miracles of Nature*: Short Nature Quotes.com, 2020.

Hanh, Thich Nhat. *Surrounded*: Peace is Every Step, 1992.

Grahame, Kenneth. *All This He Saw:* The Wind in the Willows, 1908.

Angier, Natalie. *Beauty of the Natural World*: New Views on the Nature of Life, 1995.

Thoreau, Henry David (n.d.). *Good Things*. AZQuotes.com. Retrieved 2021.

Kilmer, Joyce. *Trees.* Trees and Other Poems: Doran Publishing, NY, 1914.

Thoreau, Henry David (n.d.). *Live Each Season*. AZQuotes.com. Retrieved 2021.

Navajo Prayer (n.d.). *Walk in Beauty*: Closing Prayer from the Navajo Blessing Way Ceremony. Retrieved Aspen Institute 2020.

About Louis Valenti

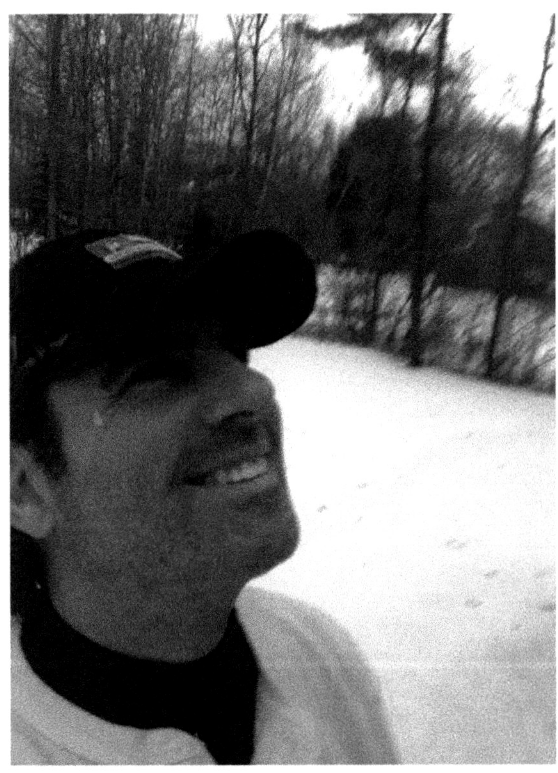

"Words can hardly describe the natural beauty and wonder of Saratoga. A photograph, an image, is different, it can capture the essence of a particular landscape; the many different sounds of the forest; and the feel of the wind and the sun and the cold. I offer this pictorial story in the sincere hope that I have conveyed the feelings and emotions and moods of the moment of each photograph."

*Through his photography, Louis Valenti attempts to inspire an appreciation and deeper understanding of the beauty and uniqueness of places such as the Albany Pine Bush Preserve, The Berkshires, Jersey Shore Beaches, Cape Cod Massachusetts, and Saratoga New York's parks, trails, and wilderness areas. In addition to photographing these American places of interest, his work includes **Seasons of the Pine Bush** (SPA City Publishing, 2021). He is currently engaged in a multi-year project photographing Troy New York's Historic District. His photographs are widely recognized in the Capital Region of New York and prints of his work are available from Louis Valenti Photography.*

For more information about Louis Valenti Photography, please visit
www.LouisValentiPhotography.com or Facebook.com/Louis.Valenti.Photography